# HAYDÉE SANTAMARÍA, CUBAN REVOLUTIONARY

*Margaret Randall*

# HAYDÉE SANTAMARÍA
★
## CUBAN REVOLUTIONARY

### SHE LED BY
### TRANSGRESSION

*Duke University Press    Durham and London    2015*

Printed in the United States of America on acid-free paper ∞
Designed by Heather Hensley
Typeset in Whitman by Graphic Composition, Inc.

Library of Congress Cataloging-in-Publication Data
Randall, Margaret, 1936–
Haydée Santamaría, Cuban revolutionary : she led by
transgression / Margaret Randall.
pages cm
Includes bibliographical references and index.
ISBN 978-0-8223-5942-5 (hardcover : alk. paper)
ISBN 978-0-8223-5962-3 (pbk. : alk. paper)
ISBN 978-0-8223-7527-2 (e-book)
1. Santamaría, Haydée. 2. Revolutionaries—Cuba—Biography.
3. Casa de las Américas. I. Title.
F1788.22.S265R36 2015
972.9106'3092—dc23
[B]
2015003794

Cover image: Haydée Santamaría. Archivo Fotográfico
Casa de las Américas

FOR HAYDÉE

# CONTENTS

# ACKNOWLEDGMENTS

WITHOUT THE ENCOURAGEMENT and always loving support of my partner, Barbara Byers, this book would not exist. For many years she experienced my need to write it, convinced me the time was right, and backed me up in more ways than I can say.

In Cuba, I want to give special thanks to Roberto Fernández Retamar and Silvia Gil, who understood the importance of the project before I even knew I had the courage to begin; to Chiki Salsamendi, who worked tirelessly to get me the photographs that make the book so much richer; and to Ana Cecilia Ruiz Lim, who held my hand throughout my fieldwork in Havana. Marcia Leseica, who was with Haydée at Casa's inception in 1959, made herself available to me for a fruitful interview in 2014. At Casa de las Américas I am also personally grateful to Yolanda Alomá, Idelisa Escalona, Juan Calzada, Jorge Fornet, Myriam Radlow, Alicia Varela, and Jorge Vivas for aiding me in different ways.

I consulted many documents by and about Haydée at the Casa de las Américas archive and was given generous access to them all. Casa's library was also extremely helpful. The Office of Historic Affairs at the Cuban Council of State was forthcoming with its valuable holdings. And the newspaper *Granma*'s document center kindly allowed me to use the photograph of Haydée's funeral procession.

With regard to the photographs, many come from Casa's archive. In most cases the original photographers are unknown and so cannot be credited. I am grateful to them for having made these images that capture Haydée in so many moments of her life.

Among the few living members of Haydée's family, I am deeply grateful to her nieces Norma Ruiz and Niurka Martín Santamaría, and to her grand-nephew Boris Javier Martín Santamaría. Norma, especially, provided invaluable help, both in Cuba and later when I was back home and bombarded her with questions about this or that detail.

Also in Cuba, Arturo Arango, Rebeca Chávez, Norberto Codina, Ambrosio Fornet, Michele Frank, Ana Maite Gil, Juan Luis Martín, Christina Mills, Aimée Vega, and Lesbia Vent Dumois pointed me in important directions, helped with my fieldwork, were there for fruitful discussions, and aided me in many other ways. Through the years, Arturo Arango in particular has always been available for friendship, resources, and consultation.

Outside Cuba, Ana Bickford, Bernardine Dohrn, Doug Dunston, Sarah Mondragón, Ximena Mondragón, Jane Norling, Rini and V. B. Price, Gregory Randall, John Randall, Robert Schweitzer, Susan Sherman, Nancy Stout, Tineke Ritmeester, and Alba Vanni were all helpful in a variety of ways. Gisela Fosado, my wonderful editor at Duke University Press, supported the book with the sort of intelligent enthusiasm that makes any writer want to do her best. Her assistant, Lorien Olive, was helpful, patient and reassuring.

Last but certainly not least, thank you Haydée, for living the life.

# 1 BEFORE WE BEGIN

Cuba is an independent and sovereign socialist state of workers, organized with all and for the good of all as a united and democratic republic, for the enjoyment of political freedom, social justice, individual and collective well-being and human solidarity.
—Article 1 of the Cuban Constitution

In these times of global economic crisis,[1] the poor and middle classes of countries calling themselves capitalist, Socialist, Communist, Social Democratic, Christian Democratic, monarchist, liberal, Islamist, conservative, or based on the principle of happiness[2] lose jobs and security while small groups of the powerful rake in more and more of the profit stockpiled by their labor. This gulf between rich and poor, between gluttonous and desperate, has become so sharp it seems irreversible. Even more troubling to those of my generation who believed we could change the world, current powers favor the reverse direction from the one we imagined.

Dramatic climate change and devastating natural disasters, the increasing interdependence of nations, a liberating but also dangerously controlling information revolution, race and gender manipulation, the intentional complexity of corporate markets with their tricky bundling and devious hedge funds, the destruction of public education and consequent failure to teach young people critical thinking, the glorification of violence, fabricated need, elaborately deceptive official rhetoric, and expertly induced fear: all combine to convince us healthy change is impossible.

Endless wars mask ordinary need and overcome our longing for peace. Obscene amounts of money buy elections. Pseudopatriotism has taken the place of reason. The mentally ill are denied the services they require, and some of them take their frustrations out shooting up schools or other public places. Whistle-blowers, once respected and protected, are now considered traitors and exiled or imprisoned. Evil is blamed on anyone different from ourselves, and a cultivated fear of difference nurtures a racist and xenophobic status quo that keeps mainstream America from asking the complex questions. Many of those we misunderstand, disregard, and treat as childish underlings hate us with good reason.

Against this backdrop and through the systematic erasure of historic memory, few Americans recall that only fifty-five years ago, a small group of rebels on a Caribbean island ninety miles from the Florida coast ousted a dictator and took the future of its nation into its hands. A successful social revolution right offshore! The United States was stunned when it suddenly lost control of one of its nearest clients. Public officials, unaccustomed to thinking such a thing could happen, weren't prepared. The US power structure wasted no time in devising ways to undermine what it saw as an incongruous and unacceptable upstart.

The United States sought and received help from regional dictators, such as Somoza of Nicaragua and Trujillo of the Dominican Republic. Members of Cuba's owner classes were afraid of losing their fortunes. Churches were nervous about an atheist imposition (which the revolution, unfortunately, did nothing to counteract). And an irrational anti-Communism made it easy for a rapid dissemination of lies and unfounded rumors to spread fear even among many in Cuba's middle class.

Inside the United States, the first two Cuban counterrevolutionary organizations were founded before 1959 had even come to an end: La rosa blanca (The White Rose) and Milicias obreras anticomunistas (Workers Anti-Communist Militia). The CIA funded them from the beginning. In March 1960, Eisenhower approved a government program aimed at bringing down the revolution. It consisted of four parts: sabotage, the introduction of paramilitary groups to spark an internal uprising, the establishment of a subversion and intelligence network, and a broad campaign of psychological warfare. In this same year, the first important group of business owners and those with large landholdings left the island.

While the US government's posture was becoming more and more criminal, many on the American Left, on the other hand, were inspired; their understanding of this new revolution varied, but they were quick to see in it the answers their diverse visions conditioned them to understand.

To the United States, prerevolutionary Cuba had been a convenient playground where high-end businessmen could go for a weekend of fun at one of the US crime syndicate–owned casinos, spend a few hours with a voluptuous *mulata*, and drink rum and Coca-Cola oblivious to what life was like for those who serviced their whims. In old Havana, a US marine had a few too many beers, climbed a statue of José Martí, and urinated on the patriot's head. Such incidents, harmless jokes in the imperialist mind, to Cubans were symbolic of decades of domination.

For them, their country was a land where a one-crop sugar economy exploited vast numbers of cane cutters who had work only a few months of the year. These people were indebted to the company store and subsisted under miserable living conditions with little access to education and health care. Sugar, tobacco, and coffee production was in the hands of US companies. Cuba depended as well on US oil and imports of all kinds. The nation's raw materials and human resources meant huge profit for foreign interests, with a bit trickling down to an ostentatious local oligarchy.

All this got much worse on March 10, 1952, when an ex-president and general named Fulgencio Batista staged a coup and took power. The left-center Orthodox Party had been expected to win the upcoming elections, but Batista put an end to even such modest dreams of reform. The United States immediately recognized the new government, which it knew would continue to protect its interests. All over the island, young people were looking for ways to take back their country.

In Havana, a young lawyer named Fidel Castro was able to rally a group that would later emerge as the July 26 Movement. The name was derived from the attack 160 of his men and two women launched against Moncada Barracks, the nation's second-largest military garrison, in Santiago de Cuba on July 26, 1953. The action was a military failure but lit the spark that became the Cuban Revolution.

The young revolutionaries, some of whom are featured in this book, gave a great deal at Moncada: brothers, husbands, fathers, lovers. They also lost their innocence—but gained immeasurably in dignity. The Cuban people learned there were those among them committed to sacrificing everything for justice. Moncada's survivors, including Haydée Santamaría and Fidel Castro, were captured, tried, imprisoned, and eventually released in 1954 and 1955. Fidel found it too dangerous to continue the struggle on home soil and retreated to Mexico. There he gathered and trained a group of less than a hundred men. He vowed they would be back in the mountains of his homeland, fighting or dead, before the end of 1956.

Embarking upon an overloaded and risky sea voyage, the secondhand yacht they called *Granma* departed from the Mexican port of Tuxpan and landed at Las Coloradas beach on Cuba's eastern coast in the early morning hours of December 2, 1956. The Santiago underground had planned an uprising to coincide with the landing and provide cover for the returnees, but choppy seas and slow going on the part of the novice sailors made for miscalculation. Most of the revolutionaries were gunned down upon arrival. Fidel, his brother Raúl, Che, and a few others made it into the nearby mountains; some have said twelve, some sixteen, some only seven. They may have been able to salvage seven weapons. With these in hand, Fidel famously declared the war won.

What followed were two years of increasingly well-organized guerrilla warfare. It would become a model emulated, with varying degrees of success, by other liberation movements throughout the next two decades. Nothing like it had been seen in the Western Hemisphere since Haiti's successful defeat of French colonialism in 1804. Finally another small country, exploited by US imperialism, was demonstrating the courage and capacity to rebel.

Cuba's revolutionaries, women as well as men, proved brave, strategic, ingenious, and extremely capable. They built an impenetrable stronghold in the Sierra Maestra mountains and a perfectly coordinated underground movement in the cities. In February 1957 they were even able to bring *New York Times* reporter Herbert Matthews safely into and out of the mountains, where he interviewed Fidel and gave worldwide lie to Batista's claim that the rebel leader had been killed in the landing.

At first the guerrillas suffered a string of defeats. But they learned from their mistakes and by the end of 1957 were winning battles, capturing military posts, and taking prisoners—whom they treated with a generosity that set them apart from their adversaries. Fidel and a number of other leaders demonstrated an unusual integrity. News of the Argentine doctor named Ernesto "Che" Guevara began to surface. Toward the end of the war, in September 1958, a woman's platoon went into battle: a first for the times.

From a motley group of visionaries—lost, hungry, and without enough weapons to go around—and in a surprisingly short period of time, the rebel army grew to thousands: several well-trained columns capable of coming out of the mountains and advancing the length of the country, liberating cities as they went. Just as important, the Cuban people supported their liberators in ways rarely seen before or since. Thousands of those who weren't directly involved warned the revolutionaries of approaching danger, hid people in their homes, supplied food and other provisions, carried messages, or simply stayed silent and out of the way.

On January 1, 1959, Batista and his inner circle fled. The July 26 Movement had won the war. It then continued the sometimes messy job of incorporating other progressive forces—those of the old Socialist Party (PSP, Moscow-oriented Communists), the Student Directorate in Havana, and other groups—into a cohesive governing body and began to construct a society that politically, economically, and socially was the antithesis of its predecessor. Had the United States observed a hands-off policy, this would have been difficult enough. Given the obstacles it devised to bring the revolution down, the task became titanic.

Fidel was the acknowledged leader, admired and beloved in almost every quarter. By February 1959, he was the country's new prime minister. In April the casinos were closed and Cuba's pristine beaches opened to the public. In May the first agrarian reform law was enacted. An urban reform law followed. In October a people's militia was established to protect a revolution already being sabotaged by the United States and disaffected Cubans. Neighborhood groups called Committees to Defend the Revolution (CDR) were also set up, creating a nationwide web of "people's eyes and ears" to guard against attack.

The next few years would see giant advances in the creation of a more just society: the nationalization of sugar mills and foreign oil interests, a literacy campaign that taught almost all Cubans to read and write, the establishment of free and universal health care, and an emphasis on putting people to work, building schools, creating day care centers, and retraining domestic workers and women who had been forced to work in the sex industry so they could use new skills to seek more dignified employment.

Coca-Cola, the iconic thirst quencher favored by a people deeply immersed in US culture, was no longer the popular soft drink. One of many commodities that disappeared or were in very short supply, it was replaced by Son, a substitute that never quite satisfied. More important, because shortages appeared and the revolution prioritized equal access, a rationing system was soon implemented. It affected almost all basic necessities, including food and clothing.

When I moved my family to Cuba in 1969, we opted for the ordinary ration book rather than the special one most foreigners had. I remember the five of us receiving three-quarters of a pound of meat every nine days, a liter of fresh milk a day for those under twelve, a can of condensed milk per person per month, three eggs a week for each of us. Coffee was in short supply. Nonsmokers, my partner at the time and I traded our cigarette ration for something more to our liking. My three older children were at boarding school all week and ate well there, so we were able to invite friends to eat with us on weekends. When one harvest or another came in, extra potatoes or vegetables appeared at market. There were lots of jokes about split peas, and lots of recipes made the rounds, often featuring something that might have been thrown away to create a new dish or making what we had last as long as possible. The knowledge that no one in Cuba went hungry mitigated the stringent rationing. I can't remember feeling deprived.

Although new global political configurations, the Cold War, and some important internal errors kept Cuba from the sort of rapid development it envisioned, making people's basic necessities rather than capitalist profit the priority enabled the revolution to fulfill dreams of universal health care, an educated population, and access to culture and sports. Even today, fifty-five years later and in its complicated transition to open markets while retaining its principal socialist gains, what has been maintained is astonishing.

In July 1960, the United States suspended its quota of Cuban sugar; the Soviet Union immediately agreed to buy that sugar at favorable prices. In September of that year Cuba nationalized all US banks. In January 1961, Washington broke diplomatic relations with Havana. The United States increased its program of covert and overt actions against the young revolution and in April 1961 launched a full-scale military attack, called Bay of Pigs in the United States and Playa Girón on the island. The Eisenhower and Kennedy administrations expected Cubans to rise up and join the mercenaries. What happened instead was that they defended their revolution and defeated the invaders in two days. The 1,200 mercenaries captured were later traded for $54 million dollars worth of medicine and baby food.

Subsequent years would see the Cuban Revolution developing its unique brand of *socialismo en español* (socialism in Spanish). US public intellectual and philosopher Susan Sontag[3] visited Cuba in 1969 and wrote perceptively: "Like all Revolutions, the Cuban one is a reorganization—and a vast release of human energy [. . .] this release of energy is experienced as 'liberating.' Even deprived of the right to go into private business or to see pornographic films, the great majority of Cubans feel vastly more free today than they ever did before the revolution."[4] Sontag remarked on the cultural nature of the revolution, differentiating it from the Old Left models in which changed relations of production were prioritized above all else. She pointed to Che Guevara's "Man and Socialism in Cuba" (1965) and its emphasis on creating a new consciousness as well as new economic relations.

From its inception, the Cuban Revolution saw itself as part of a global struggle. Even as it consolidated its own process, it looked to movements in Latin America, Africa, and Southeast Asia. "Two, three, many Vietnams" became a rallying cry. Cuba's goals were full independence and the right to design a responsive relationship between the people and their leaders. It contributed a great deal to world revolution, including the extraordinary generosity of its internationalist contingents of doctors, teachers, soldiers, and other experts still working in dozens of colonized and underdeveloped countries.

Sontag considered "the greatest discovery of the Cuban Revolution [to be] the invention of Cuban internationalism, that peculiarly intense form of fraternal international feeling [. . .]. Havana today," she wrote, after the revolution's first decade, "starkly denuded of commodities and comforts as it is, is vibrant with the conviction of being a world capital. [. . .] One feels more in the world, more in touch with events, in Havana, capital of this poor small Caribbean island, than one ever does in such genuinely provincial cities as Rome or Stockholm."

Many who have written about the Cuban Revolution have pointed to this internationalism, this sense of being part of a vast human community, this new consciousness so often mentioned by Che and Fidel, as indicative of change that is human as well as political. No one in the revolutionary pantheon embodied this spirit of politics as a set of human relationships more than the subject of this book, Haydée Santamaría.

Cuba became an example for people throughout Latin America and the world; to a great extent it still is. At the same time, its revolution never stopped aggravating the United States, its powerful neighbor to the north. A series of US presidents vowed to destroy the beautiful experiment, launching an economic blockade, a trade embargo, constant counterrevolutionary propaganda, outright military attack, and hundreds of covert military and sabotage actions aimed at bringing the project to failure.

For many years, the United States was able to prevent Cuba's natural allies from establishing diplomatic or trade relations with the island. The few nations that defied US threats, such as Mexico and Canada, served as bridges but were unable to make up for lost revenue. Cuba's adhesion to the Soviet Union saved it from early ruin but also tied it to policies that ultimately proved to be counterproductive. When the socialist bloc imploded in 1989 and 1990, the revolution once more found itself alone.

Although all these maneuvers, actions, and reactions have meant additional hardship for the Cuban people, the multipronged US campaign has not worked. The Cold War ended a quarter century ago, but this remnant of its politics continues: a woolly mammoth in a land of sun and palms. Despite the fact that sectors of the US business community and increasing numbers of lawmakers have pleaded for a different approach, a powerful but aging exile lobby continues to oppose the normalization of relations, holding US Cuba policy hostage. With slight shifts in one direction or another, the United States continued in what can only be described as a bully standoff against a country much smaller and much poorer, a country that wants nothing more than to be left alone to shape the future it has chosen. A relentless blockade and travel restrictions that are in place to this day have separated families and attempted to separate ideas.

The revolution itself has not been perfect; it is made of human beings: brilliant, creative, courageous, and fallible. All it has ever demanded has been its right, as a sovereign state, to make its own decisions, follow its own path. The Cuban Revolution's great achievements have been near-full employment, universal health care, free education from day care through university, and subsidized culture and sports. Important (although as yet inconclusive) strides toward gender and racial equality have been made. Cuba alone among nations has been able to stabilize its HIV/AIDS crisis—no meager list of accomplishments. Although it is poor, different priorities have made possible a degree of social change of which we can only dream.

Solidarity with other disenfranchised peoples and a generosity of spirit almost forgotten in the United States have characterized Cuba since the inception of its revolution. But new values are hard to sustain when faced with ongoing aggression and the exhaustion that comes when years pass and promises cannot be kept. The younger generation, with no memory of the

ravages of the neocolonialist state, has seen a return to a degree of individu-
alism and social fatigue. Some major problems, such as inadequate housing,
have eluded solution. New ones, such as exhaustion and substance abuse,
have emerged.

Currently some 36,000 Cubans emigrate each year, many of them having obtained professional degrees at no cost to themselves. Approximately a
third that many return from abroad, but these tend to be older people who
are no longer productive and require considerable state investment in their
health and well-being. As the country transitions from a socialist system to
include certain features of a market economy, corruption has also taken a
toll. The majority of Cubans, however, continue to reject a purely consum-
erist society and the distortions it brings. They are struggling to preserve
the rights and dignity the revolutionaries of 1959 sacrificed so much to win.

The Cuban Revolution's survival and the level of social welfare it has been
able to provide its people are nothing short of extraordinary. Its continued
existence seems miraculous. Mistakes? Yes, plenty of them. Wrong turns?
Some of those as well. Interested readers can consult hundreds of books on
all aspects of Cuban history and life.[5]

On December 17, 2014 US President Barack Obama and Cuban President
Raul Castro announced reestablishment of diplomatic relations between the
two countries. Ending the half-century blockade will take an act of Congress,
so the degree of real change will only unfold over time. We wait to see if this
is a change in method or in policy.

My purpose here is not to analyze the revolution's successes and failures
but simply provide some background for those who may not remember a
moment, 55 years ago, when a tiny island nation challenged a major world
power and threw off the imperialist yoke. I have begun in this way in order
to jog the collective memory, pique the interest of young activists, and set the
stage for the story I want to tell. It is the story of Haydée Santamaría, one of
the extraordinary women who made the Cuban Revolution possible.

Haydée Santamaría, 1970s. PHOTO BY MARGARET RANDALL.

# 2 WHY HAYDÉE?

... the mere mention of Haydée Santamaría signifies a world, an attitude, a sensibility, and also a Revolution, which she did not conceive of as confined to the land of José Martí but to the future of all our peoples.
— Mario Benedetti (1920 – 2009), Uruguayan poet and novelist

Haydée Santamaría was a heroine of the Cuban Revolution, a brilliant, strong but unassuming woman among powerful men. One of only two females among 160 males, she helped organize the 1953 attack on Moncada Barracks in Santiago de Cuba and fought on its front lines. Following that first military operation, when she was captured and shown her brother's eye and lover's mangled testicle to make her divulge information about their movement, she replied: "If you did that to them and they didn't talk, much less will I!"

Haydée — like Fidel, all who knew her called her by her first name — was a provincial woman who had never before left her island country. Yet during the revolutionary war she found the courage to travel to the United States, organize its Cuban community, and buy weaponry from Mafia thugs. After that war was won, despite growing up in a small rural village and never having gone past sixth grade, she founded and ran the most important cultural institution in Latin America, which drew artists and intellectuals such as Violeta Parra, Jean-Paul Sartre, Simone de Beauvoir, Laurette Séjourné, Julio Cortázar, Eduardo Galeano, Ernesto Cardenal, Idea Vilariño, and Gabriel García Márquez to visit and satiate their curiosity about that small nation with enormous dreams.

Haydée conceived of change and participated in actions—military as well as political—beyond those accessible to the vast majority of women in her time and place. She took enormous risks and avoided detection with an uncanny calm and remarkable talent for deception and disguise. She was one of the founders of Cuba's July 26 Movement and later its Communist Party (PCC), remaining at its highest levels of leadership throughout her life. Yet she had no interest in the positions of power such membership bestowed. She led by transgression.

In her work at Casa de las Américas, Haydée rendered ineffective the cultural blockade the United States tried so hard to establish, along with its diplomatic and economic counterparts, and protected and encouraged more than a few creative spirits persecuted during repressive periods in Cuba's revolutionary history. She was a courageous innovator, deeply sensitive to the needs of others, a bountiful mother, and warm friend.

Her life was also rife with contradictions. When she committed suicide, at the age of fifty-seven, Havana historian Eusebio Leal eulogized her, saying: "Haydée was Moncada's last victim." I prefer the word *casualty*. Haydée was not someone who allowed herself to be victimized by anyone or any circumstance. Yet she lived with profound loss and grief. There was Moncada, where she lost the two people she loved most—her brother, Abel, and fiancé, Boris Luis Santa Coloma—and whose brutal and sadistic deaths accompanied her for the rest of her life.

There were other losses as well: Che Guevara, with whom she shared the dream of Latin American liberation. Celia Sánchez, perhaps the only other woman who understood her completely and whose deep friendship helped her stand tall in a world of men. Other close friends, whose lives were cut short for one reason or another. Colleagues who abandoned the revolutionary project. And some dreams of social change that never came quickly or permanently enough for her vision of immediate justice.

Justice, revolution, loyalty: these were her mantras. Depression ran in her family, requiring sensitivity and compassion. Betrayals, of close comrades as well as ideals, pained her to the core. Armando Hart Dávalos, fellow revolutionary and the man she married after losing Santa Coloma, gave her a son and daughter and for a while provided love, stability and comradeship. Together they parented their biological children as well as a number of others, orphans from Latin American revolutionary struggles. When Hart left her, suddenly and without discussion, it was an additional blow. Just like revolution, marriage was forever in her worldview.

She was plagued by depressive episodes and periodically took to her bed in despair. Today we understand more about depression than we did back then: how debilitating it can be and what courage it takes to confront its ravages. Yet Haydée's work at Casa and other important projects were more than successful; they achieved a level of excellence and set standards of collectivity few have been able to match. All the children she raised described her as an extraordinary mother. She challenged power wherever and whenever she saw its corrosive damage and espoused feminist ideas long before the philosophy was accepted in Cuba. She produced and sustained more in the way of creative change than anyone I have known.

This is not a biography. I will provide enough data so the reader will have the "facts": birth, childhood, role in the Cuban Revolution, professional and family life. But my intention is to veer from the confines of traditional hagiography and probe deeply into the paradoxes, as only someone who trusts intuition as much as reason can. Further developing a genre I began to explore in *Che on My Mind*, I am interested in looking at tensions and trying to decipher how this woman negotiated multiple contradictions. This is an impressionist portrait, written by a poet rather than a historian. Mine is a rebel and feminist lens. First, I want to tell the reader why I have chosen to write about Haydée Santamaría.

I must say upfront that I loved Haydée, loved and admired her as a friend and as an exceptional twentieth-century woman: an extremely unique spirit, brilliant intellect, courageous and creative revolutionary, and generous human being. Even in death, she remains a mentor.

I first met her on my initial visit to Cuba in January 1967. I was living in Mexico City and had been invited to participate in *El encuentro con Rubén Darío*,[1] hosted by Casa de las Américas, the exemplary arts institution of which she was the director. That visit to "the first free territory in America" (as we called the country back then) was illuminating in all sorts of ways. But no part of the experience had a more profound or lasting impact than meeting Haydée.

She was a small woman and ordinary in appearance; some might even say plain. Slightly stooped and with the telltale rise in her chest common to those who suffer from severe asthma, she nevertheless carried herself with a dignity that stopped you in your tracks.

I remember her in simple pants and shirt, sitting on the floor talking animatedly with groups of visitors. And I remember her delighting in a hand-embroidered peasant dress someone had given her. She didn't flaunt the latest in elegance or fashion but was vain about her hair, often wrapping her head in a scarf or turban or indulging in one of several wigs. I imagined these as expedient solutions to bad hair days for someone I doubt had much time for beauty parlors. She always had an inhaler in her hand.

Her piercing hazel eyes didn't flinch; they grabbed you and held on, sometimes almost accusatory, always inviting. You could lose yourself in those eyes but might not be able to bear what you found there. You understood that she held you to standards you would find hard to achieve. We all knew her story; the drama she had been forced to endure might have seemed exaggerated or even macabre if she hadn't been right there in front of you, genuinely interested in every aspect of your life, conversationally at ease and serene.

You sensed she saw through you to a place you yourself might discover years down the road. But it was her voice that made the most profound impression: what she said and how she said it. She spoke directly, forcefully, clearly, often wandering and seemingly lost until she brought her discourse back to a more linear configuration. What others shrouded in hyperbole she put out there, simply, as if it were the most natural thing in the world. And coming from her it was. You believed her without question, and that proved to be a good idea 99 percent of the time. But you weren't doing the math, not in her aura. Essence was more important than detail.

Our relationship deepened after I went to live in Cuba in 1969. I was like many whose lives she touched, in that she never became the sort of close friend who frequented my home. Yet we had an immediate and deep connection, and I experienced an intimacy that has remained with me. I remember some of our conversations verbatim. I suspect that almost everyone who crossed paths with Haydée felt a similar connection, for she had an uncanny ability to see, listen, and empathize. Until 1980, when she died and I left Cuba, we shared moments that included formal interviews as well as private conversations. Her suicide still sometimes wakes me at night, bereft and shaking.

I have written about Haydée in several prose texts and poems.[2] The memoir I published about my eleven years in Cuba is dedicated to her.[3] That dedication reads: "To Haydée Santamaría, who took the secrets with her." I wasn't referring to those supposed secrets the revolution's detractors are so quick to imagine must exist, hiding this or that error or betrayal. Neither did I mean purely personal secrets, such as those we all keep. I meant a knowing that only someone as pure as Haydée possesses and projects quite naturally.

Despite its clichéd connotation, I use the word *pure* with intention. There are people for whom no other adjective fits. Revolutions—great, complex social upheavals that turn society on end and, if successful, change the way we relate to one another—are made by all manner of people. They necessarily think outside the box, are courageous, and willing to make enormous personal sacrifices. But like all humans, they also have their contradictions. Some start out with a vision that bends and erodes as time goes on. Most believe some future end justifies means that fall short of espousing their proclaimed values. When those once engaged in guerrilla warfare must switch gears and manage the affairs of state, certain compromises may become necessary. There are also those who jump ship at some point along the way, suspicious of an ideological turn, dragged down by difficult times, or unable to continue making do without the creature comforts.

In my lifetime, Vietnam's Ho Chi Minh and South Africa's Nelson Mandela have been exceptions, exceptional. Among the many good men and women of the Cuban Revolution, a few embody this purity—a particular combination of innocence, vision, courage, brilliance, creativity, inclusiveness, and genuine humility. I think of Fidel,[4] first and foremost. I think of Ernesto "Che" Guevara,[5] Celia Sánchez,[6] and Haydée Santamaría. There are others, of course, but these four names are at the top of my list. I do not mean they are perfect, whatever that may mean, only unwavering in their search for justice and profoundly principled.

Each was his or her own person, shadowed by contradictions, capable of regret or egregious error, perhaps even going down the wrong political path for a time. Each may have hurt others as he or she searched for the greater good. And each was a product of a particular place, time, culture, and historic necessity, bound by those limitations even when reaching beyond them. But all were ahead of the time they inhabited and ultimately transcended that time, place, culture, and necessity.

I had written about Haydée, but never deeply enough. I hadn't asked the right questions or ventured enough answers, which is what I hope to do here: bringing my own imaginings to the clues she left. The books and articles written by others unfortunately range from extremely partial to frustratingly superficial. Eulogies at the time of her death and remembrances on its anniversaries are among the most moving testimonies. Her closest associates and family members, including both her biological children, are mostly gone.

In order to create the portrait I hope to bring to life, I traveled to Cuba in April 2014, where I was able to research archives, interview people who had been close to my subject, visit her birthplace and childhood home, and gather material from different sources. Fortunately, I am at a point on my own journey where I consider no hero to be beyond a probing lens. In fact, I understand that only when we are willing to apply that lens will we bring them into the sort of focus that allows an honest exploration of what made them so extraordinary.

In Haydée's case, it helps to be able to go back and understand what life was like for women in Cuba at mid-twentieth century. They inhabited a narrow space, and depending on economic status, education, and culture, it might have been narrower still. As a woman, particularly one who lived at a time so constrictive to women's opportunity and agency, Haydée transcended gender, class, racial, sexual, and cultural prisons. She didn't do this through economic status, formal education, theoretical study, or by spending time deconstructing the hypotheses of her day, though all these played a role. Her childhood on an early twentieth-century Cuban sugar plantation had given her a hard look at exploitation, the inequality between the bosses and those who cut the cane or labored in the mill. She was a woman of action, and action informed her ideology as surely as Martí,[7] Marx, Lenin, her younger brother Abel, and Fidel.

She completed only a primary education, at a one-room plantation schoolhouse where a single teacher taught all the grades. Was it common at the time for girls not to seek further schooling, or was there some other reason she didn't go on to high school and university? What were the educational expectations common to her class and gender? She was certainly bright and curious enough that one would have thought a higher education was something she'd have been eager to pursue. From a traditional immigrant family, did she endure pressure to marry young?

In the early 1950s she traveled to Havana with her younger brother, Abel. Several texts emphasize the fact that she went "to take care of him," the proverbial housekeeper and cook. He as well as she made it clear that this wasn't the case. Knowing she was passionate about social change, he was rescuing her from a conservative, stultifying family life. They were both members of the leftist Orthodox Party[8] enraged by Fulgencio Batista's 1952 coup.[9] Jesús Menéndez's[10] organization of sugar workers in their native Las Villas also had had an impact on Abel and, through him, on her.

Haydée had long been influenced by her brother's ideas. In Havana she met his comrades, including Fidel Castro, "that tall guy who flicked his cigar ashes all over my clean floor," and quickly became involved in their work. She and Melba Hernández were the only women who participated in the July 26, 1953, assault on Moncada Barracks, although other women were active behind the scenes. Abel and Haydée's fiancé, Boris Luis, were tortured to death following the attack. Haydée and Melba survived, were tried, and sentenced to seven months in prison. Fidel and the other male survivors were given much longer prison terms but released through a general amnesty in 1955.

The attack on Moncada Barracks signaled the group's appearance on the political map. One hundred sixty rebels took part in that action, which was a military failure but is credited with initiating the armed struggle that would liberate Cuba five and a half years later. Although Haydée was one of the only two women directly involved, her two sisters were also part of their movement. They supported the action but stayed home to be with their parents because it seemed more than likely that many of those taking part would not survive.[11]

During the war against the Batista dictatorship, Haydée did what she had to do, creatively and responsibly. When ordered to travel to the United States to buy weaponry from the Mafia, she reported having been terrified. But she carried out that risky mission and was successful in securing what the rebels needed. Less well known is the crucial role she played in organizing the exile community, dealing with contentious differences and achieving a tactical unity.

She sewed bullets into tiny individual pockets on the undersides of the circle skirts that were popular then; that's how she got many of them into Cuba. Back home, she played an active part in preparing the uprising in Santiago de Cuba. And in the Havana underground, when it was her job to send men out to place bombs in strategic locations, she always sent those she knew would hate the task.

Of that experience, she has said:

I think it has to be difficult for people to be violent, to go to war, but you've got to be violent and go to war if it's necessary. . . . What you can't lose in that kind of situation is your humanity. . . . When someone had to place a bomb during the war, and in the underground sometimes I was the one who had to decide who was going to do that. . . . I always chose the best, the one who had the highest consciousness, the greatest human qualities, so whoever it was wouldn't get used to placing bombs, wouldn't get pleasure out of placing bombs, so it would always hurt him to [have to do that].[12]

Haydée had an unwavering belief in human beings; she appreciated them in the full range of their identities and possibilities. And she had interesting insights about the differences and interactions among groups and individuals. I remember her once talking to me about meeting Ho Chi Minh on her first trip to what was then North Vietnam. She described his small figure standing at the end of a long room and then watching him walk toward her. "I never knew if Ho Chi Minh was the kind of man he was because he was Vietnamese," she said, "or if the Vietnamese are how they are because of Ho Chi Minh."[13] She didn't need to say more. I pondered her observation for years, and when I myself visited Vietnam it was never far from my consciousness.

Following the end of the Cuban war, in January 1959 Haydée was charged with founding and heading an arts institution that would do nothing less than break the US blockade. Along with its economic and diplomatic counterparts, the United States had established a cultural boycott in order to isolate and destroy the revolution. Haydée's sixth-grade education hardly prepared her for the complexity or subtleties of the job. She had never been to college, never studied art or literature, but carried out that endeavor brilliantly, making Casa de las Américas a place where the world's greatest creative spirits felt at home. Because of her legacy, it continues to be such a place.

She looked the world's great artists and intellectuals in the eye, noticed and remembered their most intimate concerns, and gave so generously of herself that they fell instantly in love. And she was open to all their expressive manifestations. Within Cuba itself, her vision enabled her to see talent in those who were spurned by party hacks or misunderstood by correct-liners who preferred the safety of mediocrity to the uncertainty of the new. Without her patronage, the innovators of La nueva trova (New Song Movement) would not have become who they are today.[14] She sought artists and writers from among the most marginalized populations. She respected nonconformity and embraced authenticity. Inclusivity was natural to her. She resisted the clichéd socialist realist art that was being promoted in the Soviet Union. She listened, paid attention, and learned.

I don't mean to give the impression that Haydée disparaged party discipline or refused to go along with the leadership's decisions. She was part of that leadership, although without relinquishing her integrity, individuality, or capacity for criticism. She was as disciplined and loyal as the best of them but never unquestioning. Whenever and wherever she saw injustice, she challenged it. One of her attributes that most interests me is her ability to walk a courageous but fragile critical line, especially as a woman.

Another aspect of Haydée's thought process that excites my mind was her complex relationship to nationalism. I believe nationalism to be one of the most troubling tendencies of our time, provoking racist or xenophobic policies and justifying terrible crimes (such as genocide in its most extreme form).

An island is always besieged territory, and Cuba is no exception. A small island can and often does become a political football. Throughout its history, Cuba has been invaded, appropriated, and occupied by one major power after another. A heavy dose of nationalism was certainly necessary for Fidel and his revolutionary movement to win the support needed to liberate the country. Haydée, too, embodied this feeling. She often talked about Cuba's sun, beaches, and royal palms, saying that for those three things alone it was worth waking each morning. She had such a profound love of homeland, in fact, that after the amnesty of 1955 she refused to leave with her comrades for Mexico; in her own words, she was afraid she "might not be able to come home."

Yet Haydée's work at Casa involved honoring other lands and their artists, making room for their work and their ideas within the Cuban paradigm, and—precisely because she was working with a group of people known for their creative idiosyncrasies—learning to understand and respect other cultures and ways of being in the world. This is antithetical to extreme nationalism. It provides a balance, and I think in time came to temper the rough edges of the Cuban nationalism she too had embraced.

What she created at Casa was a model that the country's other institutions respected and some tried to emulate. The way Haydée positioned herself, the way she used what she learned from the world's artists to enrich the Cuban experience, offers a great deal to be analyzed and understood. In Cuba, the revolution's generous internationalism also provides a counterpoint to what might have remained a highly nationalist experience. Cold War tensions certainly favored the latter, but Fidel and the Cuban Communist Party emphasized the importance of the former.

Cuba's participation in Angola and other African battlefields began in 1975, five years before Haydée's death. She was fervent in her support of those campaigns. The schools for foreign students that existed on Isle of Youth (formerly Isle of Pines) also excited her imagination; students from some of the poorest and most war-ravaged countries studied there without cost. And the revolution made sure their cultural traditions accompanied them—in memory and relationships, music, art, and native foods.

During Chile's short-lived democratic revolution in the early seventies, there was a great deal of collaboration between the two countries. Nicaragua's Sandinista Revolution was victorious just a year before Haydée died, and she traveled there in her last months, so she also knew firsthand about the teachers and doctors and other specialists Cuba sent to that Central American nation. One of them was a niece.[15] She would not live to see the crucial aid Cuba gave to other parts of Latin America and the world. Still, at Casa and throughout the revolution in broader terms, she breathed and contributed to the internationalism that remains one of its defining features.

Haydée never let gender discrimination diminish her or prevent her from doing what she knew she had to do. Which is not to say that many of her male comrades didn't regard her with the kind of pseudo respect with which they treated women—back then and still. To a disappointing degree this formalistic approach to gender equality continues to exist—in Cuba and almost everywhere. In her personal life, Haydée went to elaborate lengths to try to make the point that gender discrimination is unjust.

She was also conscious of racial inequality. She spoke about how she was criticized as a child for befriending the black children in her community. Cuban filmmaker Gloria Rolando has spoken about the difficulties in getting her documentaries about Cuba's black history exhibited but says Casa de las Américas always supported her work.[16] This, as well as the fact that there are so many more people of color heading departments at Casa than are visible in revolutionary leadership overall, is a testament to Haydée's legacy.

Upon her death, because she chose suicide and despite an exemplary revolutionary life, the Cuban leadership failed to honor Haydée as she deserved. For years, at least in certain quarters, you could sense a palpable discomfort around the fact that she took her life. Some silently accused her of cowardice, some felt betrayed, some simply did not know what to do with their complex emotions, and many short-changed her memory in different ways. Those who worked with or were otherwise close to her mourned but were powerless to buck the conservative current. In recent years this situation has changed. Suicide does not provoke such blanket condemnation, and Haydée's undeniable luminosity has sparked a degree of reconsideration. Still, the memorial she deserves has yet to materialize.

Haydée had been a founding and highly valued member of a clandestine revolutionary organization, the July 26 Movement, previously *Moncadistas*, as many of those involved in that first action called themselves. Later she was one of the initiators of the Cuban Communist Party. She served on its politburo and remained on its central committee until her death. Yet she did what her brother Abel asked of her first and later what Fidel instructed. Until taking on Casa de las Américas, she followed rather than led. And even during her tenure at Casa, she was subject to the larger political apparatus. At the same time, often at great personal risk, she never toed a strict party line, nor could she abide the bureaucracy inherent in such organizations.

From Moncada on she participated in many of the revolution's pivotal moments. She was imprisoned following that action and, when she was released from prison, played a major role in disseminating Fidel Castro's defense speech—the programmatic text that came to be known as "History Will Absolve Me." She held leadership roles in both the Santiago and Havana underground movements and traveled outside the country to buy arms. She was indispensable on several fronts yet never, during the insurrection or following victory, achieved high military rank.

In 1967 she presided over the internationally important Latin American Organization for Solidarity Conference (OLAS), held in Havana. She was always one of the Cuban Revolution's few exceptional women; in close to sixty years their number has grown but it has yet to approximate the clear dominance of men. For too many of those years the Cuban hierarchy considered feminism a dirty word. Even, perhaps particularly, its mass women's organization, the Federation of Cuban Women (FMC), disparaged the philosophy. The Cuban Party subscribed to the international communist dictum that gender analysis would divide the working class and weaken the unity necessary to confront outside threats.

Haydée knew instinctively that this was wrong. Although she didn't refer to herself as a feminist, she was open to and appreciative of feminist ideas. I had an experience with Haydée that illustrates her concern for the degradation of women. In 1970, soon after I moved to the island, she asked me to help judge the yearly pageant to choose a carnival queen and her two attendants. I was appalled. I hated such contests and couldn't imagine validating them with my presence. But if Haydée asked, I couldn't say no.

Distraught at the task before me, I wrote a short text about why beauty pageants have no place in revolution. When the event was over, I handed it to a reporter from the official PCC newspaper, *Granma*. The next morning it appeared on its front page. Several years later, when I finally had the opportunity to ask Haydée why she had subjected me to such discomfort when she could have made any man's day by sending him, she replied: "Because I knew you would hate it, and find a way to help us put an end to such affairs. Which you did, as I remember, with your excellent article!"

Haydée's authenticity and loyalty encouraged her to take chances. She was seldom wrong but often disappointed. She rarely spoke ill of anyone. I think now of the months before her death, when 125,000 Cubans fled the island en masse and those who stayed subjected them to epithets, to psychological and even physical violence. How she must have hated those displays of vitriol and pseudo patriotism! Looking back, I am sure that the whole Mariel exodus must have caused her a terrible sadness. Could she have felt overwhelmed by this evidence of social revolution's crass underbelly?

When a close associate left the country, she was shattered; unless you were as convinced as she was that devotion to the revolution was the highest human calling, it must have been difficult to work with her. Yet her colleagues have written volumes about that privilege. They speak of the enormous attention she paid to each detail of what went on at the institution and about her far-ranging eye and profoundly democratic work ethic that made Casa a special place, unique even among other such places on the country's cultural map. It was that eye and that work ethic that make Casa, three decades after her death, a place that continues to function as the revolution itself should function but often doesn't: engaging in truly democratic decision making and inviting new generations to take leadership, thereby ensuring both continuity and change.

Throughout Haydée's tenure at Casa, artists on the cutting edge of new ideas, genres, and imaginaries visited Cuba and lent their allegiance to the sociopolitical experiment that was taking place. Since her death, they have continued to come. They write about what they see and feel. In and outside their work, they spread the word, breaking through a worn but still obstinate blockade and exposing the lies disseminated by US-based Radio Martí, sectors of the exile community in Miami, and other sources of counterrevolutionary propaganda.

The Cuban people, through Casa, come in contact with a variety of interesting ideas and with the new poetry, novels, theater, painting, sculpture, photography, dance, and music being made in other parts of the world. It is in this way that Cuban intellectuals and artists have been able to participate in the great conversations that have characterized international art and literary communities through the last half of the twentieth century and into the twenty-first. Although they live on an island, one that has been blockaded by the United States going on six decades now, Cubans are as in touch with avant-garde art and literature as citizens of Paris or Buenos Aires, Mexico City or New York, Johannesburg or Bangkok.

Much of this can be traced to Haydée's vision. A woman of simple country origin and scant formal education, she understood art as the highest form of human expression and a necessary component of social change. Even today, so many years after her death, you can go through Casa's doors and feel her presence. To those of us who knew her in life, it is a visceral experience. For Haydée art—all creative expression—was a form of revolution, one that feeds, reflects, stretches, strengthens, and pushes forward the struggle for justice.

Martí's concept of Our America—an organically unified continent—was especially important to Fidel, Haydée, and others of the Centennial Generation (the generation that came of political age around the centenary of his birth). At Casa, Haydée pierced the walls separating the countries of the Americas, even those where languages other than Spanish are spoken. She also recognized the growing pockets of Latin America that exist within the United States, paying attention to work by Chicanos and Latinos living inside "the belly of the beast" and bringing them into the great discussions about identity, ownership, and resistance taking place south of the border. In this way she also enabled them to contribute to those discussions.

Under her tutelage, Casa's important literary contest, held every year in a variety of categories, branched out to include the literatures of Portuguese-speaking Brazil, Guaraní-speaking Paraguay, the French-, Dutch-, and English-speaking Antilles, the art of dozens of indigenous cultures, Latino literature in the United States, and more. She promoted writing by women. She provided space to gay artists at a time when ignorance and fear prevented them from being accepted by the revolution's reigning bureaucracy. Each year, when the contest judges gathered to read the hundreds of entries and award prizes in a growing number of categories, she would make a point of telling them not to worry about the political message in the texts they would read. "Remember, this is a literary contest," she would insist.

Her methods were ingenious, creative, often surprising.

Her conversational style, privately as well as in public, also issued from her unique way of positioning herself in the world. She employed a simple lexicon even when putting forth complex ideas. She often failed to bring sentences to their expected conclusions, and her recorded talks are as scattered as they are emotional. But no one ever doubted what she meant to say—because she said it perfectly.

At times she rambled, but she always came back to the point she was making, her detour having pierced membranes of feeling that enriched it enormously. Her silences were as exquisite and powerful as the words she uttered. Other spokespeople for the Cuban Revolution—Fidel, Che, Raúl Roa,[17] Carlos Rafael Rodríguez,[18] and Armando Hart—gave expertly constructed lessons in history or economics. Haydée's voice was of a different timbre. And this was not only a gender issue. There were plenty of women among the Cuban leadership or at the grassroots level whose speeches were well ordered, even powerful. Haydée's discourse was informed by her magical thinking, the same magical thinking that made it possible for her to understand and embrace a myriad of creative spirits.

I have written about Haydée, thought about her, dreamed her presence, and pondered her dilemmas. She has come to me at unexpected moments, bringing a comforting word or revealing something about myself I thought I knew but didn't. Because, like her, I am largely self-taught, she has made me less inhibited by my own lack of formal education. The dimensions of her sacrifice and grief put my own in perspective. She continues to push me to risk but also to slow down and pay attention. I am constantly amazed at how advanced her thinking and action were, especially at a time when women were still considered helpmeets and servers, when precious few were able to fight their way to positions of power. Time and my own experience have also taught me to respect some of the contradictions that tore at her equilibrium.

For years I did not feel up to writing about Haydée Santamaría. Later I believed I was too old and would no longer be able to endure the fieldwork required. My partner, Barbara, convinced me it was now or never. At the beginning of 2014, I proposed the idea for this book to Gisela Fosado, my editor at Duke University Press. She supported it enthusiastically. A couple of months later I was in Cuba, interviewing those who knew my subject, going through archives, and gathering material.

I wanted to visit Encrucijada and the Constancia sugar mill, now renamed Abel Santamaría, hoped to see what she saw and breathe the air she breathed. It was encouraging to find generous support from those who loved Haydée as I do. I was moved that almost everyone with whom I spoke expected me to explore the complexities as well as the heroism.

What constitutes a hero? How to evoke the condition without resorting to stereotypes or creating a one-dimensional image? Much of the complexity inherent in memorializing Haydée, as I've said, comes from the fact that she committed suicide. It was not a choice that was easily accepted by the PCC and others, especially in 1980. As with the Catholic Church, an institution that rejects suicide because one's life belongs to God, Communists rejected it back then because they believed one's life belonged to the party. Haydée was mourned in a Havana funeral parlor, like any ordinary citizen, rather than at the Plaza of the Revolution, an honor befitting her revolutionary stature. For years after her death, her memory carried a burden of hesitancy in some quarters.

In the end, Haydée's personal history guaranteed her respect. Still, as a woman she remained an exception to the rule. Was she a token? Outside Casa, how much authority did she really have? I often wonder what went on behind closed doors when, expected to go along with some mistaken policy or witnessing opportunism, she must have disagreed with a passion that was hers alone. Yet I'm sure her party discipline was impeccable. Although she would not have voiced disagreement publicly, I cannot imagine her remaining silent within party chambers.

In her best-known talk about the origins of the Cuban Revolution, published in many languages, she says: "For me being a communist is not about belonging to a party; for me being a communist is to embrace a certain attitude about life."[19] I am interested in exploring what it cost her personally and politically to walk such an uncharted line between power and powerlessness.

Haydée described the pain of revolution by evoking childbirth:

When my son Abel was born I suffered some very difficult moments, moments like those any woman experiences when she's about to give birth, very difficult. The pains were tremendous, they tore at my entrails, but I found the strength to keep from crying, screaming or cursing. When one has such pain it is natural to cry, to scream, to curse. So where does the strength not to do so come from? It comes from the fact that you are having a child. That's when I realized what Moncada had been . . . we were able to resist because we knew something great was being born.[20]

She was close to her children and deeply concerned about the conditions under which all children lived. I remember how surprised I was when, on a visit to her home, she rather conspiratorially led me up the stairs to her bedroom, opened the closet door, and showed me a collage of photographs. There were pictures of the children of friends and colleagues, sent to her by people she knew well and some perhaps whom she'd met only casually. Right away I spotted two small snapshots of my own Gregory, Sarah, Ximena, and Ana. I had sent them to her from Mexico, just after we met. Why? Probably because I wanted this extraordinary woman to have images of those who were most important in my life. I could not have guessed she would place them, among others, on the inside of her bedroom closet door.

Haydée, as I say, gave birth to a son and a daughter, Abel Enrique and Celia María. He became a lawyer, she an astrophysicist and also, in the last years of her life, a member of the Fourth International. When I lived there, Trotsky was almost ignored in Cuban schools; the revolution was beholden to the Soviet Union, and its educational curriculum tended to follow that country's version of history. But a number of Cuban Communists who were more inclined toward independent thought read Trotsky with interest.

Armando Hart[21] had the Russian revolutionary's books on his shelf and shared them with his daughter. Before Abel and Celia's tragic death in an automobile accident in 2008, Celia gave a number of speeches and wrote some illuminating texts for international Trotskyist publications. Her adhesion to Trotsky's ideology never conflicted with her love for or defense of the Cuban Revolution or her admiration for Fidel. Her ideas in this respect, especially that of permanent revolution, bore similarities to those evident in Che Guevara's late writing.

It would be 2005 before Hart published an article critical of Stalinism, in which he pointed out that, because the revolutionary leader had never traveled outside the Soviet Union, he lacked the broad culture possessed by Lenin and others. Among many other salient points Hart makes, he writes: "In order to promote revolutionary policy, one must understand the mobilizing importance of art and culture, understand that in these the basis of our redeeming ideas reside."[22]

Despite its rejection by the Cuban party, I don't imagine her husband's critique of Stalin seemed unusual or unsettling to Haydée. I believe she shared his views. I also think she was less concerned with the finer points of ideological sparring than with how social change manifests itself on the ground. Furthermore, in her expansive reading her tendency was always to add rather than subtract.

I want to explore Haydée's relationship with her children. From what I have been able to gather from listening to Haydée and reading Celia María, she was a passionately loving mother and also expected no less from her children than the highest standards of idealism, exemplary behavior, and sacrifice. Celia María has written about receiving a box of dolls one childhood birthday, being allowed to play with them for a single day, and then being instructed by her mother to pick the one she wanted to keep and give the others to children who didn't have access to such bounty.

In this context, the way in which Haydée took her life is noteworthy. I am haunted by the knowledge that she shot herself in the home she shared with her children, both young adults at the time. Some of my interviewees told me that her son and daughter were home, others say only her son. He was the one who found her. That act, perhaps shaped by desperation and certainly removed in her mind from the impact it would have on her progeny, had to mark the latter for the remainder of their days. On the other hand, there is evidence that her suicide may have been calculated and deliberate. About her last days, Silvio Rodríguez has said: "She was saying good-bye. I got her to write a dedication in her book *Haydée habla del Moncada*. She wrote 'Silvio, understand me and love me.'"[23]

Most people I interviewed felt that Haydée was out of control when she killed herself. A few believe she was absolutely sane. One saw it as a final act of free will. Celia María, in a moving elegy, wrote:

> We have no choice but to respect those who decide they would rather be dead than alive. The old cliché about revolutionaries not committing suicide (she used to tell us this herself) is so foolish that just a few names are enough to refute it. . . . Defarge decided he was more useful to the cause of the proletariat dead than alive. . . . Who would say that Violeta didn't give "Thanks to Life" honestly, and journey into death without fear, sure of her decision.[24]

Despite her efforts to overcome them, however, the pain Celia María endured at her mother's suicide can be felt in a further fragment from this same text: "A single detail escapes me: I am her daughter or was, and objectively speaking she left me alive in her death, surrounded by other living dead. . . ."[25] I don't believe there is a way we, who do not choose that route, can decipher or make sense of suicide. It is always a mystery to those who remain.

In her personal life, Haydée was burdened with ghosts who never left her side: her brother Abel, her early fiancé Boris Luis Santa Coloma (who many told me was the great love of her life), and scores of other comrades who had been killed during the struggle to overthrow Batista. Year after year, every time she was called upon to speak about Moncada, her first words were for those she had loved and lost. She emphasized their immortality in struggle and reiterated that without their sacrifice the revolution would not exist.

But those who heard her tell the story knew that each comrade's face was indelibly seared into her memory. Rather than time healing those wounds, they remained open, raw. She could rise above them when her duties demanded, and she did. But once out of the public eye and alone again, I'm sure she heard their voices, saw their faces, relived the pain of their absence.

For two decades, Haydée Santamaría and Armando Hart had what appeared to be the perfect marriage. Dedication, struggle, and survival had brought them together. She often said that during the insurrectional period Armando was so bad at clandestine life she wished he would just stay in prison—where she knew he'd be safe. He was clearly the theoretician, one of the architects of the country's 1961 literacy campaign, and responsible for a number of welcome shifts in Cuban educational and cultural policy. She was illuminated, passionate, spontaneous. Separately, each played an important role in the construction of the new society. Together they seemed an example of what a revolutionary marriage could be. Whatever else Armando Hart may have been to Haydée, he provided comfort in a long relationship that had seen many dramatic moments.

And then he left her.

Looking at a relationship from the outside, we can never know what issues unite or create divisions, what failures of one member of a couple become intolerable to the other, what may finally make life together impossible. Midlife crisis? A younger woman? Rumors abounded at the time. I preferred to ignore them then, and they seem superfluous to me now as well. Two people of such proven trajectory and unquestionable brilliance clearly also had their frailties and passions. As deeply as I loved and admired Haydée, I can imagine that living with her may not have been easy. Their separation took place shortly before Haydée took her life and may have weighed on her decision, but it never seemed to me to be the central reason for that act. I don't believe a single event, but many, compelled Haydée to choose death. It was as if she had come to the end of a journey.

Other possible "reasons" were whispered from Cuban to Cuban during the terrible days following her suicide. She had been devastated by Celia Sánchez's death from cancer earlier that same year. Celia, another great woman of the Cuban Revolution, had been a close friend. In terms of integrity and in other important ways, they were like identical twins in an inner circle in which women were rare. For Haydée, Celia's death meant not only the loss of that friendship but also the disappearance of the person closest to Fidel. According to her daughter, Celia María, "Above all else, between one tear and another, [my mother] told me, 'Now we must worry about Fidel. Who will care for him like Celia did?'"[26]

There had been other excruciating losses, such as Che's death a dozen years earlier, and with it a delay in the dream of Latin American liberation they shared. An automobile accident several months before the end had almost taken Haydée's own life, leaving her with chronic pain. Disillusionment with certain tendencies evident in the revolution at the time may also have troubled her. And then there was the ongoing exhaustion from so much loss, what today we call post-traumatic stress disorder (PTSD). I will leave further speculation for later.

Haydée (in foreground), possibly on the occasion of her
first Communion with siblings Aida, Abel, and Aldo.
PHOTO COURTESY CASA DE LAS AMÉRICAS.

# 3 EARLY LIFE

Life on a sugar plantation was limited back then, even for a rural family
of the petite bourgeoisie . . .
—Haydée Santamaría

I am going back in time, moving through layers of legend, memory, through
stories both apocryphal and real.[1] Most stories are some combination of
both. Three or four decades don't seem like much when looking for a woman
whose imprint on history was so great. Some of those who knew her are still
alive and some, like me, continue to hold her piercing eyes in ours, preserve
the sound of her voice, feel her presence at unexpected moments. Each of
us carries a different set of memories, and some have faded unevenly—as
memories do—their images eroded by time, weight, relationship to the
roads we've traveled. Shifts in meaning make for a thickening transparency.

As the great Colombian novelist Gabriel García Márquez once said, "What
matters in life is not what happens to you but what you remember and how
you remember it." This is true in our own life and as we try to remember the
lives of others. But the larger those lives, the more room there is for myth
and memory layered upon memory; until warp and weave flow together in
a fabric that may defy decipherment. I am a code breaker now, fleeing even
my own preconceptions, places that feel too familiar or not familiar enough.

I'm headed for the municipality of Encrucijada, in cane field–blanketed central Cuba. When Haydée was born and grew up, this was Las Villas province. Since the administrative reorganization that took place in 1976, it is divided into Cienfuegos, Sancti Spíritus, and Villa Clara. It was to what we now call Villa Clara that Haydée's Spanish immigrant ancestors arrived from Galicia and made a life for themselves and their descendants. She was the oldest child of her generation, born at a sugar refinery called Constancia, near the village of Encrucijada, on December 30, 1922.

Or was it December 26 or 31? There has been some confusion. Her government-issued certificate records her birth as having taken place on February 26, 1923. It is her baptismal paper that has the correct date. Haydée liked to celebrate on December 31 because it was the more festive occasion. She was known, throughout her life, for an aggressive certainty. Once she'd made up her mind, it wasn't easy to sway her. Growing up in a family of strong women, she came to this trait easily.

There is a story about her paternal grandmother, María Pérez de Castro, having suffered a coronary thrombosis that kept her out of commission for several days. When she came to on December 31, 1922, and discovered her granddaughter had arrived, she proclaimed that to be the child's birthday. Into adulthood, Haydée herself was uncertain about exactly when she came into this world: "You know, I only found out I hadn't been born on the thirty-first when I got married and saw my birth certificate. I went to my parents and said, 'Wasn't I born on the thirty-first?'"[2]

Her older sister Aida said their mother had a little notebook, in which she wrote: "Haydée was born on December 30, 1922 at 9 a.m."[3] And Aida's daughter Niurka also told me her aunt was born on the thirtieth.[4] I believe this to be the date.

Haydée continually invented and reinvented her life as her curiosity, need to escape "a good but conservative family,"[5] and relentless pursuit of justice demanded. Secrets came easily to her. She pulled them on and took them off like a comfortable pair of shoes. But they also held the allure of fantasy and often became the kernel of an elaborate joke or bit of playacting that delighted those around her. From childhood on, family and friends loved her mischievous nature. Remembering her today, many recall that nature as evidence that she grew up happy and her later experiences alone brought on the bouts of depression.

Much later, her facility with secrets served her in another way. With the demands of clandestine struggle, her capacity for changing her appearance,

Haydée at Encrucijada, 1940s. PHOTO COURTESY CASA DE LAS AMÉRICAS.

apparent age, social status, and culture helped her carry out dangerous missions and then disappear, often in plain sight of those hunting her down.

Joaquina Cuadrado and Benigno Santamaría had five children. For whatever reason, they wanted to give them all names beginning with *A*. They may not have realized that Haydée commences with *H*, since that letter is silent in Spanish. The local official who recorded the birth may also have had his own ideas about the spelling. And so their firstborn was unique, even insofar as her name is concerned.

The story around Haydée's name doesn't end with the addition of the *H*. It seems that her mother wanted to call her Aida, but her mother-in-law, through thrombosis and all, favored Haydée (she had read *The Count of Monte Cristo*, and Haydée was the name of one of its female characters). This mother-in-law, not a woman to be trifled with, usually got her way. Joaquina had to content herself with naming her second daughter Aida.

Joaquina and Benigno married in Cuba on April 5, 1922. Haydée was born on the next-to-last day of that year. Her sister Aida Maximiliana came into the world on April 27, 1925; Aldo Miguel on September 29, 1926; Abel Benigno on October 20, 1927. And then, eleven years later, on February 24, 1938, when Joaquina was fifty, she gave birth to Ada.

Since first meeting Haydée in 1967 and learning that she was born and grew up on a sugar plantation in the Cuban countryside, I'd had dreams of visiting that bucolic place. Encrucijada was founded in 1850 and incorporated in 1910. I longed to see what her eyes saw, although I imagined it might look different with so many revolutionary changes over the years. One of the most interesting things about revolution is precisely what changes and how.

Then again, landscape always retains something of its original character. I wanted to breathe in the sweet, molasses-impregnated atmosphere of the mill, listen to the machinery that still deafens as it presses juice from the cane, and watch the smoke rising from a tall brick chimney through layers of languid air. I wanted to see the house at Encrucijada where Haydée and her brother Abel were born and the other, closer to the mill, where they spent their early years, learning about exploitation from the inequalities in their own community.

It would be decades before my dream became reality. In April 2014, while in Cuba to do the fieldwork for this book, I had the opportunity of traveling to Encrucijada and Constancia—the latter now renamed the Abel Santamaría Sugar Refinery. Ada's daughter Norma, one of the few remaining members of the next generation, accompanied me; so too did Norma's son Abel and his girlfriend Claudia, members of the one that follows. Juanito Cabeza drove the van Casa lent us, and the institution's director of international relations, Yolanda Alomá, came along as well.

For five hours we moved steadily eastward from Havana on the dilapidated eight-lane central highway bordered by cane fields and other crops.

Che Guevara Memorial and Crypt, Santa Clara. PHOTO BY MARGARET RANDALL.

Juanito drove slowly so as to avoid the many potholes. Occasional glimpses of sea reminded me this is an island. Stands of royal palm brought back Haydée's frequently stated affirmation that if only for the beaches and palm trees, it was worth opening her eyes each morning—until it no longer was.

We passed the city of Santa Clara, where Che Guevara and his men derailed an armored train at the end of the revolutionary war and where an imposing monument to him stands upon a hill. This is where the remains of Guevara and some of his comrades came to rest when they were finally unearthed 30 years after their deaths in Bolivia.

A few visitors had climbed the marble steps and were walking along the base of large bas-relief stone slabs upon which scenes of Che's struggle are embossed; some of his iconic texts catch the midday sun. The memorial's architecture projects a sense of decision, a well-founded confidence in a better, more equitable future, set against intense blue sky. I thought of Haydée, who shared so much with the man, and imagined her gazing up at this monument she didn't live to see.

Finally we were in Encrucijada, still a sleepy village although probably quite a bit larger than the one Haydée knew. Today the surrounding area claims 33,640 inhabitants. Like the rest of the country, with its aging population, it is shrinking. In the village we were met by local PCC officials; the

Santamaría Cuadrado home, now Abel Santamaría Museum, Encrucijada. Haydée's niece, Norma Ruiz; head of international relations at Casa de las Américas, Yolanda Alomá; and Juanito Calzada standing before the house.
PHOTO BY MARGARET RANDALL.

party's headquarters are next door to the Santamaría Cuadrado home, now a museum. It was thrilling to observe how moved everyone was to welcome Norma; someone from the family clearly provides a living link to the revolutionary heroes whose memory they preserve so lovingly. No one we met is old enough to remember Abel, and few knew Haydée. This small town is absolutely ordinary in every way but one: two people were born here who changed their country's history.

The museum was closed both because part of the roof had fallen in and due to a general termite infestation. But the on-site historians hastened to open it for us. A large home by local standards, it is a simple wooden construction on a corner, with only a few small rooms and a wraparound veranda. A number of photographs were on the walls, along with a smattering of historic objects. Still in boxes was the bulk of what will be exhibited here when there are money and materials to restore the building. But one of the historians, Amparo Vila, hastened to open some of those boxes.

From one she extracted the old radio around which the family gathered to listen to the evening news. I thought of that July 26, 1953, when dramatic

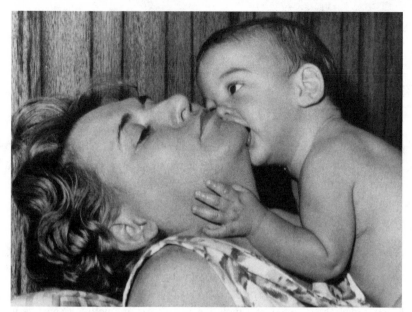

Photograph of Haydée and her son, Abel Enrique. PHOTO COURTESY CASA DE LAS AMÉRICAS.

dispatches and uncertain rumors began to circulate about a rebel attack in Santiago de Cuba. The announcer said there were many dead. Perhaps Joaquina and Benigno heard the still-confusing stories on this very radio. Joaquina is said to have known immediately that her son was involved, perhaps also her daughter.

From another box Amparo carefully removed a simple but beautiful old mantle clock encased in fine wood. As she lifted it from its cardboard protection, the pendulum began to swing and chimes sounded. We all gasped and looked at one another, conscious of a vanishing span of years, family tableaux silhouetted against the transparency of time, lives lived, presences among us. Several objects, such as this clock, may have come from the old country.

Amparo pointed out a half-dozen pieces of furniture, including a small desk on which Abel wrote some of his political texts. A couple of items had been made by Haydée's father, Benigno, master carpenter at the mill. Haydée was present in photographs, one in which her infant son is biting her chin. Norma remembered that after Haydee's death she took some of these objects from the Havana house and brought them to Encrucijada. She said she felt they belonged here.

A few miles distant, it was an ordinary day at the sugar mill. Men and women—old and young, black and white—were operating the machinery that extracts the juice from the cane. An ancient locomotive engine sat on narrow tracks, as if fossilized in time. Hot water and steam fed into a pool outside the mill. Our hosts told us the harvest wouldn't be good this year: "There's plenty of cane but climate change has affected its growth. Still," they said, "we hope to meet our production goal."

The house where the family lived at Constancia is also a museum: the same tired wood but painted pale blue instead of yellow. Despite their importance to revolutionary history, I don't imagine these small country museums attract more than a few visitors—maybe an occasional group of schoolchildren or someone like myself.

I thought of Haydée and Abel as mischievous children, "borrowing" the rusty gandy dancer car that now stands idle on the old track and heading for the beach. I tried to imagine what life in this quiet village must have been like for two brilliant, passionate, and decisive young people in the first half of the twentieth century, infuriated by the crooked politicians of their day, frustrated by the society into which they were born, and willing to give their lives to change it—though as yet unsure how they would accomplish that. Abel, being male, must have believed a different future was possible. I wondered if Haydée did as well and how her process of self-confidence unfolded.

Western women at mid-twentieth century straddled painful stereotypes, burgeoning expectations, and challenges frequently beyond our reach. In most moderately advanced countries we had won the vote but had much less formal education than men and made up minuscule percentages of the paid labor force—yet worked two or three shifts, most of them unpaid. We were privy to few reproductive rights and subject to a broad number of limiting social conditions. We were still more servant than agent of our lives. A hypocritical propriety not only defined us but made it possible for our male counterparts to indulge in reckless "boys will be boys" behavior. World War II, which took so many men into battle, required new initiatives of women. But after that war, women who had occupied men's places in industry and the professions were forced back into domesticity.

Cuba is an island, with the insular qualities islands encompass, culturally as well as geopolitically. For women, this often meant an exaggeration of mainland prejudices and limitations. Alternatively, it sometimes permitted a certain sort of exceptionalism. Despite a history that includes outstanding

Santamaría Cuadrado house at Constancia. PHOTO BY MARGARET RANDALL.

female figures in all areas of human endeavor, Cuban women overall had few real opportunities back then. Stereotypical images included the playgirls working at the famous casinos, the prostitutes who were also endemic to that exploitative scene, and the housewives and maids who—like servants everywhere—kept the unacknowledged underside of the economy going. "Good" women, irrespective of their class and race, dressed and groomed themselves unobtrusively, thereby separating themselves from the image of the sexually provocative *mulata* who dominated prerevolutionary billboards and tourist advertising. "Good" women also saved themselves for marriage.

One thing no Cuban woman, of any social class or culture, was supposed to do in prerevolutionary Cuba was take part in armed political struggle. The very few who had, such as Antonio Maceo's mother Mariana Grajales, were exceptions. And Grajales is remembered not for fighting on the front lines but for managing the rebel camps. In my first interview with Haydée, she told me: "My own mother was the kind of woman who thought that men were the only ones who had the right to make revolutions."[6] It wasn't only what she was fleeing—the provincial life of a sugar plantation—that set Haydée apart. It was also, perhaps especially, what she was moving toward.

From her earliest years, those closest to Haydée called her Yeyé; the diminutive may have come from her younger brother Abel's inability to

The former Constancia (now Abel Santamaría) Sugar Mill. PHOTO BY
MARGARET RANDALL.

pronounce her name when he was learning to talk. Throughout her life, her
family, close friends, and a few of her colleagues at Casa de las Américas
continued to address her by that endearment. One of my interviewees, Chiki
Salsamendi, who worked closely with her for the last twenty years of her life,
told me: "Soon after I started working at Casa I began calling her Yeyé. I don't
really know why."[7]

Haydée's father, Benigno Santamaría Fernández, was born in the municipality of Melón, between Pontevedra and Lugo, in Galicia, Spain. He came
to Cuba as a child, acquired the scant education available to someone of his
immigrant status, and became foreman and master carpenter at Constancia.
His own father, who arrived as an adult and worked his way into this position, bequeathed it to him. Benigno wasn't one of the wealthy landowners
who profited from the sweat of cane cutters and laborers who are able to
count on a meager income only three months out of every year; but neither
was he one of those impoverished workers. Aida has said: "My father was
the one who managed the money in the house. I don't think my mother ever
knew how much he earned. And he was very frugal."[8]

Later in life, Haydée spoke on several occasions about how hard it was for her to pinpoint her class origins:

My family enjoyed a good economic situation, well, not that good, but you know . . . my father had a car, he worked all year round. He was the foreman at the mill, he earned a decent salary, at least enough to live in a place where the vast majority only worked three months out of the year . . . three months. So you could see the difference. Most families like ours had Christmas gifts, clothing, shoes. My other little friends had nothing. When you get to be seven, eight or nine years old, you begin to ask: Why? Why do the Three Kings visit some but not others? You realize the Three Kings don't exist, because if they did they would visit everyone.[9]

Perhaps because theirs was a large family, perhaps because her mother was frequently ill (with severe attacks of asthma) and needed expensive medication, perhaps because her father, in contrast with his more prosperous brothers, was generous with those who needed help, or perhaps out of an immigrant frugality brought from the old country, Haydée and her sisters remembered certain differences that kept them from the lifestyle enjoyed by their peers. They rarely had new clothes, each younger sister having to make do with those handed down from the one a couple of years older. Shoes could be purchased only once a year. Haydée couldn't remember receiving many gifts or having more than a few toys in her childhood. Money was always tight.

As was true for all middle-management families at the mill, the male Santamaría children could expect to work their way into positions of confidence. In this context, when he was only nine years old Abel started sweeping the company store after school—not because he had to but because that was the traditional way male offspring began acquainting themselves with the business. He was never bitter about this; rather, he prided himself on doing a good job. Soon he was given more serious work. His father was a foreman. If he proved himself, in time he could expect to earn a similar position. But Abel always knew that wasn't the life he wanted.

On the other hand, working at the company store informed Abel's social consciousness from a very early age. Haydée explained:

One of our uncles by marriage was the mill's bookkeeper. Abel began to understand how the bosses stole from the small peasant, the small cane farmer. They refused to mill his cane, but carried his account. What I'm saying is that they let him accumulate debt until he wouldn't have been able to pay it off in fifty years. Then they would tell him: Okay, we'll settle your debt in exchange for that small piece of land. But that piece led to another piece, and that piece to another . . . and that's how two or three people came to own all the land, and they only milled the cane on the land they owned.

Abel began to discover how all that worked, the evil of it, the terrible way they exploited the sharecroppers. And then when they took away their land they also took away their shacks, made of palm boards and thatch, and those families had to figure out how to get another parcel of land so they could build another place to live. And they ended up having to go back to land that had once belonged to them, but now they were paying rent. Abel saw how all this worked, not because of his position or because he read Marx, but because of his human sensibility.[10]

In rural Cuba, daughters were expected to marry and raise their own families or, if they remained single, settle into the dull routine of household management, charitable deeds, and caring for the children of others. Neither Aida nor Haydée envisioned that life for herself, Haydée least of all. Ada, born so much later, had a different set of options. Aida did marry and live at the mill for a while, before making a life in the capital. We know how Haydée escaped provincialism: Abel brought her to Havana. And then the revolutionary war—initiated by Fidel, Abel, Haydée and others—cut through this family like a knife, giving and taking away and then giving again, changing its history as it changed the history of Cuba.

Haydée's mother, Joaquina Cuadrado Alonso, was also from Galicia, from the region of Salamanca, and like her husband came to Cuba as a child. She was a strong woman: dominating, opinionated, willful. Her offspring described her as someone of conservative values, although after the revolution she became a fervent defender of the new society and a powerhouse in her community. She even joined the Communist Party. Such women shaped this family: from Haydée's grandmother María to her mother, then to her and her two sisters. I saw evidence of that same strength and determination in the women of the next generation with whom I spoke.

Haydée and her mother had a particularly contentious relationship, probably because they were both so strong willed. Both were known for defending their positions, right or wrong. Both insisted on having their way. Aldo said all the siblings had similar disagreements with their mother, but Haydée was the only one who gave voice to them:

The tensions were always greater between our mother and Haydée, because she answered back, she rebelled. She wouldn't take anything lying down, nor would she subordinate herself easily to anyone. She had such a strong nature, although she was also very sweet, very maternal, very sentimental and generally fair. She would confront any problem, even if she knew that doing so would create another. Abel and I, on the other hand, tended not to answer back. We didn't argue, but we went ahead and did what we wanted.[11]

Aida has said:

Because she always wanted to help people, Yeyé often got in trouble with Quina—that's what we called our mother. She wouldn't ask for things at home because she knew they wouldn't give them to her. She just took them on the sly. She didn't give things away simply because she wanted to, only to people who really needed them. But the thing is, we weren't a family that had a lot. Our father was a salaried worker, and although we weren't hungry we endured hard times. We each had a single school uniform, for example: one change of clothes for the morning, another for the afternoon, and one when we had to dress up . . . that's why Mother was often exasperated with Yeyé.[12]

The men in the Santamaría Cuadrado family have been described as kindly but of few words. Aida has said that she cannot remember their father spanking or even raising his voice with any of his children. Others have commented on his gentle nature, his penchant for joking around, celebrating a job well done, and encouraging his offspring—in his own quiet way. Aldo, too, was said to have had a tranquil demeanor, although he was also active in the struggle, became head of Cuba's Navy after the revolution came to power, and has given some very moving testimony about his sister. Abel, who would become Fidel Castro's second in command at Moncada and died tragically in that action, was more verbal: from his earliest years he had something important to say.

As a parenthesis, I can't help but note that this family, like the Kennedys in the United States, suffered an exceptional degree of loss. In terms of their economic and social status, the families couldn't have been more different. Politically and culturally they were worlds apart. But the Santamaría Cuadrado siblings also died much too young. Haydée took her own life in 1980, at the age of 57. Ada died of cancer in 1991 at only 53. Her daughter Norma told me that her decision, too, was a form of suicide: she had been depressed since her older sister's death and didn't tell anyone about the cancer until she was sure it was too late.[13] Aldo died in 2004 during an operation that shouldn't have taken his life. And Aida, the oldest, died of dementia in 2005.

In a continuation of family tragedy, Haydée's two biological children, Abel Enrique and Celia María, were killed in an automobile accident in 2008. The accelerator got stuck on the Volkswagen Beetle Celia María was driving, and they hit a tree. Aida's oldest daughter died of a brain tumor when she was still a young woman. Other family members, too, have left before their time, and several have suffered from mental illnesses, which at times can be a sort of death in life. Do some families attract tragedy—perhaps because their members are so numerous, perhaps because they are prone to taking risks, or perhaps because of some characteristic more difficult to define?

María Pérez de Castro, the grandmother who decided upon her first granddaughter's birth date when she rose from her sickbed, came from the village of Prexigueiro in Orencia, Galicia. She was dominating and not easy to get along with. No one except Haydée cared much for her, and she also favored Haydée. She would ply the child with special treats, which Haydée then shared with her siblings when her grandmother wasn't looking. But she was a pillar, and many subsequent females in the family bore her name: Haydée María, Celia María, and others. María was also the name Haydée used in the underground and throughout the war.

Both sides of Haydée's family were part of the great migration that fled a stagnating Spanish economy in the early years of the twentieth century to seek a better life on the American continent. This particular wave of Galician immigration never reached the mainland but staked its claim on the island of Cuba. Rugged, hardworking women and men brought with them their customs and habits from a much colder climate and dissimilar culture: heavy clothing and heavier food, both inappropriate to the tropical island heat, and a strict hand when it came to child rearing.

They also brought strength of character, ingenuity, and determination. Perhaps it was the predominant mix of hardy Spanish immigrants and Africans brought over in the Middle Passage that gives Cubans their unique strength and resourcefulness. At the Cuban Revolution's initial battle, the attack on Moncada Barracks, 70 percent of those who took part were of Galician heritage.

Haydée's grandmother, María Pérez de Castro, with her immediate family. Photo taken in Spain before their immigration to Cuba. PHOTO COURTESY NORMA RUIZ.

All the Santamaría Cuadrado siblings were close, the three women insep-arable in their later years. People who interacted with the three of them told me that each had a particular role to play: Aida was the one who brought order and equanimity into any situation, prevailing upon her sisters to con-sider the consequences of what they did. Ada was fun loving and rebellious. Haydée, of course, was the heroine and also the sister who had suffered un-speakable wounds. But from the beginning, Haydée and Abel shared a devel-oping social consciousness and growing concern for the exploited that gave them a special bond. All the sisters and brothers were revolutionaries, each contributing to the struggle in her or his way. But Haydée and Abel didn't join an existing movement; they created one.

Early in Joaquina's and Benigno's marriage, while he was still trying to get his family on a comfortable footing, they lived with his mother, María. Both women were strong willed, and Joaquina wasn't happy with the ar-rangement. Aida said Joaquina and her mother-in-law detested one another, a strong word given the respect that predominates in Cuban families.[14]

Benigno moved his family to Havana for a few years to see if he could do better there. But the capital city proved difficult, and he was unable to get ahead. So he decided to return to Encrucijada. Joaquina, however, refused to

Santamaría Cuadrado family. Left to right, standing: Benigno, Ada, and Joaquina; seated: Abel, Aida, Haydée, and Aldo. PHOTO COURTESY CASA DE LAS AMÉRICAS.

go with him. She wasn't going back to living with her mother-in-law, and so she remained in Havana with two of their children. Only Aida accompanied her father. Aldo was sent to Spain, where he lived for a few years with his maternal grandmother. Ada had not yet been born. Joaquina told Benigno she wasn't coming back to Encrucijada until he was able to provide them with a house of their own. About a year later he did, and she returned, no longer subject to her mother-in-law's domineering ways.

Aida's daughter Niurka told me that although Haydée was still a small child during that year she spent with her mother in Havana, the experience was formative for her. She was extremely observant, noticed everything, asked questions, and must have filed away for later use some of the things she learned in the big city. She would return to Encrucijada all too quickly, though.[15]

Growing up in rural Cuba during the 1920s and 1930s marked Haydée. The village of Encrucijada and the nearby Constancia sugar mill were a world apart from city life, with its more cosmopolitan culture, educational opportunities, and connection to the outside world. The mill owners enjoyed a measure of provincial luxury. Everyone else, including middle-level management and even many of the laborers, knew each other by name. You might say they were friends. People shared food, helped each other out, and cared for one another in times of need. But Haydée would come to think of her place of origin as one in which questioning the status quo—thinking at all— was frowned upon:

> You know how the people at a sugar mill are . . . the first thing they ask when they get up in the morning is: How did you sleep, what have you had to eat, how are you? Because at a sugar mill everyone knows everyone else. Even those who have a certain status—I'm not talking about the owners, of course, just those who live a little better than the rest. And there's solidarity among the families. At a sugar mill, when you cook someone will say: If you're making something today, bring me a little.[16]

Haydée also often talked about the limitations of that life: the willingness to accept a traditional mentality, the reluctance to question or challenge ignorance or conservative values.

Racial prejudice was a given. Children of European descent were not supposed to speak to or play with black children, the sons and daughters of the cane cutters and mill workers. Abel and Haydée ignored this unwritten law and were often criticized for fraternizing with children of color—especially Haydée, because her gender required greater decorum. There is a story in which a black teacher at the rural schoolhouse tried to convince Abel that his position as a teacher showed that blacks really could get ahead. Abel told the man: "It's true, you are black and you are a teacher, but because you are black you will never go beyond this one-room schoolhouse."[17] Even today, after more than five decades of revolution, there are few blacks in high government or party positions.

The great Cuban trade unionist Jesús Menéndez, also black, was born in Encrucijada and organized throughout the area. He was a member of Cuba's old Socialist Party and active in the struggle against President Grau San Martín's administration. Menéndez secured some benefits for the disenfranchised cane cutters. Grau San Martín tried to give preferential sugar pricing to the United States, something opposed by Menéndez and his movement. Abel and Haydée knew this rebel leader, and he influenced their early political thinking. He was murdered in January 1948 and his death had a great impact on Abel and his sister.

In an interview in which she talked about growing up in Encrucijada, Haydée said:

I didn't know what communism was back then, but people called me a communist . . . because with my social status, talking to a black person, or just conversing in general with the field hands, befriending other little girls who weren't like me, made you a communist. They called me a communist because I talked to black people. I was everyone's friend. I didn't know what discrimination was. . . .[18]

The truth is, Haydée's childhood and youth at Constancia helped form her class consciousness. She said:

Cuban sugar mills, at least the one where I was born and grew up, are places where class differences are blatantly obvious. These are small places where the same families live for years . . . their children grow up and have children, and those children have children and so forth. . . . Everyone knows one another. All the children go to the same school, the children who have nothing and those from the dozen or so families who have more, who seem almost rich, although when you think about it they aren't. They are just a little better off, with a better house, a car, maybe they dress a little better or eat all year long. . . .[19]

Cuban poet Roberto Fernández Retamar,[20] who worked closely with Haydée, spoke about her younger years in a heartfelt tribute:

As a child, when she played house she curled up inside the hen house like one of the family hens and subjected herself to their angry pecking. Some years later, after her teacher taught a lesson on Cuban history, although she was the daughter of Spaniards she invented a *Mambi* grandfather (Cuban freedom fighter) for herself . . . [still later] she joined the ranks of the Orthodox youth with her brother Abel. . . .[21]

Everyone who knew Haydée as a child has testified to the ways in which she broke through the confines of plantation life. She loved to read, and her sister Aida said she often imagined herself the protagonists of the novels she devoured. Her brother Abel gave her historical and political literature, which she also read avidly. He introduced her to the writing of the great Cuban patriot José Martí, later considered the intellectual architect of the revolution.

Fernández Retamar, who is also a noted Martí scholar, has written movingly of the country girl turned heroine's early reading habits:

Haydée at Casa de las Américas
with image of José Martí, taken
during the filming of *Vamos
a caminar por Casa*, by Víctor
Casaus, 1979. PHOTO COURTESY
CASA DE LAS AMÉRICAS.

I don't know, among the many rural readings that consumed her (often
from clearing to clearing, like Don Quixote), whether she read Unamuno;
I know she would have found the tormented Basque's agonized medita-
tion on death familiar. But [. . .] I have no doubt she would have found
more to her liking that other great woman of similar talent, known in her
century as Teresa de Ahumada, and today as Santa Teresa de Jesús, who
with her brother read of exploits of dreams and justice and tried to make
them real, undertaking in her time all that was revitalizing and brave.

Like her Cuban counterpart, even as she was exuberant in her love
of life, Santa Teresa desired death. It is known that Martí also read this
indulgent mother of Avila. In 1905, at only twenty-one years of age, Pedro
Henríquez Ureña, the father of twentieth-century Latin American criti-

cism, said that at times Martí's style "possesses the emotional intensity of Teresa de Jesús." And 25 years later, he added that Martí wrote "with the candor of Santa Teresa, from whom he learned that one who feels as he did, should not have to hold back."[22]

As a young woman, Haydée also had an active social life. She loved to go dancing and was passionate about horseback riding. This joyous nature, though, could turn wistful without warning.

Today, when we know so much more about depression, it seems clear that the condition affected more than a few members of Haydée's family and plagued her throughout her life. Historians point to her experience at Moncada, certainly cruel and indelible enough to cause permanent trauma. What psychiatrist or psychotherapist would have been capable of understanding those wounds? But my research also made me wonder if her depression didn't have its origin many years before that brutal battle, in which she lost her beloved brother and her fiancé simultaneously, and after which she was shown their mangled body parts in an attempt to get her to talk.

At her trial she felt she couldn't display the slightest sign of vulnerability. Those experiences would have been enough to push anyone over the edge. In Haydée's case they may have been adding insult to an injury already present. I am sure she struggled throughout the rest of her life between giving full rein to her exuberant creativity and keeping those horrendous images from overwhelming and destroying her. It is tragic to think of her having to cope with the depression itself and also with the ignorance and dismissive misconceptions that surrounded the condition back then.

Haydée finished sixth grade at that one-room country schoolhouse and then, because she loved learning and had no possibility of going on to middle or high school, repeated it three or maybe four more times. She was fortunate to have an exceptional teacher who, despite their provincial surroundings, made his students understand that they were not just from Constancia but belonged to a nation with a great history of struggle. From him she learned about Céspedes,[23] Agramonte,[24] and Maceo.[25] And she was able to read Martí, who wrote for children as well as adults.

I wondered if poverty, convention, or both prevented her from continuing her education. Surely her parents must have recognized her unusual intelligence. Couldn't they have sent her to a nearby town or city where more schooling was an option? From what I had been able to gather, in interviews with the few who remain, both the family's economic situation and Haydée's gender ultimately precluded her from further study. Sending her away wouldn't have meant tuition alone; she would have had to board somewhere, and that was beyond the family's means.

But Niurka told me that Haydée's parents did recognize their oldest daughter's gifts and paid for a tutor who would help her get ready to enter nursing school.[26] Clearly, she was drawn to the helping professions. Haydée herself said: "To study nursing you had to be well prepared. Especially for someone who didn't have political pull. . . . I had to take the train to Encrucijada at eleven in the morning and didn't get home until seven in the evening. At the time, my mother wasn't against my trying to get into that school."[27]

She tried to enter nursing school, but her unwillingness to butter up the local political strongman finally got in the way. She decided to become a teacher instead, until that dream, too, crumbled beneath the difficulties of time and place. So Haydée, now a young woman, began to make a life for herself at the mill in the only way available. She began attending to neighbors when they were ill, becoming the person known for giving injections, teaching hygiene, and the like. She was an expert seamstress, with a particular talent for embroidery.

People from Encrucijada in their eighties and nineties remember her making the rounds of her community, giving advice, helping people with their problems. Some say that from the age of fourteen she had been giving injections to her neighbors. Her sister Aida, just a couple of years younger, married and had a child. Abel joined the Orthodox Youth, excited by Eduardo Chibás's political ideas, and the sister who identified so closely with him followed suit.[28]

Haydée felt she was suffocating in the provincial atmosphere of her youth. Nevertheless, she kept on trying to make herself useful in the community. Her good nature and creative impulses helped keep her going. There is an anecdote that illustrates her unique sense of humor; it has to do with Don Mamerto and his wife, Doña Juanita.

This couple had come over from Spain, as Haydée liked to say, "very young, recently married, wearing rope sandals and totally illiterate. Some years later, and not by luck or chance, Mamerto had five sugar mills." He was the patriarch of the Luzárraga family that owned Constancia. As Haydée told the story:

Don Mamerto's wife Juanita made sweets she sold on saints' days. By the time I was a young woman she had declared herself a marquesa. She actually claimed she was a marquesa, with a title and everything. One day they built a little church in the village. It seemed huge to us. And the Bishop of Cienfuegos came to inaugurate that church in honor of Juanita's title. This might sound like a joke, but I swear it's true. When we found out, I went right over, I went to mass, and I asked: "But who died in Spain so Juanita could start calling herself marquesa?"

The thing is, I had a pretty little German shepherd puppy I also called Marquesa. And that dog was a well-known troublemaker in Constancia. . . . At home no one knew why I had named my dog Marquesa, until one day, when I called "Doña Juanita" and Marquesa didn't come running. My mother asked: "What do you mean, Doña Juanita?" And I said: "Well, I'm calling Marquesa Doña Juanita now!" They thought it was subversive of me to call my dog that. Poor dog.[29]

And so life dragged on for a brilliant and sensitive young woman who was born and grew up in a place far removed from the centers of power but whose inhabitants suffered from their trickle-down policies. She must have felt more and more frustrated.

When Abel moved to Havana, determined not to follow in their father's footsteps at the mill, she lost her best friend and closest ally. She was desolate. When, a few months later, he sent for her to come and live with him in the capital, it must have felt like salvation. He not only introduced her to a world of struggle that would define her and change her country's history; he would save her from mental and emotional death.

# 4 MONCADA

I didn't die at Moncada, but I left my life there.
—Haydée Santamaría

The small apartment on the sixth floor at 164 Twenty-fifth Street in Havana's Vedado neighborhood is known simply as 25 and O. I stand before the unassuming building, its light blue facade and symmetrical balconies giving no clue to the discreetly momentous activity that took place here in the early 1950s. Abel had come to Havana in 1951 or 1952. Back then no one was conscious of the importance of keeping a historical record, so the exact year remains in question.

Abel got a job at the Pontiac dealership, studied at night, and rented a room on Virtudes Street. As soon as he was able, he sent for his sister Haydée. He, better than anyone, understood her desperate need to escape the confines of their family home and stifling plantation atmosphere. It must have been just before her arrival that he moved to 25 and O. He paid $50 a month for the apartment, quite a bit at the time but worth it because of its excellent location. It would quickly become one of the gathering places for a growing number of young people intent upon liberating their country.

For as long as those young people knew—in historic memory as well as in their own experience—Cuba had been humiliated by foreign powers. First England, then Spain, and now the United States, in conjunction with a

Living room of apartment at 25 and O, Vedado, Havana. Now a museum.

PHOTO BY MARGARET RANDALL.

corrupt local oligarchy. Each new day brought insults, large and small, that riled all those with a sense of national dignity.

And things were about to get much worse. On March 10, 1952, a general named Fulgencio Batista staged a coup d'état and wrenched the Cuban government from President Carlos Prío Socarrás. The United States immediately recognized the dictator, as it has so often in other countries before and since. Abel Santamaría not only hated Batista for his dictatorial stance; he despised the man for having ordered the murder of Antonio Guiteras, the revolutionary student leader who had impressed him in the 1930s.[1] Guiteras had believed that liberation could be achieved through violent confrontation with the established order but simultaneously held firm to an ideal of democracy. Abel's generation of revolutionaries admired him deeply.

Haydée was living with her brother by the time Batista's coup imbued them and other revolutionary youth with an intensified sense of urgency. Havana was only one center of activity; Santiago de Cuba, Manzanillo, Artemisa—all over the country young people were beginning to organize. Fidel's presence in the capital lent authority to what was going on there, but dissatisfaction was widespread, and there were palpable links with earlier struggles as well. One day Abel met Fidel Castro, a young lawyer with similarly radical ideas about social change. He brought him to the apartment at 25 and O and introduced him to his sister.

Haydée is famously remembered as having complained about "the tall man who flicked his cigar ashes on my clean floor." But she too was profoundly impressed with Fidel's revolutionary ideals and focused brilliance. Brother and sister agreed that this was the leader capable of changing Cuba's destiny. *Guevara* From then on, 25 and O became a meeting place for those who would initiate what came to be known as the July 26 Movement. The teacher and poet Raúl Gómez García and others, including Jesús Montané, Elda Pérez, and Ernesto Tizol, frequented those two rooms. Some survived. Most did not.

Today the apartment is a museum, moving in its austerity. I could imagine the small living room, tiny kitchen, single bedroom, and bath, overflowing with the men and women who gathered there more than six decades earlier. Haydée cooked for them all and was often quoted as saying that nothing later ever tasted as good as those meager portions of Spanish omelet or *congrí* (black beans and rice). The books they read are on display in a glass-fronted bookcase, Martí prominent among them.

Dolores Pérez Resta ("Lolita"), a collaborator from those times whom

Melba Hernández and Haydée Santamaría in their cell at Guanajay prison, 1953. PHOTO COURTESY CASA DE LAS AMÉRICAS.

I interviewed in 2014—she was eighty-seven, rail thin, and as sharp as if the years had touched her only lightly—told me how after the attack on Moncada she went to the apartment and removed everything that could have been incriminating: books, the mimeograph machine on which the revolutionaries produced their clandestine newspaper *El acusador*, even a wall calendar featuring an image of Martí. She kept all of it safe until after the war.

A word about the newspaper shows the sort of leadership brought by Fidel. Abel and his friends had at first called it *Somos los mismos* (We Are the Same), implying continuity with earlier struggles and identification with ordinary Cubans. Fidel was the one who suggested they change its name to *El acusador* (The Prosecutor), reflecting his legal training and denoting a more combative stance.

When I stopped by, the apartment had recently been repainted. The couch on which Abel slept had been refinished in a fabric as closely resembling the original as possible. A framed swatch of that earlier upholstery hung on the wall just above it—physical evidence of the reverence and attention to detail with which Cuba remembers its heroes and martyrs. When I asked the young historian who welcomed me if the museum gets many visitors, he said mostly groups of school children. I thought about time and how easily it can obliterate a consciousness of struggle unless that struggle is kept alive in ways that spark the imagination of new generations, who naturally have different reference points and rapidly changing interests.

I stood quietly for a few moments, taking in every detail of those historic rooms. I could see Abel, Haydée, Melba Hernández,[2] Elda Pérez Mujica, Boris Luis Santa Coloma, Fidel with his ever-present cigar, and others—dead and alive, their spirits still inhabiting this space. I thought of them as they must have been back then, young people who believed enough in what they had to do that risking their lives was not an impediment. I thought of the many who died, the few who lived to take part in the war, and the fewer still who survived that war. Each one had been sure that whatever his or her personal fate, a free and independent Cuba was worth the sacrifice.

While certain epic events can remain ignored or vague, due to the prejudicial points of view of the writers of history, the attack on Moncada is iconic and so has been thoroughly mythologized. It is best known as "the military failure that nonetheless sounded the opening salvo of the Cuban Revolution."

Without Moncada, the people of Santiago de Cuba would not have witnessed the rebels' heroism or been aware of this group of determined revolutionaries. Fidel Castro would not have been captured or sentenced and would not have represented himself in the extraordinary defense speech known as "History Will Absolve Me." That speech, smuggled out of prison in fragments, printed and distributed by Haydée and Melba, contained the revolution's goals and early program. It became the organizing tool for a movement, a successful war, and—five and a half years later—a resounding victory.

The Cuban insurgency foreshadowed decades of Latin American revolutionary efforts and for many years remained the only successful revolution on the continent. More than half a century later—in a dramatically changed world—its continued existence is stunning: tenacious proof that change is possible.

Along with Moncada, a smaller group of revolutionaries set out to attack another garrison, Carlos Manuel de Céspedes, in the city of Bayamo. But Moncada is revered as the event that started it all. Because the young revolutionaries met such a brutal response—Batista vowed to kill ten rebels for each dead soldier, and his men carried out his orders with particular sadism—it is also remembered as a trial by fire. One-third of the rebels who attacked Moncada either died in battle or were murdered by the regime.

One aspect of the action that has received less attention was its absolute audacity. The group of men and two women who went to Moncada were young and had few resources. Their average age is said to have been twenty-six. Most of them were laborers or peasants who experienced exploitation in the form of palpable daily privation. Fidel, from a bourgeois family and already a lawyer, was in the extreme minority; most had minimal formal educations. If we think of what they set out to do and the sense of absolute confidence with which they carried out every part of the plan, it seems nothing short of extraordinary.

Although audacious, the attack on Cuba's second largest military garrison was carefully and discreetly planned. This discretion, along with the compartmentalization of information—no one knew more than he or she needed to know—and the fact that so many involved were killed, probably accounts for so little having been written about the planning itself. Abel Santamaría, the young movement's second in command, was murdered after the attack, as were many of the others who took part. Fidel was captured, tried, and imprisoned. Following Moncada, all attention necessarily focused on the next stage of struggle.

Now I imagined Haydée, thirty years old, freshly arrived from the conservative ambience of her rural upbringing, fully involved in the feverish task of revolution. Other young women came to their country's capital city to study, look for work or a husband, get ahead, raise a family in an atmosphere that offered more advantages than rural life. It is true that Haydée was seeking

HAYDE SANTAMARIA CUADRADO

Photo from Haydée's police file, 1953. PHOTO COURTESY CASA DE LAS AMÉRICAS.

personal release from a suffocating family situation. But very soon her life was consumed by the complex work of profound social change.

Over the year or two leading up to Moncada, the sister and brother returned often to Encrucijada. They arrived by car, impressing family and childhood friends. They showed up on holidays and the occasional weekend. They understood the dangers inherent in what they were planning and didn't want to lose touch with those they loved. Haydée, especially, wondered if she would live to see her older sister Aida's little girl grow up, celebrate her fifteenth birthday, marry. Aida had come to Havana to give birth in a clinic, and the child had lived her first weeks at 25 and O, sleeping in a bureau drawer. All the comrades loved holding her.

Just before the July 26 attack, Abel and Haydée stopped in at Constancia. They got to hold that niece, Carín. It must have been difficult for them not to let slip any mention of what they were about to do, kiss the baby girl, and then go off and take part in an action that would separate forever many of those brave young people from their own sons and daughters—even while they were confident that what they were doing would usher in a society in which every child would be happier, healthier, with greater possibilities for growth and development. It takes enormous faith to hold onto an image of something as yet intangible in the face of almost certain death.

Physical places hold the essence of every breath, sentiment, and action that has inhabited them, layer upon layer. Back in 1967, after attending *El encuentro con Rubén Darío*, I stayed on in Cuba an extra week and accepted my hosts' invitation to travel to Santiago de Cuba, where the revolution began. We were a small group of poets, maybe eight or ten. Our knowledgeable guide was Ada Santamaría, Haydée's youngest sister, who also worked at Casa then. She was only fifteen when her sister and brother attacked Moncada Barracks, but the event was deeply engraved in her memory.

From one moment to the next Abel had gone from big brother to martyr, Haydée from caring older sister to someone forever changed by loss. Her parents and remaining siblings had been thrust into unspeakable life changes. And then came the war years—in which Ada, too, played a central role—and finally victory. On the occasion of my first trip to Santiago, the revolution wasn't yet a decade old.

I retain vivid memories of that journey. We traced the *Moncadistas'* route from the small farmhouse at Siboney to the barracks and hospitals that had been their targets and the scenes of such unequal conflict. Ada pointed out to us where the various groups of revolutionaries entered the garrison, where the major confrontations took place, where a doctor on duty that night refused to attend to a dying soldier, and where another found the courage to respond to pleas by Haydée and Melba, begging him to do right by his Hippocratic oath.

Like all the dictatorship's major military barracks, Moncada was now a school. Turning sites of repression into those of joyful learning was symbolic of the young revolution's promise to remake society—with the motto always in mind that "los niños son los mimados de la revolución" (children are the spoiled ones of the revolution). Boys and girls in wine-colored jumpers or pants and sharply pressed white shirts sat in classrooms or ran on the playground, their bright red neckerchiefs denoting membership in the *Pioneros*

Police file photo of
Haydée, 1953. PHOTO
COURTESY CASA DE LAS
AMÉRICAS.

(youngest contingent of Communist Youth). One small corner of the main building had been designated a museum. Photos of those who fought and died there, as well as a few articles of clothing and other relics, were on display.

I remember leaving Moncada and driving back toward Siboney. Every so often we passed a small monument to one or more of the revolutionaries who had been hunted and gunned down as they retreated along that narrow road. Silent, I gazed through the car's window at the filmstrip unfolding before me. I can still feel the strange heat emanating from those markers; they seemed alive. Each had the job of representing a man who had died in that frustrated attack, offering himself selflessly to a cause that must have seemed all but unobtainable.

The next few years, though, would show that it was obtainable: a flare had gone up, and unspeakable sacrifice had provided the spark that drew enormous popular support. First thousands, then tens of thousands. Those who died—those who were tortured to death at Moncada—had done their job. And those who lived continued to do theirs.

Although it always brought her visible pain, in the years to come Haydée spoke often about Moncada. After the end of the war and as each July 26 approached, she and other survivors visited schools, workplaces, military units, neighborhoods, and collective farms, telling their story again and again. They wanted the younger generations to know what it had been like: the cost of victory, the detailed human stories that go so much farther than heroic proclamations in keeping history alive.

Haydée always started those gatherings slowly, appearing almost hesitant. She would say that public speaking wasn't her strong suit. She would say that Melba was the one who remembered dates and other details; what she remembered were the feelings. Her style was conversational, often circuitous. But once the first memories surfaced, it was as if a floodgate opened. She was off and running: passionate, wistful, anguished, sure—and compelling as she relived each unforgettable moment. For a while, at least, the distance between those who initiated the revolution and those who were born long after its victory narrowed appreciably.

As the years unfolded, though, one had the feeling that repeating this story became more and more difficult for Haydée. In July 1980, a friend of mine who worked at a Havana radio station had the privilege of listening to her talk. In the restroom, after she'd finished her presentation, my friend overheard the heroine confessing to someone how painful it was: "I just don't know if I can do this again," she heard her say. She would kill herself two days later.

Haydée's conversation at the University of Havana's Political Sciences Department on July 13, 1967, was particularly comprehensive and evocative. This conversation, that included questions from some of the students, became the book *Haydée habla del Moncada* (Haydée Speaks about Moncada), published in Cuba and translated into dozens of languages throughout the world. It still offers some of the richest memories of the experience:

> Whenever we talk about anything, insignificant as it may be, we tend to say: "that happened before," or "that happened after." And that before and that after are before Moncada and after Moncada. After Moncada, we underwent a total transformation. We might have been the same person, the same person who went to Moncada filled with passion, and who

continued to be a passionate person. But the transformation was huge, so huge that if we hadn't really understood what we were doing it would have been difficult to keep on living, or at least to keep on acting like normal human beings. [. . .]

On another occasion, she went even deeper into what that "before" and "after" meant to her:

That's where my life began, after Moncada. I realized who I would never see again, the ones who died and I could never bring back. [. . .] Those minutes one doesn't know how they will transpire: heroic or cowardly [. . .] and it was after Moncada that one understood who had been lost, and who remained. One realized then that Moncada couldn't be allowed to die. That's where the "after" began. The struggle for life, the struggle for the lives of all those comrades, for Abel, for Melba, for everyone, and for one's own life as well. And not knowing where Fidel was, if he was dead or alive, the terrible agony of that. . . .[3]

In the talk at the Political Sciences Department, she continued:

We always remember when Abel told us: "After this it will be harder to live than to die, and so you are going to have to be braver than us. Because we are going to die and you, Melba and Haydée, must live. You're going to have to be stronger than us. Our role will be easier than yours."[4]

Haydée and Melba had both been afraid that when the time came for the movement to carry out that action they would be left behind. Neither they nor the other subordinates had any idea exactly what the action would be, or where. The women had followed every order without question. They had developed multiple skills and shown their capacity for absolute discretion. But the era's gender assumptions led them to question, privately, if they would be allowed to participate.

Fidel and his second in command, Abel, made good on their promise and took the two women into battle. But Abel was clearly conscious of the likelihood that he would die while his sister and Melba might survive. Were these simply the words he chose to instill courage, to convey the fact that, should he and the others be killed, the women had an important job to do? Or was he, too, counting on the gender differences of the time, believing that the women, even if captured, might be treated less brutally?

The women were in fact treated differently. No sooner had the gunfire stopped than Abel and Boris and a number of others were taken off and tortured to death. Haydée and Melba were isolated, burned with lit cigarettes, and shown the gruesome evidence of the tortures endured by those they loved in an effort to get them to reveal Fidel's whereabouts. They kept silent counsel, hearts undoubtedly pounding out of their chests but heads held high. Each played his or her part to perfection. Later, in prison, Haydée and Melba were housed with more than a thousand common criminals. The authorities assumed those hardened criminals would harass and abuse them. Instead, they protected them from their real abusers: the prison guards.

Haydée spoke as well about the months and days and hours prior to the attack. She remembered how she and Melba had waited patiently in Havana for the instructions they would have to follow leading up to the trip. When they were given the go-ahead to travel, they asked what clothing they should pack and for how many days, hoping for some clue to their destination. In both cases the response had been "just bring whatever you want."

They traveled separately and, until the night before each departure, had no idea of where they were going. Haydée rode the train to Santiago de Cuba accompanied by a large trunk filled with weapons. It was carnival time in Santiago, the most popular carnival in the country, and lots of people were making the trip. The train was crowded. A soldier sat next to Haydée, and she struck up a conversation with him, even making plans to meet and go dancing when they reached their destination. When he asked what was in the trunk, she said books. He offered to haul it off the train for her, and she continued to flirt as she gratefully accepted. Abel was at the station to meet her. When he caught sight of the soldier, he wondered if the weapons had been detected. But Haydée gave him one of her confident looks as she introduced her travel companion, assuring her brother the man's company had made her trip ever so much more enjoyable:

> In order to buy a rifle, to buy ammunition, we had to limit the food we could afford to buy. Our comrades had to go without cigarettes; they had to go without the little cup of coffee that cost three cents. To be able to purchase those meager weapons and what ammunition we could get, we literally had to go hungry. But the thing is, we never felt hungry.[5]

Many years and so much history later, Haydée's daughter Celia María added her own lucid commentary to her mother's passionate reminiscence. I've found no better analysis of what Moncada and the Cuban Revolution as a whole meant in Haydée's life and what Haydée meant to the Cuban Revolution than these words from Celia's prologue to a 2005 edition of *Haydée habla del Moncada*:

> This Revolution, that came through the narrow door of that apartment at 25 and O, that apartment she kept so scrupulously clean, was the reason for her existence. This same Revolution that now, fifty years later, has become the world Revolution, changed its first wet diapers in the soul of that woman who, as chance would have it, also happened to be my mother.
>
> She often told me that she believed in Fidel from the very beginning, and that for her and for Abel, Fidel had to live for a long long time. None of us doubt that now, but half a century ago only the special light that shone in the eyes of those Santamarías reflected the importance of Fidel Castro to the Cuban Revolution.
>
> This is clear in the letter she sent to my grandparents from the women's prison at Guanajay [. . .]. With an almost infantile innocence she invites her mother to feel joy in Abel's death, and she promises *enormous and profound* changes for my grandparents, changes that did in fact take place: my grandmother, a conservative Spanish woman, lived out her days fighting with energetic fervor for her Constancia sugar mill, and joining the ranks of the Communist Party.
>
> Even with all of this, Moncada was only the tip of the iceberg. I don't believe that anyone who knew her well could conclude that "Haydée wasn't able to survive Moncada," that she wasn't able to survive Abel's dead eyes floating in a basin. After that, she was much richer internally, and she did a great deal more. Abel's death was the death of her first great love, and it made her stronger, never weaker. She was aware that she lived in the eye of the storm, like all the *illuminated ones*.
>
> For this woman, Moncada, Boris and Abel were only the beginning. I can't imagine, for example, how Fidel ever thought he could have prevented her from going to the civilian hospital, dangerous as that was. From the moment her delicate woman's hands ironed the combatants' uniforms, she was part of that history. She had more than enough room left in her life to know and weep for other loves.[6]

In the final hours before the attack, at the Siboney farmhouse the leaders of the movement distributed the weapons they had been able to accumulate,

Photos from Haydée's police file, showing length of sentence. PHOTO
COURTESY CASA DE LAS AMÉRICAS.

and Fidel spoke one last time to those about to go into battle. He told them
they could still back out for whatever reason and that no one would think less
of them. No one took that option. The cars left the farmhouse roughly in the
order decided upon by the leadership, although there was some discussion as
to which car Haydée and Melba should ride in and what their specific destination should be. Someone said they would be useful at the civilian hospital,
and that chance suggestion allowed Haydée and her brother to be together
as the attack unfolded.

So much has been written about this historic battle, so much testimony
exists from those who were present and survived: not only the rebels but
also several doctors and nurses who were caught up in the attack, as well
as a few townspeople who happened to be nearby and heard the gunfire.

When momentous events succeed one another in a relatively brief period of time, as occurred in the history of the Cuban Revolution from Moncada to the trial and imprisonment of Fidel, amnesty and exile to Mexico, return on the poorly outfitted boat called *Granma*, war in the mountains and city undergrounds, and exuberant victory of January 1, 1959, a lot can get lost.

Fortunately, Cuba's revolutionaries made a point of telling and retelling the stories, and we have enough verifiable testimony from a range of participants to be able to piece the history together. Although Armando Hart had been active, along with others, in trying to build a viable opposition to Batista, he was not part of Fidel's group, nor did he take part in the Moncada attack. He would join Fidel soon after that action, participate in the founding of the July 26 Movement, and he and Haydée would marry and live together until shortly before her death. His bystander's description of the assault's intention and of how Fidel managed to escape torture and death is succinct and useful:

> On July 26, 1953, the country was shaken by news of the heroic events. [. . .] These actions aimed to capture by surprise attack the Santiago and Bayamo garrisons, as well as the Provincial Court and Civilian Hospital, in order to then summon the entire country to a general strike. [. . .] If the attack was defeated, the plan was to try and continue the struggle in the mountains. And that was the alternative Fidel put in practice when [it] failed. He was arrested, however, by a military patrol under the command of Lieutenant Pedro Sarría,[7] who acted with a dignity highly unusual in that army and took Fidel to the municipal jail to face trial, rather than handing him over to Chaviano, the commander of the Moncada garrison. Fate worked this time in favor of the Revolution.[8]

Haydée's voice, with its exquisite mix of breadth and depth, memory and passion, is without a doubt among the most evocative. She has said:

> My final moments with Abel are vague. I was able to talk to him at the Hospital, then they took him away and after that I can only imagine. So I can't really be sure which were our last moments. Perhaps they were when he was no longer alive. Because in that sort of situation everything happens so fast. And we were combatants, trained to go into combat whenever that became necessary. Later, so many things go through your mind that you can't be sure if you dreamed them or they really happened . . . the time

comes when you want to think and believe that's the way it was. That's why I've often been afraid to write about all this, because you just don't know. Images get confused with reality. Tremendously.

And so I will say that our last moments were probably when he instructed Melba and me, when he told us what was going to happen and how the two of us should conduct ourselves. That was really our last encounter, because that was when we received Abel's final instructions, when he prepared us to go on living. Because Abel was always sure we would survive and he wouldn't. I don't know why. For him that was absolutely clear, and he prepared us much more to be able to keep on living than to die. If he'd believed we were going to die, he would have prepared us for that. So that was our last meeting . . . his last message . . . where our gazes remained, our thoughts, those fragments that might have been fragments or not, but who cares. That's another story.[9]

While waiting for their trial, Haydée and Melba remained at Boniato prison. Excerpts from a letter she wrote to her parents give some sense of her state of mind, although it is clear she wrote in a way she felt might soften the situation for them:

> Dear Parents, I don't know what to tell you, because I know nothing I say will help, you've suffered too much, but life is like that, those who least deserve it suffer most.
>
> Don't feel bad for me. I'm doing very well. Even though we are isolated we are fine, and our health is good. I have enough clothing. [. . .] Melba is fine, very well really, she doesn't even have a cold. The doctor here is good, and he's prescribed two types of vitamin B for me, not because I am ill but because he says I need to gain weight. [. . .][10]

Haydée Santamaría's file bore the number 148/953. She was charged with "sedition against state power." She was listed as being 1.61 meters tall (5'3¼"), weighing 101 pounds, with a pale complexion, white skin, light brown hair, a medium forehead, straight eyebrows, natural eyelids, hazel eyes, a straight nose, small mouth, fine lips, medium-sized ears, and an oval face.[11]

When Haydée, Melba, and the other survivors—except for Fidel; he was brought before the magistrate separately—were tried in Santiago de Cuba, among the three dozen or so reporters permitted to be present at the proceedings of Cause no. 37 was a sixteen-year-old journalist from Havana. Marta

Haydée and her mother, Joaquina Cuadrado, on Haydée's release from the prison at Guanajay, 1954. PHOTO BY CONSTANTINO ARIAS, COURTESY CASA DE LAS AMÉRICAS.

Rojas, an intern at *Bohemia* magazine, was acutely observant and deeply touched by Haydée in particular:

> I expected to see a subdued group of ruffians, half destroyed by what they had been through: a sad and dramatic scene. I expected to find them dirty, in shabby clothing, and also filled with hatred. [. . .] I was surprised to see beautiful faces, the faces of perfectly normal young people, like those you might see anywhere. They were clean, with neatly ironed clothes [. . .] but their faces were what I noticed first. They moved me tremendously.
>
> It was just a flash, a few seconds. They entered the courtroom in a group, with a sort of rustling sound, nothing out of the ordinary but there were a lot of them, and since they were handcuffed you could hear the jangle of the cuffs. And the handcuffs were shiny too, which reinforced the sense of some sort of splendid occasion.[12]

Marta Rojas, the young black reporter from Havana, noticed Haydée. And Haydée, in the midst of her agony, noticed Marta:

> She began writing everything down, everything about the trial, in a little notebook. But what did she do then? She tore each page out and hid it. She always wore a skirt with lots of pockets, and I noticed that what she left in the notebook were notes that wouldn't seem like anything out of the ordinary if they were confiscated at the door: So and so gave his testimony at 3 p.m., things like that. But she was always writing, writing and tearing out pages and putting them in her pockets. And that's how so much of that trial has been preserved. I tried to retrieve my own testimony and couldn't. I think they made sure it got misplaced. And she had copied it almost word for word. At the time she had only a journalist's consciousness, and probably thought no one would publish what she wrote anyway. But it's clear she had an intuition for history. . . .
>
> I kept looking at her because her face didn't seem to me to be the face of someone who supported the dictatorship [. . .] after I got out of prison, she told me that when I kept staring at her like that, she lowered her head; she said she imagined I must think badly of her, and felt ashamed. That's why, when they were taking us out and she stepped forward to say hello, she was afraid I would brush her off. [. . .]
>
> They let us receive some clothing when we went to trial and my mother had sent me a handkerchief—I have this habit, I don't know if it has to do with nerves, but I have this habit, when I speak, I have this

habit of holding a handkerchief or something in my hand, and [. . .] she'd noticed that handkerchief because I twisted it constantly. And when she approached me, so as not to have to say hello—because she didn't know how I'd react—she said: "What a pretty handkerchief!" And I said: "Do you like it? Here, take it." And she did.[13]


In the July–August 1973 issue of *Casa de las Américas* magazine, the institution to which Haydée gave so much paid tribute to the twentieth anniversary of the attack on Moncada by publishing a series of interviews with its founder that had been conducted by Marta Rojas and other journalists. In 2013, on the sixtieth anniversary of Moncada, the magazine reprinted parts of those interviews. Haydée herself had been gone for more than thirty years. Her daughter, Celia María—such a wise interpreter of her mother's life—had been gone for six. The years pass, survivors die natural and unnatural deaths, and memory is ever more threatened by silence.

Haydée's testimony contains the intelligence, feeling, precise weight, and extraordinary poetry that so palpably evoke that moment that changed history—the history not only of Cuba but of all of Latin America. I offer fragments of that testimony here, as the very best way of conveying an event almost too large to be constrained by words:

When we went to Moncada in the last car, one of the cars in front of us had taken a wrong turn. It wasn't headed to the Civilian Hospital or to the Military Hospital, or to the Court, or even to the barracks. We got confused, and for a few minutes we were lost. And we began to wonder if we could get to the hospital, because we had already begun to hear gunfire. Lost as we were, it seemed crazy to try to reach the hospital.

I don't remember exactly how the other comrades reacted. But I remember my reaction. I thought: Abel is there, and if we don't make it to the hospital I won't be with him. That moment, in which one of the cars got turned around, causing us to get briefly distracted, was so terrible that it lived in me for years and years. So much so, that it was what made me refuse, much later, to leave Cuba for Mexico.

When Fidel and the others were about to come back on the *Granma*, on two or three occasions he wrote asking me when I was coming to Mexico. I put him off, again and again. And it wasn't even conscious. Those moments in which I didn't know if I would be able to get to the hospital had traumatized me to the point where each time he told me "come to Mexico," I thought: What if I can't get on the boat? What if I get seasick? If I can't land? Or they imprison me in Mexico? How will I get back here then? I knew that in Cuba, wherever Fidel managed to land I would find him. This gives you an idea of how terrible those moments were for me. I don't know if it was ten minutes, five, four. I don't know.

But I do know that in that car there was a discussion about whether or not we should even go to the hospital. There was a moment when someone said we should just stop anywhere within the garrison, what difference would it make? But my goal was the hospital. [. . .]

I insisted and insisted that we find the hospital. If I'm being absolutely honest I have to say that I wanted to find Abel. I remember a brief conversation in the car about it being crazy to wait until we get to the hospital. And it really was crazy, because there was gunfire all around us by then, and we could get caught in the crossfire.

When I saw "Saturnino Lora," I said: Here it is! And I jumped from the car and began to run. I looked at Melba, as if to say: "Come on, let's go!" The others didn't move, because it was clear there was a firefight going on. But I told myself I had to reach Abel. Not because I was more revolutionary than the others, or because I had a greater desire to fight than they did—because we could have fought in any of the other locations. I wanted to get to where Abel was. I wanted to die with Abel or live with Abel. [. . .]

At the hospital I remember we took two or three prisoners and stuck them in a room. They had their hands up, pleading with us that they weren't going to do anything and that we should just let them hide there. I think one of them was a woman. [. . .]

Later I went looking for Abel. I don't remember what we said when we found one another. I know he was happy, contented. He was pleased with how everything was going. [. . .] The most important thing was not to let the enemy take our position. If we weren't going to be able to capture the garrison, what reason did we have for remaining there? The only reason, I think now, was that for Abel it was very important that we keep fighting so the enemy wouldn't realize everything had ended, and Fidel would have more time to get into the mountains as we had planned. [. . .] Abel knew we hadn't taken the garrison, but he went on firing to hold their attention, so they wouldn't think the battle had ended. This wasn't something we had planned. This was something that occurred to Abel at that moment.

In any case, those who fought at the garrison had to find an escape route. They couldn't stay where they were because it was as if they were in the street, in plain view. We were inside the hospital. We had two options: we could go out or stay where we were. I think we chose the worst of the two options because we didn't know our way around Santiago. That was the first time we'd been to Santiago de Cuba, at least Melba and I. Abel was the one with the experience, he'd been coming to Santiago for a while by then. But he was so concerned that Fidel have as much time as possible to make it into the Sierra, that he didn't say anything. From the time the shooting ended until the moment of our capture must have been an hour and a half or two hours.

I'm still confused about exactly how the comrades who fought there were captured. My memory is not very clear about that. They told us, and all the data seems to confirm it, that the person we suspected was the one who gave us away. But I didn't really remember. In fact, [after the war] when that person went on trial, they didn't execute him because I wasn't absolutely sure I recognized his face. I only remembered one face, and it was Abel's. In 1959 I had to identify several nurses. The only one I remembered was the one who bandaged Abel's eye. She was engraved in my mind because of her connection with Abel. [. . .]

Humans can be unpredictable! A doctor I called to help us save one of the wounded, one of the wounded who wasn't ours but one of the dictatorship's soldiers—he was a sergeant or a lieutenant, I can't remember—that doctor told me flatly no. He wasn't going out there. If we dragged the man inside, he'd take a look. The man was lying in the patio and we wanted that doctor to see if he could help him, or at least tell us if he was dead or alive. And he said no, that if we brought him inside he'd see what he could do. We told him we couldn't lift the body. Gómez García and I had already tried. [. . .] I had put my hand on his heart and everything, but I couldn't tell. And that's when I went back to get that doctor, and he refused to come with me. I tried arguing with him. I asked him what kind of a doctor he was to let a man bleed to death. He said: "But he's not even one of yours."

Then the other doctor said: "Okay, I'll go." And he crouched down and accompanied me. For a second time I dragged myself to where the wounded soldier lay. [. . .]. When we got there, that doctor looked at him, then at me, and said: "There's nothing to be done. He's dead. He died instantly. There's nothing we can do." [. . .]

*Moncadistas* and family members, upon Fidel's release from the prison at Isle of Pines, 1955. Left to right: Raúl Castro and his sisters; Melba's mother, Elena; Melba Hernández; Fidel; Haydée. PHOTO COURTESY CASA DE LAS AMÉRICAS.

Melba, Fidel, and Haydée. PHOTO COURTESY CASA DE LAS AMÉRICAS.

Later, during the trial, they took opposite positions. Their roles were reversed. The judge asked: "Is it true that you saw two women, and the blonde one let one of the soldiers bleed to death?" That doctor responded by pointing to me: "Yes, that one." It was the doctor who had accompanied me to look at the soldier.

And the doctor who had refused to go with me, who didn't want to take the risk, when the judge asked him: "Did you see a woman approach a wounded soldier?" he responded: "There was a young woman who came for me and asked if I would help her attend to a wounded soldier." He testified to that, and it was a courageous thing to do. [. . .] For me it was very important that the people of Santiago didn't see me as a beast, as someone without feelings, because that accusation had been terrible.

That doctor was very brave at the trial. So I don't know which of the two is worth more, because each had his moment. We'd have to find out who they are today in order to be able to analyze which of them is worth something and which isn't. Because the one who is the bravest, the one who is worth more, would be the one who is with the revolution. In any case, I was tremendously relieved when that doctor said: "No, she came looking for me and tried to make me go with her." For me that was a gift.

Those they took down [a flight of stairs] were never seen again. Those who went down those stairs . . . not even the soldiers witnessed what they didn't want them to see. When they brought us up, I remember one of the soldiers saying: "You're lucky, because not everyone makes it back up here." I'll never forget that little staircase, because when he said that I thought: So Abel's not coming back up. When they brought us up those stairs, the boys were in very bad shape, very bad shape. They were finishing them off.

At trial I felt a tremendous euphoria. I thought I might see Abel. Then, as soon as I said the words *my brother*, I suddenly thought to myself: But Abel is dead! It was just a fraction of a second. The judge said: "If you want to take a break, you can." That's when I recovered, and said: "No, he told me I had to live to tell what happened." That gave me a lot of strength. "He told me I had to live to tell everything, and I'm here and I want to tell everything." That helped me get through it.

When I stopped talking I returned to my seat filled with pride. Not pride in front of all those people, just to show them who I was, but pride because I was able to recover my strength when I talked about Abel and

Boris, about what they did to them. And then, right away, I felt like I was being pulled apart inside. I felt like something was ripping me in two. My declaration wasn't very long. And I had planned what I was going to say, but didn't say any of what I had planned. I didn't say anything I'd planned, but I said everything. [. . .] That's when I realized that what I had been through could shut me down.

In the hospital I lived because Abel was there. Later, in the barracks, when I realized they weren't going to kill me I thought: I have to live until I know that Fidel is alive, I can't die until I know he isn't dead. Then Fidel appeared, and I told myself I have to live in order to help Fidel. Furthermore, Fidel doesn't know if Abel is dead or alive, and I have to tell him Abel is dead, but that's okay. . . . I had to tell Fidel that Abel loved him, what Abel felt for him. I had to tell Fidel that Abel didn't care if he died as long as Fidel lived.

Then I thought: I have to stay alive until the trial ends, because at the trial I have to tell the world how Abel died. It has to be me. I have to live for that. I got through the trial, I finished my declaration, and told myself: Now I can die. [. . .] If I hadn't been able to get to the hospital, what would have become of my life? I don't know. It would have been unbearably sad. [. . .]

And I love life. Because I'm telling you, not a second, not a minute of that last night at Siboney escapes me. I was conscious that it was a decisive night for me, whether I lived or died. That's why I remember it as the most marvelous night of my life. [. . .] What's not possible is to live knowing you've left something undone. This is what makes life worthwhile. It's the only thing that does.

For me, [all the important moments] have been like that night at Siboney. Then it was also nine o'clock, and Frank wasn't there. Like July 25 of 1953, when it was nine o'clock and Abel hadn't arrived. Like that November 29, when I looked at Armando and thought: What if we never see him again? Like July 25, when I looked at Boris and thought: What if we never see him again? This is so hard. It's very difficult to live through moments like those, if you don't go through them with comrades, if you don't go into them in love with life, determined to give everything or achieve everything.

Later we were in the mountains. I looked at Camilo, saw his beautiful smile and thought: If we lose that smile, like we lost Abel's. . . . Even later, in normal times—I mean after 1959 when we were no longer underground—when I looked at Che, I still thought: If we never see that smile again, what greatness will have been taken from us!

Moncada existed because there were dozens of young men who the people of Santiago saw tortured to death, murdered. Because the people of Santiago felt their pain, they came to understand people differently. Because they knew that not everything had gone to ruin here. They knew there were people willing to be tortured to death shouting *Viva Cuba!* All of that took root in Santiago de Cuba. And the help the people of Santiago gave those in the mountains was decisive, the help they gave the underground was decisive. [. . .]

This happened in Santiago de Cuba. What gave birth to it? . . . Of course, the nobility of the people of that city, no doubt about that. That was what enabled them to understand Moncada. Because there was a greatness, a nobility, in that city that made it possible for the people to understand those who went to Moncada, for them to understand the caliber of those who died and those who lived. [. . .]

And so, without the courage of those who died, and without the firm resolve of those who survived, Moncada would have been an attack on a military garrison, but it wouldn't have been Moncada. [. . .]

The essence of Moncada lives on in those comrades who didn't fail to show up, in those who lay buried in Santa Ifigenia, or in any patch of Santiago's earth. Although we always say they're in Santa Ifigenia, that's not really true. Some of them might be anywhere, wherever. That never concerned or troubled us, because where any of those heroes is buried, even in the most impoverished or nondescript grave, a beautiful *mariposa* flower may bloom on that spot, and maybe without anyone even planting it. And so Moncada is everything. Even that *mariposa*—such a Cuban flower—reminds us of Moncada. Moncada is those who died and those who will live forever. It is everything that came later: Che, Camilo, the people, the Revolution, Fidel. The one thing we cannot imagine is Moncada without Fidel.

And this is the only thing we have to teach our young people: that life is more beautiful than anything, and that life is beautiful when you live it like that. You cannot really live it any other way.[14]


I want to say something else. It doesn't describe or explain Moncada as much as it demonstrates the honesty with which Haydée explored her own relationship to struggle. Sometime in the 1960s, preparing for yet another anniversary of the historic attack, she suggested that singer-songwriters Silvio Rodríguez, Pablo Milanés, and Noël Nicola might be inspired to write a song about Moncada and perform it at that year's commemoration. They said they were honored but hesitant. How could they hope to create a song that would say anything new or do justice to such heroism?

Haydée told them not to be afraid. She would help by sharing some of her own memories of courage, fear and cowardice: the range of sentiments and attitudes manifest in the attack:

> I told them I didn't think it should be so hard, because they could sing about anything, anything at all, and they would be singing to Moncada. I said it wouldn't be hard because if they sang about life, they would be singing to Moncada, if they sang about death they would be singing to Moncada, if they spoke about joy, if they spoke about pain, if they spoke about courage: Moncada was all of that. And maybe if they spoke about cowardice they would also be speaking about Moncada. Because how many of us who were there may have been more cowardly even than those who didn't show up? Cowardice isn't defined in a single moment any more than courage is. I can tell you there was hardly a comrade who participated with me, not just at Moncada but in other actions as well, who remembers me acting in a cowardly way. And yet if I am sincere I must say there were many times in which I experienced a terrible fear.[15]

As was customary, during the 1954 holidays visitors brought toys to the prison, to the children who lived with their mothers incarcerated for nonpolitical crimes. Marta Rojas, the same reporter who had taken notes at Haydée's trial, took advantage of the occasion to snap a picture of the two *Moncadistas*. Forty years later, in September 1996, she was working at *Granma*, the Cuban Communist Party newspaper. On December 25 of that year she published an article, accompanied by that picture. Not much later, she received a letter, sent to her office by a young woman named Maritza. Some of that letter's most relevant paragraphs read:

> I am one of the little girls who appear in the photo that accompanied your article. I am the one on the right, seated by Haydée. I lived at Guanajay with my mother, who had gone to prison for homicide, and I was there from the age of a few months until I was five. I remember a lot from that

January 6, 1954; visitors to Melba and Haydée bring Christmas gifts for the children living with the nonpolitical prisoners. PHOTO BY MARTA ROJAS, COURTESY CASA DE LAS AMÉRICAS.

Melba and Haydée leaving Guanajay Prison, 1954. PHOTO BY CONSTANTINO ARIAS, COURTESY CASA DE LAS AMÉRICAS.

time, but my family never wanted to talk about that period in our lives. It was shrouded in silence. [. . .]

Maritza's letter goes on to describe how she suffered as a child at the prison, how the guards used her as a toy and her mother had to carry her around when she was forced to scrub the long halls. After the revolution mother and daughter's lives changed radically. For a long time she was ashamed to talk about her past, but Marta's story made her feel pride rather than shame. When she wrote to the journalist she had been a teacher for many years.[16]

In an interview she gave in 2008, Rojas explains how she managed to get that photograph:

On Three Kings Day, society women here were accustomed to giving gifts to the common criminals' children. Since journalists were allowed to photograph the event, I talked to my boss, Enrique de la Osa, about the possibility of getting a photo. I asked Melba's mother where the women's cell was located, and told her to tell them to be sure to stand at the bars until the end of the act. I went with Panchito Cano. [. . .] He had two cameras. And we began to take notes as if we were writing up the story. When a group of children had already received their toys, I told them: "Go over there and see that blond lady." I asked Panchito for a camera (we'd planned it all beforehand), and followed the children. When they got close to the bars I took one picture. When I was about two yards away, I said: "Stand up," and I raised the camera and took that one. It was published for the first time in January 1959.[17]

# 5 WAR

She was an exceptional creature in her passage through life, possessed of a volcano's force and flower's delicacy, hurricane's beauty or mountain dawn, the astonishing ability to fight as she loved and to love with the ferocious intensity of combat.

—Editor's note, *Casa de las Américas*, no. 273 (October–December 2013): 3

The July 26 Movement knew that armed struggle was the necessary, even inevitable, way to depose Batista and to create a society based on justice. Its leaders didn't take that struggle lightly. They developed modalities that avoided unnecessary danger. They were generous in victory.

War was painful and also strangely natural for Haydée. Painful because she hated violence and because she lost so many people close to her, beginning with her brother Abel and fiancé, Boris, and including in rapid succession all the others who died at Moncada, in the underground, in the Sierra, and even after victory. Frank País. Camilo Cienfuegos. Che Guevara. Celia Sánchez. Each name was a world, and these are only the most prominent among them.

War was also uncannily natural to this woman, whose character was such a mix of passion and calm. She knew all other routes had been exhausted and never doubted her commitment or what she had to do to give birth to the

January 27, 1953. After depositing a floral wreath at the José Martí statue,
Havana's Central Park. Left to right: Boris Luis Santa Coloma, Haydée,
Elda Pérez, Melba Hernández, and Jesús Montané.

In the Sierra on the occasion of the leadership meeting of the July 26 Movement, 1957. Left to right: Ciro Redondo, Vilma Espín, Fidel, Haydée, and Celia Sánchez.
PHOTO COURTESY CASA DE LAS AMÉRICAS.

Cuba of her dreams. And she possessed every skill necessary for that delivery. She was fearless when in greatest danger.

Nancy Stout describes Haydée, Armando Hart, Vilma Espín, and Frank País on their way to a clandestine meeting of the movement's leadership in February 1957.

> In Havana, as soon as directors Armando Hart and Haydée Santamaría found out that Fidel wanted the leadership to assemble, they simply went to the airport and took the first plane to Santiago. [. . .] Vilma Espín drove the big three—Frank, Haydée, and Armando—over the mountain highway from Santiago to Manzanillo. Stopped at all checkpoints, they were completely conspicuous in the Red Threat [what they called Vilma's car], but to the soldiers they appeared to be two happy couples in a new red Dodge.[1]

Haydée could also change her appearance instantly:

> It's always been easy for me to gain weight. When I wanted to, I could put on 20 pounds without any trouble at all. And when I wanted to take them

off, I could do that just as quickly. That, and changing my hair, cutting it or letting it grow, and I looked like another person.[2]

With these ruses or through other disguises or by pretending to be a peasant woman, aged or pregnant, she carried out operations that were difficult if not impossible for her comrades.

She could be serene in the midst of great drama. On April 15, 1957, US journalists Robert Tabor and Wendell Hoffman came to Cuba seeking a television interview with Fidel. Haydée picked them and all their equipment up in Havana and delivered them to the Sierra. Armando Hart and Faustino Pérez descended from the car they were all in and were arrested before her eyes. But she managed to get away and continue to carry out her mission. Although Armando was already her husband, she never looked back.[3]

Haydée insisted that she developed this sort of serenity in the face of danger because she had to.

Moncada was behind us, and I was worried that the publicity had made me too familiar a face, that they wouldn't allow me to keep on acting. And that participation was terribly important to me; it meant more than life itself. I needed to keep doing things, move freely, work on every front. Because if I couldn't, why had I lived? Having survived imbued me with a profound tranquility.[4]

Haydée told the following story, clearly one of many.

I remember one night when Vilma [Espín] and I were hiding at the Ruiz Bravo's house. We got wind that the police were in the neighborhood. Vilma always had a bag [. . .] it was a brown paper bag in which she kept Frank's correspondence, and later Daniel's [René Ramos Latour]. The police arrived and I said: "Vilma! Vilma, run, take the bag!" Vilma grabbed the bag and lit out of there. She climbed over a rooftop and I could hear her shouting, "Yeyé, Yeyé, come on!" I told her: "I'll be right there!"

When I realized that Vilma had jumped—I don't know how she managed not to break a foot, because she jumped quite a long ways down—I told the others in the house: "Let me go to the door." I opened it and welcomed the cops: "What can I do for you, Officers?" "We've been told there are people hiding here." "Well, come on in. Would you like some coffee? Anything else?" And I gave them something to drink.

The people who owned the house were all right there. The police began to search the premises, and I followed them from room to room: "Do what you have to do," I told them, "so we don't have to go through this again tomorrow." If they missed a room or a closet or even a bed, I'd say: "Come on, don't you want to look over here?" Of course there were some places where I knew we had hidden things—documents, letters—but I would open doors before they could get to them: "Look here, make sure you look over there."

I had some letters from Armando. I can't remember if he was in prison then or in the Sierra, but I know he wasn't in Santiago. I had hidden those letters in the folds of a drape, so of course I didn't direct their attention there. They finished searching, and asked for more coffee. I served it to them, we shook hands, and my parting words were: "Okay now, you guys, you know there's no problem if you have to come back."

When the police were gone, Esperanza, María, Ramona, the whole family almost passed out—and I should say that the mother, father, and all seven or eight children belonged to the movement. I felt calm as could be. On the outside, of course. Because inside I was . . . well, you can imagine. Only later did we realize that all of us had received the cops in our nightclothes.

Vilma returned a while later, sure that I had escaped as well, and when they told her I'd welcomed the cops, given them coffee, and everything that had taken place, she was . . . ! I'm telling you, I was calm the whole time, because I really never thought anything would happen to me. Nothing happened to me at Moncada, nothing happened in so many other situations, I don't know: I just didn't think I was vulnerable. And I felt even less vulnerable after making it through that night.[5]

Haydée said that for years Batista's police were unable to catch her at anything or anywhere:

I operated all over Cuba, and they never caught me. I kept on transporting arms to the Sierra, and they never caught me. I went up into the mountains and came down again, and they never caught me. I can tell you, I had a lot of experience, much more than all those people in Miami combined, whose only experience was living well, the experience of not caring how many people in Cuba were dying. They did what they did for status. And I, who had status here, did what I did so my comrades would have the arms they needed.[6] [At the time of this talk, Haydée was particularly angry at Miami's exile community, which continued to launch damaging covert actions aimed at destabilizing the revolution.]

In 1958, Armando Hart was imprisoned at Boniato, the same place where Haydée herself had served time not that many years before. The April strike had just taken place, and she wanted to inform him about decisions taken by the movement leadership regarding that strike, as well as to tell him she was being sent abroad to carry out a mission for the revolution. She also knew he was suffering the recent death of his brother, Enrique, who had been killed when the mechanism on a bomb he was placing failed and exploded too soon.

In order to visit him, she changed her appearance completely and registered with the prison authorities as his sister, Marta Hart. Armando was stunned when he caught sight of her. None of the guards recognized her, although she said she remembered a number of them all too well. She would never forget those faces.

Between 1955 and the end of the war in December 1958, Haydée traveled the island with impunity. Along with a few others in the leadership, she prepared the complex November 30, 1956, uprising in Santiago de Cuba that was planned to coincide with the *Granma*'s arrival. The idea was that generalized fighting in the city's streets would divert attention from the return of Fidel and his men from Mexico (they were expected to land on the nearby coast). Unfortunately, as high seas and other unforeseen problems brought the boat in several days later than planned, the calculation failed.

But Haydée also proved key to saving lives that fateful day. Her experience of having been trapped at Moncada had taught her that when a battle was doomed, the most expedient measure was to effect an immediate retreat. She had to argue with Frank País, then head of Action in Santiago, but was able to convince him she was right. A small group of those who arrived on the *Granma* managed to make it into the mountains. As Fidel later famously said, with those few men, victory was assured.

Haydée played an essential role in both the Havana and Santiago undergrounds. She recruited hundreds of people to the rebel cause, acquiring safe houses and transporting and hiding those who needed refuge. She was a contact for foreign journalists, picking them up in Havana and accompanying them to their mountain interviews with Fidel. She traveled into the Sierra and returned to the cities time and time again, never once getting caught. Sometimes she was the only one in a group of comrades who didn't. She traveled outside the country, reluctantly but with extraordinary resourcefulness,

Haydée and Fidel in the Sierra, 1958. PHOTO COURTESY CASA DE LAS AMÉRICAS.

successfully carrying out every task she was assigned. Most important, she was part of the movement's leadership, fully involved in its analysis and decision making.

Nancy Stout writes about Haydée, in her leadership position, being consulted about an important movement decision.

> Celia, learning of Fidel's determination to come [back to Cuba] within the year, made a quick trip to Havana to ask Armando Hart and Haydée Santamaría for permission to fly to Mexico and return on the *Granma*, accompanying Fidel and his soldiers in the landing. She pointed out that she knew the coast better than any others who would be onboard, could guide the crew into any of the harbors, and could then be there to coordinate the truck drivers. Haydée was supportive; Armando talked the idea over with Frank [País]. Fidel was consulted, and was ambivalent about the dynamics of having a woman on the trip. It was Frank who made the decision: Celia was in command of the landing, and should be there, on the coast, directing the preparations for it, not on the vessel en route from Mexico.[7]

Armando Hart was looking for the leader he believed could defeat the dictatorship. It was Haydée who recruited him to Fidel's cause. Hart writes:

> As soon as I got out of prison, I contacted Melba and Haydée. They talked to me about what Moncada represented and told me of the work carried out by Abel Santamaría and the group of *compañeros* who together with Fidel had prepared the action. They also explained Fidel's ideas and program, as well as his fundamental opposition to the traditional parties. I came to the conclusion that, if united, the supporters of García Barcena,[8] the students, and the *Moncadistas* could provide a solid foundation for the development of the Revolution we aspired to.[9]

The apparent ease with which Haydée moved from city to mountains and from foreign countries back to her own was due, without doubt, to her conviction, discipline, and flexibility. She also had an inclination to trust her intuition, something that saved her on more than one occasion. This highly developed characteristic continued to serve her throughout her life. Nothing was too difficult for her. But those skills were cultivated and undoubtedly took their toll.

Little has been written about Haydée's prison time following the attack on Moncada Barracks. The fact that she and Melba were together proved

Haydée resting in the Sierra, 1957. PHOTO COURTESY CASA DE LAS AMÉRICAS.

extremely important and comforting to them both. They were close friends and comrades but very different in background and temperament. Melba was from an upper-middle-class family in Havana; her mother was also an important movement collaborator. And she was a university graduate, with a law degree. Haydée, with her primary school education, was from a conservative immigrant family in rural Cuba. Although a quick study, she was largely self-taught. Both women were equally committed, but Melba must have felt she had to take on a mothering role when Haydée seemed, at times, to sink into the haze of mental exhaustion.

At first the women were isolated at Boniato Prison. After their trial, they were sent to Guanajay. During those first days and weeks, Haydée suffered long periods of sleep deprivation, not directly imposed by her jailors but due to a kind of emotional paralysis. One morning, after she'd finally managed to get a few hours' sleep, Melba looked at her and began to sob. She couldn't stop crying. Haydée didn't understand, now that she'd been able to sleep, why Melba was so upset. "Because you look like you're ninety years old," her comrade said.

Haydée described periods, during her time in prison and right after she

Haydée and Celia Sánchez in the Sierra, 1958. PHOTO COURTESY CASA DE LAS AMÉRICAS.

was released, when she felt almost catatonic. She would stare into space, her mind blank. Or once out of prison, she would gaze at something in the natural or material world and feel an intense sadness that Fidel and the others who were still behind bars couldn't see what she was seeing. Sometimes she thought of her beloved dead, who could no longer see those things. She suffered from a sort of mindlessness. And she had to will herself back to her former energy level.

Were these states simply the logical residue of what Haydée experienced at Moncada, her wrenching losses and the supreme effort she was forced to make in order not to let the pain she was in destroy her? Or did they also have something to do with her singular integrity, even in seemingly playful situations? Even in much less dramatic circumstances she was supremely principled. I always had the sense she wouldn't let a racist, sexist, or homophobic joke go unchallenged.

Before and after Moncada, being one of such a small group of women among so many men also demanded a rigorous calm. How do we cope with such wounds, such challenges? Where and how do the fault lines open up between mind and body? Where does the psychological landscape end and political expediency begin? Throughout Haydée's life it seems clear that her internal borderlands remained profoundly contested.

Haydée also occasionally spoke about her other experiences in prison. She remembered an old woman serving a thirty-year sentence for having killed a man who seduced her daughter:

> She was a good person, and sympathized with us. In that prison the women could have their children with them. And in that dirty, often violent, atmosphere, those children, who went from newborns to adolescents, were subjected to all sorts of obscenities and immoral acts. This only reinforced my conviction that we needed a revolution to put an end to all that.[10]

When they were released from Guanajay, one of the first tasks Haydée and Melba were assigned was locating the comrades who had been with them since 25 and O but were now dispersed. Some had managed to escape the bloody battle and had disappeared. Some had made it into the nearby mountains; others had been able to leave the country:

> We had to find out where each of them was, and as far as possible bring them together in one place; I can't remember if it was Mexico or Guatemala. And we had to locate those who for one reason or another hadn't been able to participate in the attack—because they lacked a weapon, or had family problems, whatever the reason. Those comrades, especially, felt traumatized, profoundly affected by all that had happened.
>
> As it turned out, we didn't even have to look for those comrades. They came looking for us. Some even risked visiting us in prison, although we told them not to. What I'm saying is that Melba and I didn't have to try to find them. They came to us on their own, because they couldn't stand the thought that they hadn't been able to participate on July 26 and they

Haydée and Celia Sánchez in the Sierra, 1958. PHOTO COURTESY CASA DE
LAS AMÉRICAS.

wanted to act. This is how what we later called the movement began to
take shape.[11]

Still incarcerated, Fidel produced a document he called *Mensaje a Cuba que
sufre* (Message to a Suffering Cuba). He wrote with lemon juice between the
lines of ordinary letters, carefully numbering pages and using code names to
indicate the beginnings and ends of sections. He exposed the way so many
valuable lives had been cruelly massacred at Moncada. He described a country that had just lost its most promising young men, but also one that suffered
terrible poverty, class oppression, and increasing political repression from
the dictatorship. Haydée and Melba took on the job of copying and collating

those smuggled pages, raising the money to have them printed, and distributing them throughout the country and abroad.

Soon came the even more important task of doing the same with *La historia me absolverá* (History Will Absolve Me), a reconstructed version of Fidel's defense at trial. This latter, much more than just a powerful courtroom speech, was a full-fledged political program—and a very detailed one. For the first time, the people of Cuba and the world learned that the rebels who had gone to Moncada weren't simply lashing out against a dictatorship; they had a serious platform that contemplated almost every area of political, economic, and social change. For Haydée, printing and distributing the important document became the reason for her existence until the men—Fidel and his brother Raúl Castro, Ramiro Valdés, Jesús Montané, and others—were released from prison in the general amnesty of 1955.

Nor was Haydée absent from the intense struggle to achieve that amnesty.

This was another activity that contributed to broadening and reinforcing our organization. Every time there was one of those campaign rallies the bourgeoisie calls a "political" act, we had a group of comrades there shouting "Amnesty! Revolution! Amnesty! Revolution!" Shouting "Revolution!" while our comrades were in prison was risky, because it could affect how they were treated. But Fidel never sent word for us to stop, even though he and the others suffered the consequences. Fidel liked it better when we shouted "Revolution!" than when we shouted "Amnesty!"[12]

When Fidel was released from Isle of Pines, Haydée was at the prison gates to meet him. On the ferry that took them back to the mainland, they talked through the night. This was a moment of serious discussion.

We began exchanging ideas, and Fidel said it was time for us to decide on a name for our organization. He listened to each person's opinion, and I'm almost sure he was the one who suggested we call it the July 26 Movement.

I wanted to call it Moncada. I was used to people calling us *Moncadistas*, and I felt proud when the cops referred to us as "those damned *Moncadistas!*" Melba and I were detained on several occasions after we got out of prison, and each time they would say "those damned *Moncadistas!*" [. . .] So I really thought that should be our name. Fidel's argument was that using the name Moncada was too narrow, too much about the group of us who had attacked the Barracks. [. . .] We finally agreed on July 26

Movement. Before that we had just talked about the kids or the comrades: the kids from Artemisa or the kids from Santos Suárez. . . .[13]

Speaking about being a woman in that world of men, Haydée had some interesting things to say.

Throughout the entire revolutionary struggle I had very advanced ideas. But I was very careful. I was careful of what people might say about me as a woman, because I felt I had to protect Abel, Boris, the movement in general. Today a different way of dressing and acting is considered normal, even how things should be. But back then that appearance and those attitudes were completely off limits for me. I was never just Haydée. I was Abel's sister, Boris' girlfriend, someone linked to Fidel. Any pretext for showing me in a bad light would have reflected on the movement as a whole.

For example, we often met in those cheap hotels where couples go to make love; they were called *posadas* back then and I think they're still called *posadas*. I was careful about being seen there, because I knew what the police would say. How would they portray me? How would that reflect on Cuban women in general?

On the other hand, when I had to go to the United States, I had to frequent the worst sort of places. [. . .] I had to meet with the Mafia, wherever they told me to go, and for the first time in my life I was forced to escape from one of those meetings with a pistol in my hand. Here in Cuba I never had to carry a pistol for self-defense. I'm telling you, when I'd leave those meetings in the US, even if I took three or four showers I felt dirty. I don't want to give the false impression that any of those gangsters took advantage of me; they weren't interested in a kid who barely weighed 90 pounds. But I was always afraid they might try to kidnap me in order to get money from Fidel.

Those gangsters robbed us of millions of pesos, millions of pesos intended for Cuba. We didn't even receive the weaponry we paid for, or the planes. We ended up with little enough, and most of what came from outside the country didn't even come from the US. The ammunition we got we were able to smuggle out due to the courage of Cuban women, who traveled with it sewn into their skirts. In those days circle skirts were popular, those skirts that looked like big plates, and we tried to make them as broad as possible with individual little hidden pockets so the bullets wouldn't clang against each other. And our women comrades couldn't even travel that often, because if they did they would have been discovered.[14]

Although Haydée spoke often about her abilities, she was also forthcoming in admitting her fears.

I was always afraid of leaving Cuba. So much so, that I refused to leave. I always felt the need to be here, in my country, whatever the circumstance. [In contrast with Celia Sánchez, who had wanted to go to Mexico and return on the *Granma*—and her sister in arms had supported her in that desire—Haydée left Cuba only reluctantly.]

Fidel knew how I felt. But there came a time when my refusal made it difficult for the two of us to talk. I sensed that, and so I accepted. The truth is, I wouldn't have accepted it from anyone but him. He told me he had to ask something very difficult, and that he'd chosen me because I knew the conditions they were facing in the Sierra at that time. I told him: "All right, Fidel, if there's no other way." He said: "Well, I really need you to go, I have confidence in you. . . ."

And so I went to Miami. The only thing I asked was that he let me decide how to make the trip. I told him not to worry, no one was going to capture me. I wasn't going to take refuge in an embassy or seek asylum. I thought that would have made it even more difficult for me to return. Details, because when you're going to fulfill a mission, what's the difference? I went to Camagüey, then Santiago, I talked to Daniel—who was in charge of Action by then—and I traveled with Marcia, Léster Rodríguez's wife. She was a very young woman but with nerves of steel. We'd already gone on a few missions together.

I got to the airport first. She followed. The plan was: if something happened to me, she wouldn't get on the plane. If everything went okay, she'd board after I did and we'd continue on together. When I got to the airport and handed over my passport—one with another name and another photograph—the kid who took it looked at me, looked at the name and the photo, looked at me again, and said: "Stay right here."

I managed to get close to Marcia and I said: "Look, I think they're on to me. Go to the end of the line, so if something happens you can get away." I was wondering if I should stay there or not. But after the line moved some, that young man returned. "Come this way," he said. I started protesting: "Hey, people are already getting on the plane. . . ." And he said: "Yes, but there wasn't any room, and I've found you a seat." He grabbed me, and took me through a back way. He took me right to the plane, avoiding all the other immigration checks. Marcia, who saw what was happening but couldn't hear, ran behind us yelling at that guy: "Hey, they just told me I couldn't board, and now I see you're boarding this woman who was behind me in line!" She pretended to be upset: "So there are no seats left, huh?" But the kid told her: "Okay, you come too, come on!" She was still pretending to be mad.

When I was about to go up the steps to the door of the plane, he took my hand. He seemed a bit flustered. Then he said: "Good luck!" Fifteen years later, not long ago in fact, I ran into that man in Camagüey. He greeted me, and said: "Haydée Santamaría, you don't remember me do you?" I stared at him, because I forget names but rarely forget a face: "You remind of me someone, long ago. Are you from my village? Are you from Encrucijada? You remind me of someone in my childhood. . . ." "I'm the guy who shook your hand when you took that plane to Miami. Do you think you had me fooled?" "No," I said, "we said good-bye to each other and everything!" Then he told me that at that airport the employees would take passengers to the front of the line in order to make some money off them, and he had used the pretext that he was going to do that with me, because it was a much safer way of getting out; you didn't have to go through all the checkpoints.[15]

The woman who never wanted to have to carry out a mission outside Cuba, because she feared not being able to get back to her beloved homeland, found herself in the United States on the night of December 31, 1958, when Batista fled the country and the revolution triumphed. It was her birthday or at least the day on which she had always chosen to celebrate it. She knew victory was imminent but had many reasons for feeling nostalgic, among them the absence of those closest to her and her own physical distance from home in those final nerve-wracking moments.

The thirty-first is my birthday and it's also New Year's Eve. I was at Yuyo de Valle's house [in Miami]. Logically, I was very sad, but I don't like showing sadness in front of people. [. . .] There were a number of Cubans there

Haydée, Celia Sánchez, and Fidel in the Sierra, 1958. PHOTO COURTESY CASA DE LAS AMÉRICAS.

that night, those who were closest to us and wanted to ring in the New Year together. My presence there was like a little bit of the Sierra, a little bit of Fidel, a little bit of Moncada, of Cuba. . . . I knew I represented all that for them [. . .] and so I tried not to appear sad because there were a lot of kids there too. [. . .]

I knew I wasn't going to be strong enough to put on a credible act. I was thinking of Cuba, of those who were there and those who were no longer there. [. . .] I knew they were planning on singing our national anthem— naturally it wasn't going to be the classic New Year's Eve party. We were a group of Cubans awaiting our freedom. And it was too much for me. But I didn't want to inflict my anguish on the others. So I said I was expecting a call at a quarter to twelve. [. . .]

Yuyo knew I received certain calls, because there was a lot of communication by then. We had telephone connections with certain countries, among them Venezuela. I would get encoded messages from the Sierra via Venezuela. [. . .] I said I was expecting an important call from Cuba, so at quarter to twelve I'd have to be alone in my room. [. . .] "So you go on and celebrate." [. . .] I remember I even said: "If you're religious, pray. If you believe in the babalawo,[16] ask for his blessing." And I didn't leave my room at twelve or twelve-thirty or even one. Everyone knew not to disturb me. That was the only time I lied so I wouldn't have to celebrate with the others.

At 2 a.m. the phone rang (I heard the news before many Cubans did!). And the person on the other end of the line said he was the Cuban consul (the consul representing Batista's government). I don't know how they got my telephone number. [. . .] He said: "Are you so and so?" "Yes, hello?" "Do you know if something has happened in Cuba?" "Of course I know," I responded. "What should I do," he asked, "what should I do?" "Stay calm," I said, "and wait for instructions."

The truth is I had no idea what had happened. So I called Llanusa. I told him about that call, and I called Oscarito as well. [. . .] I said: "Let's go over there, something's happened. The consul asked what he should do, and he also told me he's been in that job for forty years and he's not a politician. I didn't even ask him his name.[17]

Haydée wanted to go to the Cuban consulate, but her two Cuban comrades, Oscarito and Llanusa, persuaded her to stay put. They'd go, they said, and call her as soon as they knew something. It was Miró Cardona, who was also in

Miami at the time, who finally called her to say there was a rumor that "the Man" had fled Cuba.

Haydée's creative mind was now in overdrive. She immediately thought of the commercial Cuban planes parked at Miami International Airport. She knew all too well that the United States would waste no time in trying to put obstacles in the way of the revolutionary government, confiscate what it could, initiate all sorts of propaganda campaigns and destabilization programs. She sent comrades to the airport to occupy those planes and get them back to the island.

It also occurred to her that Fidel might need some magistrates to formalize the establishment of the new government. A number of Cuban lawyers, members of the Supreme Court, and other judicial officials were also in Miami. She got them all together and told them Fidel needed them. They should fly to Havana immediately. One of those Cuban planes would take them. She wanted to tell them to go to the Sierra but knew that would frighten them. So she got hold of a Cuban pilot, a member of the movement, and told him to fly that group of aging men to Santiago de Cuba. "Tell them you're taking them to Havana," she said, "or else they'll die of fright."


A book twice this size would not be big enough to describe all the different decisions and actions in which Haydée participated—often assuming a leadership role—between her release from Guanajay in 1954 and the revolution's victory in the final days of 1958. She wasn't the only woman. Celia Sánchez, Vilma Espín, Melba Hernández, Asela de los Santos, Elsa Castro, Lidia Doce, Clodomira Acosta, Zoila Ibarra, María Antonia Figueroa, Aida and Ada Santamaría, Rebeca Chávez, Isabel Rielo, Teté Puebla, Mirta Rodríguez Calderón, Marcia Leseica, and Marta Rojas make up a very short list. Hundreds of others were central to the war effort in the cities or did support work. Thousands protected the revolutionaries in one way or another. Celia Sánchez was one of the principal organizers of the July 26 Movement in eastern Cuba, the first woman to join the rebel army as a combatant, a member of its general staff, and Fidel's closest confidant and aide. Celia had a legion of women as well as men working in the resistance.

In terms of gender, Cuba was no different from most of Latin America at mid-twentieth century. In the 1950s it was one of the more economically developed countries on the continent, yet by 1953 only 13.5 percent of its adult female population labored outside the home. Many of those women didn't even earn a salary; 70,000, many of them black, were domestic servants. Women were discriminated against in higher education, the workforce, and professional life. Poor women and women of color were doubly or triply oppressed. Almost no women held political positions, and the few who did were meant to be more decorative than influential.

The Cuban Revolution took women's equality seriously, insofar as its ideology at the time permitted. Emphasis was placed on enabling women and girls to study, and they soon filled classrooms at all levels and took predominance in a number of fields previously dominated by men. Equal pay for equal work provided new job opportunities, although for several decades the revolutionary government had a list of jobs women were not allowed to perform, in line with the idea (prevalent back then) that they would prove injurious to female reproduction. Abortion was legal and free, as was all health care.

The 1961 literacy campaign, special programs to provide sex workers with new skills and retrain domestic servants, day care centers, workplace dining rooms, and a great body of new law aimed at bettering women's lives all improved the situation for women—and for society overall. There was even a certain amount of mass education around the "second shift" and the need for men to do more at home as women entered the workforce in greater numbers.

The 1974 Family Code famously stipulated that husbands shoulder 50 percent of housework and child care. When my son and his partner married in 1983, the judge who officiated read that part of the Family Code into the ceremony. (I remember how thrilled I was to hear her words and then how startled by the joke she made moments later when she pronounced them man and wife: "You can take your merchandise now," she told my son and laughed.) By 1981, 44.5 percent of Cuban women were incorporated into the salaried labor force, and by 2008 the figure was 59 percent.

The Cuban Communist Party's early rejection of feminism and its consequent failure to encourage a gender analysis of society that would enable it to look at its power structure in greater depth unfortunately slowed the progress of women's emancipation. Great strides had been made in education, health care, and labor, but the issue of the complex power differential was relegated or purposefully kept at bay. Later, during the 1991–1995 Special Period caused by the dissolution of the Soviet Union, a precarious economy also sent many working women back into the home.

In 1993, a small group that called itself *Magín* broke with traditional constraints and produced a gender analysis that revealed some startling gaps in the revolution's progress in this area. Most of the *Magín* women were journalists. They were troubled by the sexist images of women that still predominated in the Cuban media. *Magín* did important work, but the Federation of Cuban Women (FMC) never accepted its validity and opposed the group until it could no longer function. Some members remained in the country; others emigrated.[18]

All these equations have since shifted, most for the better. There is much more openness and acceptance of a broad range of viewpoints. Raúl Castro's daughter Mariela runs CENISEX, a sex education and outreach institute that advocates equality for Cuba's LGBTQ community. As she has created important spaces for everyone in the gay community, she has been a strong voice for implementing more inclusive law. Some gay Cubans feel that these initiatives still come too much from above and are trying to promote more organic change. The country has not yet managed to legalize marriage equality, but many old barriers are crumbling. There is no doubt in my mind that Haydée, had she lived, would have supported all these efforts.

While she was alive, during the war that succeeded in bringing to power the first enduring twentieth-century revolution in the Americas and throughout the hard years that followed, she almost automatically assumed positions, with regard to gender and every other issue, that were advanced for her time. During the war and against entrenched discrimination (more endemic to Cuban society in general than to Fidel and most members of his high command), Cuban women demanded their place in struggle. They sewed uniforms, collected funds, distributed propaganda, nursed the wounded, ran messages, attended to safe houses, served as drivers, gave orders, and traveled outside the country to keep contact with supporters and collaborators. They were active in the underground and in the Sierra. Many were armed, but others were not (making them even more vulnerable). A few were in the movement leadership.

Women in the Sierra, especially, felt they deserved to be allowed to fight. In the last months of the war, a group headed by Isabel Rielo demanded the opportunity to establish a women's platoon. Fidel was enthusiastic about the idea, always believing women fought as well if not better than men. But he had to confront the doubts (misogyny) of several military officers who didn't think it was a good idea to allow women onto the battlefield. He established a women's fighting force in September 1958, calling it the Mariana Grajales Platoon and placing one of its most vociferous detractors,

Eddy Suñol, in charge.[19] After only a few military encounters, in which the women acquitted themselves bravely and with consummate skill, Suñol was thoroughly convinced.

Following victory, the Mariana Grajales women gave themselves to the hard work of building schools in the mountainous region of eastern Cuba. A number of women were named to important postwar positions, most of them political in nature. Women believed the revolution was making their lives better and organized massively to participate in a variety of ways. More women were educated. More women worked outside the home. Women had better health care (including attention to reproductive health) and much better conditions for raising children. For several decades this progress seemed satisfying, even extraordinary. In time, in the context of both life on the island and global change, Cuban women saw that they needed more. Their struggle continues, aided by many of the tools they acquired through their revolutionary experience.

Haydée, as I say, was always at the forefront of change. I believe that were she alive, she would identify many of the remaining challenges and be fully involved in what comes next.

It is worth pointing out that, during every phase of struggle—the preparation leading up to the attack on Moncada Barracks, the exile and return of movement leadership, the careful construction of an underground movement, the difficult unification of several progressive organizations, the war in the Sierra and final military campaigns that swept the length of the country and forced Batista out—Haydée was the single female constant. She was the thread that linked one moment to the next, the presence that provided continuity. No other woman had been present in every one of those periods, in every arena. Celia Sánchez was the other woman who was always there, but she entered the struggle after Moncada. Moncada, in fact, was what brought Fidel and his movement to her attention.

Although Armando Hart abandoned his marriage when Haydée was abroad and without so much as a conversation, an act many have called cowardly and some believe influenced her decision to take her life, their history—intimately combining revolutionary struggle, romance, and joint parenthood for so many years—cannot be denied. Together they raised two children of their own and others adopted from throughout Latin America. They shared memories only they could know. And after victory they worked in

Armando Hart and Haydée. Wedding photo, 1956. PHOTO BY CELESTINO PÉREZ, COURTESY CASA DE LAS AMÉRICAS.

the important fields of education and culture, fields where they both contributed brilliantly.

I requested an interview with Armando Hart but was told he is too ill to converse. He sent word that if I sent him a few questions, he would be happy to respond. I formulated a brief questionnaire. What I received in return were not specific answers to my questions but possibly something more moving: a few paragraphs about their life together and a copy of a letter she sent him from Miami in October 1958, during the last months of the war. I have come across almost identical versions of his text in several published books but reproduce it here because I feel it opens a window on their relationship, both political and personal, during the years they spent together:

> During the second half of 1955, Haydée and I became close, and our relationship gained such depth that it is very difficult for me to describe the exquisite and marvelous woman I knew. My personal memories of that time, and of course of subsequent years, are permeated by that relationship. It would take an immense talent to be able to put into words the images I carry with me. Our lives were intertwined with, or formed an integral part of, the great revolutionary and historic task we both embraced. I felt that nothing in me was apart from her. The intimate and historic

aspects of what I remember are so deeply linked that it is hard for me to separate them. We were almost the same person, and worked together without political or ideological differences. She was my other half, as I was hers. This is a memory I will have with me always.

I have so many beautiful stories, that it would be hard to know which ones to choose; I would need to be a poet to do them justice. But here is one: When she came down from the mountains and was headed outside the country on a mission Fidel had asked of her, I was imprisoned at Boniato. When she passed through Santiago, she came to see me. It was the same prison where she herself had spent several months not that many years before. She was taking a serious chance of being arrested again. Seeing her there frightened me. She was risking her own freedom in order to give me some information regarding decisions taken in the Sierra following the April Strike. She also thought I might need consoling because I had recently lost my brother Enrique.

She carried out her mission abroad magnificently, but that visit to the prison, like other moments too numerous to enumerate, is permanently engraved in my memory.

I also want to say something about her work after the victory of the Revolution. Her innate love of justice led to her passion for these values: Fidel, Cuba, Latin America, Fidel's interpretation of Socialism, and culture. She had a very clear vision of the role culture plays in the quest for justice. Now that culture has become a political priority, I often think of Haydée and her immense dedication to Casa de las Américas. Even without mentioning any of her other revolutionary merits, it alone would assure her of a place of honor in our country's history.[20]

And this is her letter:

Armando: I bought you this book seven months ago. I had hidden it because I wanted to surprise you, give it to you some morning as I woke you with a kiss as always. That hasn't been possible. Although it might seem strange, I give it to you with even more love, and with two kisses, with infinite sentiment and delight, there on that island where Martí was imprisoned and much later Fidel, and you, like them, are without sun, without light, although the light of the Teacher and his student illuminate you.

Fidel was less alone than Martí. He had ideas, books, and the task that Marti wasn't able to bring to fruition. You have more than Fidel, because you have the light both left us, and you have something else neither of them had. You have your Yeyé. You have her and will always have her. You will never have to go through the agony that befell our Martí, our Fidel, that terrible pain, the loss of their *Ismaelillos*.[21]

You will always have me, and if one day we are able to have our own *Ismaelillo* no one will be able to take him from us the way they took him from Martí and so many years later Fidel.

If life gives us our *Ismaelillo*, when he is old enough we can give him this book. We can give it to him with our heads held high, and tell him: Son, we have you, we are alive, but we will never fail to do our duty, even to save our own lives or yours: we were faithful to the Teacher, and to Moncada which is to say Fidel.

Then perhaps we will have some time for ourselves, and even if we don't, if we are as close as we are today, as we have been up to now, I am sure no one has had so many years of happiness. Your Yeyé[22]

Haydée, 1964. PHOTO COURTESY CASA DE LAS AMÉRICAS.

# 6 WITNESSES

She had a hunger . . .
—Norma Ruiz

In my dream she appeared in a loose-fitting peasant shirt, bell sleeves covering her arms to the wrists, expressive hands moving every which way beneath them. The hair that so often pained her in life looked perfect to me: free-flowing honey. Her expression was earnest yet kind. The fingers of one hand grazed my shoulder as she told me she was glad I was finally writing this book. Before us a grove of trees stood in a broad clearing, beams of sun descending between new leaves. Two or three horses grazed close by, raising their heads from time to time to look at us, their large brown eyes compassionate.

I was younger by many years, and held the old Nikon confidently. "I want to make some pictures," I told her, "sit over there." I indicated a spot at the base of the largest tree, and she danced toward it, spread a piece of richly embroidered cloth on the ground and settled herself. One of the horses, a creamy mare, looked up, then made a soft throaty sound of welcome.

I must have snapped the shutter a hundred times. She changed position and when she did it was like a moving sculpture, filled with grace and power.

Then, very slowly, everything faded. When I awoke, I knew it was all right. I had the approval of the only person who mattered.


In December 2013, Haydée would have been ninety years old. She'd been gone more than three decades. Her father died in 1964, her mother in 1977. She lost her brother Abel at Moncada, although his vision and heroism made him one of those who live forever. She preceded her four siblings in death, but they're dead now as well. Her biological children, Abel Enrique and Celia María, perished in an automobile accident in 2008. I've often thought it was fortunate, within such a tragic paradigm, that she didn't live to have to add those losses to so many others.

New generations of grandchildren, great-grandchildren, and cousins once and twice removed know about Haydée and the whole of their extraordinary clan—not because they remember them; most were born decades later. They didn't grow up in the same houses, share meals at the same tables, take vacations together or go to one another in times of trouble. Their relationship to family stories is more and more distant. But something of that rare spirit lives in each.

As Aida's grandson, Boris Javier Martín Santamaría, told me: "I knew my family was special, but not because I heard that at home. It was at school where I first learned something about my uncle and aunt's lives. But I remember knowing about Moncada before I knew how to read."[1]

Boris is a historian, which gives him an edge in terms of his interest in the family: he is trained to think about it analytically, and he also experiences it from the inside and is personally familiar with its dynamics. When I asked him about the sort of conversations that take place when he and his cousins get together, he said they often find themselves talking about the dead: "Not in any macabre way, but simply because there are so many of them."[2]


Niurka is Aida's second child. Her older sister, Carín, was the little girl Haydée thought so much about on the eve of going to Moncada. She died a few years ago, after a debilitating illness. A brother is also gone. Niurka is the only remaining member of the next generation in her mother's line. She is a large woman, whose expressive eyes are reminiscent of her aunt's. Boris Javier arranged our meeting, which took place at the home of Norberto Codina, a

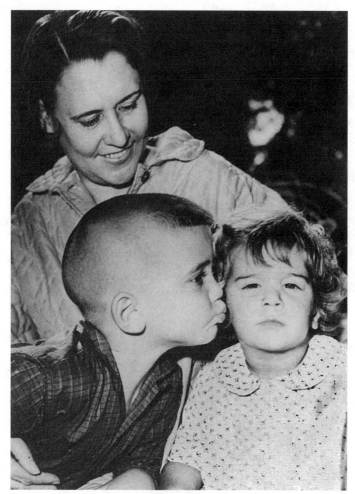

Haydée with her son Abel Enrique, and daughter, Celia María, 1964.
PHOTO COURTESY CASA DE LAS AMÉRICAS.

friend from the 1970s. Norberto, his wife, Gisela, and daughter Jimena made us comfortable in their ample living room, then retired to other rooms in the apartment. Niurka settled herself, the familiar blue plastic asthma inhaler at the ready. I turned on my little digital voice recorder.

Niurka began with her teenage memories of Haydée. She was always close to her aunt, and they spent many hours together. She described Haydée's impetuous nature, how she would arrive at a family gathering or just show

Niurka Martín Santamaría. PHOTO BY MARGARET RANDALL.

up at your house with energetic ideas about what a fun evening might be. If you were cooking black beans, Niurka told me, Haydée would say "No, why don't we make red!" If you'd arranged your living room furniture in a particular way, she would begin shifting it around, sure you'd agree it looked better the way she had in mind. And she could change plans on the spur of the moment, with such infectious enthusiasm that it was more exciting than frustrating.

Niurka said:

> Once I was feeling down: romantic problems or something. I called my aunt, and she said: "Stay where you are. I'll be right over, and I'm going to take you out." She came by and took me to the funeral parlor at Calzada and K! A filmmaker at ICAIC named Saúl Yellín had died, and my aunt had to attend the wake. The place was filled with artists and intellectuals. Imagine, I was a young girl and I was fascinated. I listened for hours to their conversations, my depression forgotten. When we left, my aunt looked at me and said: "I must be crazy! I wanted to cheer you up and I've had you all day long at a funeral!" But the thing is, she really had cheered me up.

> She read a lot, and she was always inventing stories. From the time she

was a girl herself. And she was so ahead of her time. All the women in the family were like that: Haydée, my own mother, and Adita. That strength and verve come through the Cuadrados, because the Santamarías were good people but much quieter, more staid.

Niurka told me she was twenty-two or twenty-three when her aunt committed suicide. And she was especially close to her at that point in her life. She had been married, divorced, and recently remarried. Haydée always had a hard time with divorce: "She reproached both my mother and Ada when their marriages fell apart. And me as well," Niurka said. But she was there for her niece. For both her weddings, she was the one who stitched the dress, made all the arrangements, threw the party. "She fixed up an apartment for my new husband and me, right next door to her home. She made it comfortable. And we spent a lot of time together."

These memories brought us to the months and days leading up to her suicide.

I had been on an internationalist mission to Nicaragua. I was teaching in the mountains there—I remember my aunt told me: "This is your Moncada, you must go and do your best!" But when I returned, she had changed. I could see that she was very agitated. I remember I sat my mother and my aunt Ada down and told them: "You haven't noticed, because you are with her everyday. But I can see how much she's deteriorated. You've got to do something. . . ."

So many, in hindsight, wished they had been able to do something: the haunting residual when someone you love takes her life. Niurka also had an additional story. She said that she and her new husband often spent evenings at Haydée's, playing parlor games. Once, not long before her death, they were playing a game called Guess What's in the Box. Haydée's box contained a pistol. Everyone was shocked, because they knew that her security detail had discreetly disarmed the pistol she usually carried; clearly by then they were afraid of how she might use it. And now she had a new one. She said it had been given to her by a friend. Was she announcing something? Asking for help? Daring or challenging the other players? Or simply dropping a clue to the inevitable?

By this time Celia Sánchez had died of cancer. Armando had left her. She had struggled with a difficult recovery from the automobile accident that had her in a great deal of physical pain. I asked Niurka if she thought that accident had really been accidental—some I spoke with believed it might have been a previous suicide attempt—but she was sure it had not been intentional.

> She was coming home from a Central Committee meeting. It was late at night and she always drove herself, a car with an automatic shift. They had been doing some roadwork at one of the *rotundas de La Playa* (Playa traffic circles), and she hit a pile of rubble. It was a terrible accident. They had trouble getting her out of the car: one leg was hanging limp, her sternum was broken, her jaw was mangled, her face badly damaged. Ramiro Valdés was coming along behind her and recognized her car. He was the one who called Fidel.

In answer to my questions about the possible depressive effect of painkillers or discouragement in the face of this new problem on top of so many others, Niurka was adamant:

> No, she faced rehabilitation like she faced everything else. I remember how painful it was for her to chew, they had to liquefy everything for her, but she told them to cook each food separately and then puree it because she wanted to savor the tastes. After the accident she made an official trip to Nicaragua. And like I said, I was there. She sent for me and I accompanied her everywhere on that visit. She was her old self, energetic, animated.

Soon after Niurka returned from Nicaragua, her husband was transferred to Cienfuegos. She wasn't enthusiastic about leaving her whole family so soon again, but her aunt counseled her to go. She remembers going to see her one evening, looking for support around her desire to stay in Havana for a while. And she remembers Haydée's definitive argument: "Your place is with your husband." She went right home and packed her bags.

"This wasn't that long before her death," she said, her eyes beginning to fill.

> In Cienfuegos my husband and I were living in a protocol house, because our own place was still being painted. The phone rang and he answered. His face went white. "We have to leave for Havana right away," he said. I remember our headlights were out and we drove the eight-lane in the dark, very fast. We went right to the funeral home. And there were thousands of people there. I found my mother and asked her what happened. She told me: "Daughter, she was just so tired, so tired."

At first I didn't want to see her. I wanted to remember her as she was in life. But after a while, I don't know, I decided to go into the small room where the casket was. I wish I hadn't. They had wrapped her head in a red turban, one she used a lot. It covered her forehead. I wish I had never seen her like that.

Niurka's grief turned to rage as she spoke. She was sobbing now, and Boris—who had come into the room moments earlier—handed her a handkerchief. "I was angry at her for years," she admitted.

And angry at the Revolution, at Fidel, at everyone who should have realized what a state she was in, should have gotten her the help she needed. At the end they couldn't really see her, couldn't take full measure of her situation. And I was furious that they laid her out in that funeral home, instead of in the Plaza de la revolución where she belonged. I was angry at Armando; I'll never forgive him! At the funeral home I wanted to throw everyone out I felt didn't belong there. I did tell some people to leave. For years I was angry, angry. . . .

Norma Ruiz is Ada's daughter. In many ways I think of her as my closest link to Haydée. Not only because she has taken it upon herself to be the repository of family papers and memorabilia, but also because she worked closely with Celia María in the last two years before her death. They had plans to make a film about Haydée. Celia's greatest desire, according to Norma, was to demystify her mother's life, write something or create a film that would depict her as she was—brilliant, energetic, joyful, but also with her depressions and contradictions. Celia did write some exquisite tributes to her mother, but her sudden death in 2008 left Norma with the task.

Another reason why talking with Norma gave me a sense of closeness to the family as a whole and to Haydée in particular, was that she lived with her aunt from the age of six until she turned fifteen. She was with her a couple of hours before she killed herself. She could have been any one of the many children Haydée and Armando took into their home. Norma's mother, Ada, divorced when Norma was a child and soon thereafter went on an internationalist mission. As naturally as Haydée did with all her children—biological or adopted—she brought her youngest sister's daughter to live at "the house in Flores."[3] And Norma looks like her mother, Ada, whom I

Norma Ruiz. PHOTO BY MARGARET RANDALL.

remember from that long-ago visit to Santiago de Cuba; she has the same ruddy complexion, piercing eyes, and playful expression around her mouth.

There were times when there were fourteen of us sitting around the dinner table: Abel Enrique and Celia María, of course, and then children from Venezuela and Uruguay whose parents were involved in liberation struggles in those countries. There might have been a child from Santiago de Cuba who'd come to Havana to study: anyone who needed a home. We all called her Mama. And she taught us to eat, walk, attended to us when we were sick, answered all our questions. . . . I always felt like she had a special relationship with me, though, because I was her baby sister's

Haydée presiding at OLAS Conference, Havana, 1967. With Rodney Arismendi, among others. PHOTO COURTESY CASA DE LAS AMÉRICAS.

daughter, and she had been like a mother to my own mother. Then, too, I had eye problems, I had to have an operation, so maybe she coddled me a bit because of that.

Norma and I talked at Casa de las Américas. We found an empty room, and I recorded our conversation. We also talked on other occasions and went together to Encrucijada. So what she gave me in the way of memories, analysis, and the answers to my many questions wasn't limited to this single interview. Norma is forty-nine, married, divorced, and remarried, with a son and daughter. She is of the generation born shortly after the revolution came to power—and born into a family like no other.

Mama taught me what it meant to be Cuban. She taught me solidarity, what constitutes a good person. And about family. Family was so important to her! She read voraciously, anything from Readers' Digest (yes, it's true!) to Marx. She read Martí's complete works. And no one told her to; she discovered him on her own. My mother, Ada, always said she thought her sister had an extra cavity in her brain: she was so smart. It might have been her limited formal education that made her so voracious to learn. She had a hunger.

I wanted to know how Norma thought Haydée had time to do all that she did: running an institution like Casa de las Américas, keeping up literally hundreds of relationships with artists and writers all over the world, her party obligations, the duties of motherhood. Everyone I've spoken with has told me the same thing: that she was an extraordinary mother. Norma didn't have to think before answering.

> She did everything very fast. She did more in a few minutes than others do in an hour or a day. And she honored special times, like meals. When we were little she always told us to eat everything on our plates, because children in Latin America and Africa were hungry. I remember once Abel Enrique asked if he couldn't just take all his food and put it in a bag and send it to those hungry children. . . .

I wanted to know if Hart was also at the table for all those meals. Norma's response was immediate.

> Yes. She made sure he was. And he was an excellent father, an excellent uncle, although some may say differently. And he was a true visionary. Of course I was mad at him for years, because of how he left her. He did it in the wrong way. And marriage was so important to her . . . that loyalty. But Celia María was the one who made me see that every page has two sides.
>
> His leaving her might have been a trigger, a detonator. My aunt was such a passionate woman. She was anti-church, anti-everything of the old order, but she was old-fashioned about divorce. But there was also a lot going on, so many things. There was that automobile accident. She suffered so many different injuries. And she had such a painful period of recuperation. I remember she was also frustrated, terribly frustrated. She had a hard time sewing those tiny stitches of hers. And a hard time writing. And you know how many letters she wrote, to everyone.
>
> Then, at the time we were all adolescents. That can be a complicated time in any household. And there was Celia Sánchez's death. Of course before that there had been Abel's death, and Boris's, at Moncada. Boris was the great love of her life. She once said: "To live is such a good thing, one's partner should be able to share its beauty. And it's difficult to find that kind of love, very difficult when you are involved in struggle. I did find it, and nothing came between us. But the enemy destroyed it."[4]
>
> And then there was Che. But Haydée and Celia had a very special re-

lationship. Celia was the only one who could handle her when things got rough, when she got agitated. She would call and tell her: "Yeyé, look here. . . ."

I was with her that last afternoon, maybe two hours before she killed herself. And I remember she was very upset because she was trying to thread a needle and couldn't. Celia María had gone with her boyfriend to Armando's house. And she told me: "Come on, I'll take you to see your grandparents," my grandparents on my father's side. She always made sure we kept up our relationships with all the relatives. You know, the Santamarías have a saying: *Conmigo o sinmigo* [with me or against me]. But I remember she was preparing the clothes she was going to take to the beach the next morning, because we were supposed to leave for our yearly vacation at Varadero. I just don't think she had planned on killing herself. No.

Everyone felt guilty, for years. Celia María because she wasn't there. I because I wasn't there. My mother because she hadn't visited her that Sunday. Everyone. And then we didn't know how to deal with suicide back then. So the way her death was handled was also hard, very hard. All the Santamarías suffered. You know, the three sisters were so close. And each had her role to play. Aida was the one who put order into everything. She had to be at all the births; you couldn't give birth until she got there. She died of sadness, that's the truth. And my mother, Ada, she committed suicide like Haydée. It wasn't that obvious, but she was diagnosed with cancer and refused to get treatment until she knew it was too late. She said she was "going to see Yeyé, Abel, Boris."

And then, after Haydée died, we didn't see the children for a while. You know they sent Celia María to Germany, where she studied astrophysics. Celia María began thinking about nothing but vindicating her mother. Vindication isn't really the word, because Haydée has always been revered in spite of everything. What she wanted was to demystify her mother's life. For people to know her as she really was: passionate, joyous, loving to play tricks on people and make them laugh. She always found ways to give funny presents, even in the times of greatest scarcity. She loved serving you a rubber egg that looked just like a real hard-boiled one, and then watching you bite into it and exploding in laughter.

I asked Norma if she remembered the time Haydée showed up at a Central Committee meeting dressed as a man. She confirmed the truth of the story.

And she said it wasn't just once. Guayaberas were considered formal dress for men in Cuba, and Haydée always wondered why women couldn't wear them too; they were so comfortable. She never missed an opportunity to make a point about justice.

We talked about singer-songwriters Silvio Rodríguez, Pablo Milanés, and Noël Nicola. I knew Haydée had made a space for them when they were starting out and protected them from the narrow-minded hacks who couldn't see how truly groundbreaking and poetic their lyrics were. Norma described a moment she witnessed at her own mother's house. Her aunt asked Silvio what he wanted for lunch and he said an omelet stuffed with plantains. She made him the biggest, most delicious, omelet he'd ever had. When he finished eating he sat down and wrote "Canción del elejido" (Song of the Chosen One), his hymn to Abel. Nora said that she and her cousins referred to it as the omelet song.

They often used to gather at Ada's house because she was the one who attracted *cultura pegada al piso* (a relaxed party atmosphere, in the home of someone who was not so high in the revolutionary structure). "But," she told me, "all three sisters took care of Silvio, Pablito, and Noël. Aida mended their clothes. Ada cut their hair. And Haydée shielded them from the repressive forces of the day, so they were free to write their wonderful songs."


Rebeca Chávez is someone I'd wanted to meet since attending the Cultural Congress of Havana at the beginning of 1968. Che's guerrilla force had been defeated in Bolivia less than three months before, and the iconic leader himself summarily executed. More than a thousand intellectuals, writers, artists, philosophers, community organizers, scientists, religious and political personalities, indigenous leaders, musicians—in short, a broad range of creative minds from sixty-six countries on four continents—met in Havana to share our diverse visions of struggle. We knew that Cuba had planned the event as a way of rallying support for Che's efforts in Bolivia; now, unexpectedly, it became a dramatic commentary on that effort. I remember strolling through *Del tercer mundo*, the impressive exhibit at Pabillón Cuba. Chávez, a young filmmaker at the time, had helped conceive the script.

Fast forward to April 2014. Several people had suggested I interview Chávez about Haydée. They agreed I would hear opinions well out of the mainstream or at least unlike those I was likely to hear from others. Rebeca

Haydée and Silvio Rodríguez, playing his guitar and singing, 1969. Also present are Pablo Milanés, Noël Nicola, and Sergio Vitier, among others. PHOTO BY ASTUDILLO, COURTESY CASA DE LAS AMÉRICAS.

was punctual (not always a Cuban attribute). We borrowed an empty office, made ourselves comfortable, and began to talk as if we had known one another for a while. I felt an immediate identification: the same people and books excited us, and we discovered we felt similarly repelled by certain hypocrisies and other pretenses. Quickly, we fell into a sort of shorthand communication. Rebeca is a small woman, vivacious, with intelligent eyes and infectious energy. She dove right in:

> I was born in Bayamo, but my family moved to Santiago de Cuba when I was very young. I owe everything to that city: my values, everything. What might have been a typical adolescent rebellion became a political one. It happened that I lived on the same street as the País brothers, in fact just a few houses away.[5] I remember once catching sight of them out in the middle of the street; the police had them there in their boxers. Other neighbors were being routinely assassinated. The struggle was heating up. Much to my parents' consternation, at the age of twelve I became involved. I was known in my family as *Segobierna*, that's what they called me: she who rules herself. At thirteen I spent some time in prison.

That's how my participation in the July 26 Movement began, there in Santiago. I knew about Luis Bravo's house, and I knew the whole family was involved. We called them *las muchísimas* because there were so many of them. And I'd seen Vilma.[6] I never actually saw Haydée, although I heard that she spent a lot of time at that house. I heard the name María, but only found out much later that María was Haydée.

And, well, I was always interested in photography and film, from the time I was very young. I wanted to be a filmmaker. After the war, it turned out that one of the first films made at ICAIC,[7] *Cuba 58*, was taken from a short story called "Los novios." I was told that story was loosely based on my own. It portrays a young girl who spends a whole day going around the city with a revolutionary to provide him cover. Saúl Yellín came to Santiago to research the film. Sergio Corrieri[8] had the leading role. And so I met some of those people. I told them I wanted to work in film, but they said I needed to finish my education first, go to university if possible.

I wanted to go to university, and I did. But I also wanted to work, to have that experience, to be able to contribute money to my family, to be independent. So I came to Havana, where film production was happening. I met Lisandro Otero[9] and others. Here I got involved in all sorts of projects, including a cultural magazine we started in 1967. That was important because around that time we were beginning to prepare for the Cultural Congress of Havana that took place in January of the following year. I ended up working on the script for the big exhibit called *Del tercer mundo* (From the Third World) at the Pabellón Cuba. Maybe you remember. That script was based on texts by Che Guevara.

Around this time I met Haydée, and the same thing happened to me that happened to you: she swept me off my feet. One of the first things I noticed was how she looked at you, without taking her eyes from yours— that gaze! Aida was really the sister I knew best, my great friend. Some of us used to hang out at her office in the afternoons. She would give us lunch and we'd talk about fixing the world (though of course we couldn't really fix it). Haydée would sometimes come around, and that's when I first began spending time with her.

You know, she radiated a kind of magnetism. I never heard her give an academic talk. She just spoke from the heart, and it was magical. The Cultural Congress highlighted so many different tendencies. And Alfredo

Guevara, at ICAIC, and Haydée at Casa de las Américas: both of them promoted that diversity. Alfredo always believed that culture was the highest
form of politics—not cheap political maneuvering, but profound political
thought. He imbued ICAIC with that view, and Haydée did the same at
Casa. The moment you came through the door, you breathed that respect
for art, that diversity, that beauty. It's no coincidence that during the times
of most abysmal narrowness and repression, both ICAIC and Casa were
places where important creative spirits found a home, a space in which
to work freely.

I remember Haydée at Aida's house. And Ada was there as well. People
called the three sisters *las sancua*, short for Santamaría Cuadrado. Haydée was always fooling around, playing elaborate tricks on people. She
delighted in that. She dressed up a lot, wore disguises. There was the time
she cut a hole in the wall at Aida's house, stuffed it with jewelry and pretended she'd found a treasure. And I remember we were all eating once,
a meal she had prepared, and she casually mentioned we'd just eaten cat.
It was really rabbit, but she loved playing that sort of trick on people. She
would laugh until she cried.

I have a particular memory of accompanying Santiago Alvarez[10] to
Casa. We were making *La guerra de Nicaragua* and wanted to interview
Haydée for the film. But she was more concerned about Santiago himself.
His wife had just been killed in a terrorist attack on an airplane, and she
was worried about how he was dealing with his loss. I found myself in the
middle of that.

Rebeca had many other stories about Haydée, always emphasizing the magical aura that surrounded her. She shared her memories of events at Casa,
especially those revolving around the yearly literary contests. One year she
had been a judge. She remembered Roque Dalton,[11] Chico Buarque,[12] María
Esther Gilio,[13] Carlos María Gutiérrez,[14] Ernesto Cardenal,[15] and many others: engaged in profound discussions and then partying with abandon. "I
remember Benedetti[16] staging table tennis tournaments, and people dancing
the *milonga*,"[17] she said. "Haydée's energy was always contagious. Casa is full
of ghosts, beautiful ghosts."

I remember coming to a meeting here, and casually sitting down on the
edge of a table. Some functionary came up to me—I forget his name—
and pointedly asked if there weren't enough chairs. "No," I told him,

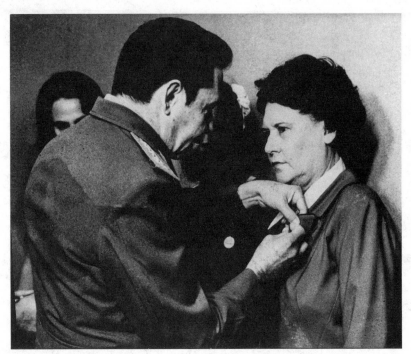

Raúl Castro pinning Armed Forces xxth anniversary medal on Haydée. PHOTO
COURTESY CASA DE LAS AMÉRICAS.

"there are plenty of chairs." Of course I knew what he was getting at.
Then he launched into a little speech about a series of behaviors that
supposedly were unacceptable at the institution. The director had these
rules, he said. Women couldn't come to work with their hair in curlers. I
said that seemed logical to me. Why would anyone want to wear curlers to
work? Then he said women couldn't come to work in pants. "And why is
that?" I asked. "Well," he said, "if they're fat they don't look good in pants."
"Well, maybe fat women don't look good in pants, but I do," I said. In fact,
I doubted that Haydée had made any of those rules. It wasn't her style.

Rebeca and I talked about Armando Hart and the shocking way he left Haydée. "It was ugly," she said, repeating the word two or three times. She talked
about having begun to work with Hart on a project of his. He was writing a
book about his own pathway to revolution and had called to get her advice.
But when she read a first draft and realized that Haydée figured in his narrative only politically—he had made no mention of their personal relationship,

their children, the life they shared—she withdrew. "I couldn't be part of that," she said. But when I asked how important she thought their estrangement had been in terms of pushing her to the edge, she didn't think it played as great a role as others did:

I remember Marta Rojas and I talked about it at the time. She told me Haydée was in a bad way for other reasons. Celia Sánchez's death, for instance, was a huge loss. Celia took emotional care of Haydée. She was there for her in a way few others were able to be.

As was true of everyone who lived through that terrible moment in 1980, for Rebeca, Haydée's suicide was a shock.

And the way it was handled was unconscionable. Holding the wake at a funeral home, as if she were just anyone! But I don't think her suicide was an act of madness. No. For me, it was an act of freedom. Haydée always practiced liberty. She always sought genuine freedom, for herself and for others. From the time she was a child. The provincial woman from the sugar plantation, the woman without a formal education, who founded and ran the most important cultural institution on the continent: she always sought freedom. For me, her suicide was her last great act of freedom.

She was a complex person, and fortunately she wasn't perfect. Fortunately she wasn't perfect.

Rebeca repeated the statement, then fell silent for a few moments, clearly pondering the value in human imperfection. Then she spoke again.

She was passionate and, above all, just. Imagine, she could have had all the power in the world, but she never wanted that. She and Alfredo were different from the rest. I believe Fidel understood that Casa and ICAIC were alternative spaces and always respected that about them. And they functioned as such. In that sense they balanced whatever narrowness or ignorance threatened to affect the revolution's cultural development from time to time. Think about it. He never suggested either Alfredo or Haydée for the role of Minister of Culture, because he knew they represented alternatives, important beachheads rather than hierarchy.

"No, Haydée wasn't mad when she killed herself," Rebeca insisted. "She may momentarily have lost her center, but she wasn't mad. She simply rejected

Haydée on the Cuban TV program *Comentarios económicos*, channel 4, June 1960.
PHOTO COURTESY CASA DE LAS AMÉRICAS.

the painful state of depression that had accompanied her for so long. She didn't want to go on living, so she chose freedom. Haydée's conduct was always exemplary, and so very much of her own making. In a way I think it was good for Che that he just disappeared. Camilo too. Like her, they were unique beings, who didn't fit the conventional mold."

> The sad thing is that the younger generation, Cuban kids in their teens and twenties, don't know her legacy. Her story hasn't been told as it should. And she wasn't a painter or a writer, so she didn't leave works that could speak for her. Her art was her extraordinary conduct, her brilliance and creativity, the way she developed Casa, the respect, the diversity, the working collective. But we're afraid, here, to talk about our great figures in their human dimensions, the small details that make up their lives. It's true with all of them. What do we know, for example, about Celia's personal life? Those stories are off-limits.
>
> Maybe it's because I'm a filmmaker, but for me life moves from dilemma to dilemma, history moves from one conflict to another. If we

want to preserve and pass on the real history, we can't be afraid of the contradictions. Haydée was part of a deeply dysfunctional family. And she was a genius at life, a great creative spirit. It's no coincidence that Pablo Milanés, Arturo Arango, and so many others of our generation named their daughters Haydée.

Casa de las Américas, Havana. PHOTO BY MARGARET RANDALL.

# 7 CASA DE LAS AMÉRICAS

Always remember, the strongest weapon with which you can help your
people is your voice in song. . . . Create beauty from all that pain. . . .
How many times have I wanted to sing to life, to the struggle, to the pain,
to those who are no longer here? And when I opened my mouth, all that
came out was a moan.
—Haydée Santamaría to Isabel Parra

There is no place quite like it. Brushed by decades of moist sea air, it sits
at the bottom of G—also called Avenida de los Presidentes—its pale gray
facade familiar to artists and intellectuals throughout Cuba and the world.
Above the main entrance is a map of the Americas. A line of flagpoles adorns
the roof ridge, ready to fly the emblems of the continent's diversity of nations.

But the physical properties of Casa are not what have made the institution
unique, a reference for such a broad range of cultural activities. It is what
happens within its walls: a yearly literary contest; several excellent magazines that reintroduce forgotten pages while presenting and analyzing the
new; a publishing program with hundreds of books to its credit; a specialized
library; Rayuela, the welcoming little bookstore bearing the name of Julio
Cortázar's[1] greatest novel; galleries filled with paintings, posters, sculpture,
and photography; lecture and performance halls; departments of literary
criticism, the study of women in literature, and indigenous cultures; ground-

breaking exhibitions and festivals; and an almost daily series of events, all free and open to the public, in which men and women of international artistic stature and the Cuban people interact and feed one another.

The year begins in January, with the famous literary contest; winners in each category have their book published under the prestigious Premio imprint and receive US$3,000. The importance of the prize can be judged by the fact that even well-known authors submit their manuscripts, eager to be able to publish in Cuba and list the coveted award on their résumé.

In February, Casa hosts a yearly Colloquium on Women's Studies and always has a booth at the Havana Book Fair. March brings the musicology prize one year, alternating with a music composition prize in April of the next. Live music from throughout the Americas can be heard in the building's concert venues.

May is Theater Month, with the attendance of theatrical groups from many parts of the world. In July and August *Verano va* (Summer in Full Swing) enlivens the premises. In November one week is devoted to the work of a particular author. As of a few years ago, a young people's gathering, *Casa tomada* (Occupied Casa), takes place during the second semester but without a fixed date. There have also been photography and print contests. Each year unfolds in this way.

No less important is what goes on behind the scenes, where a master designer may be producing an innovative poster to advertise a Casa event, someone from the publicity department is interviewing one of the institutions many prestigious visitors, or a specialist in a great poet's work is compiling the definitive volume on the subject. Compelling art hangs on every floor. The last time I was there, a rich exhibition of Latin American photography could be seen throughout the building, and Silvia Baraldini[2] addressed a riveted audience one afternoon. One of Casa's singular attractions, permanently installed on the third floor, is an enormous *Tree of Life*, gifted to the institution by the Mexican artist Alfonso Soteno Fernández. Original art from throughout the Americas, contemporary as well as traditional, is everywhere in the building.

All this was Haydée Santamaría's creation and remains her legacy. In April 1959 she accepted the revolution's challenge to found and run an institution capable of breaking through the cultural blockade. As soon as the revolutionary war ended, the United States began a relentless campaign of economic, diplomatic, cultural, and military attacks—covert as well as overt. More than half a century later, through a long succession of Democratic and

Haydée in her office at Casa de las Américas, 1966. PHOTO COURTESY CASA DE
LAS AMÉRICAS.

Republican administrations, policies have shifted slightly in one direction
or another, but the cruel barrage essentially remains in place. For simply
choosing a future of which the United States disapproves, Cuba is blockaded,
vilified, attacked, lied about, and isolated in more ways than the average US
citizen can imagine.

Fidel Castro believed that Haydée, a woman born and raised on a sugar
plantation in central Cuba, whose formal education went only as far as sixth
grade but whose life experience had given her an insatiable curiosity and
special sensibility, was the ideal person to head the effort. It was a stroke of
genius.

To those who didn't know her, Haydée might have seemed a strange
choice. Cuba has always had a much larger number of prestigious artists
and intellectuals than a similar-sized population might have been expected
to produce. And as most of these men and women supported the revolution,
most stayed. There were luminaries of the worldwide stature of Alejo Carpentier,[3] Fernándo Ortíz,[4] Alicia Alonso,[5] Nicolás Guillén,[6] Mirta Aguire,[7]
and Wilfredo Lam.[8] All supported the revolution but none of them was
tapped for the job.

Haydée wasn't an artist or critic. But she loved art. She understood people
of all cultures. She approached them through their humanity as well as
through their work. She had long been a voracious reader, and now her read-

ing went in new directions. She was curious about absolutely everything. She also loved people, especially those whose vision and talents led them to create something meaningful. She rejected, as impoverished and spent, the socialist realism that was being promoted in the Soviet Union. She understood that the arts are necessary for social change and that culture is the highest form of politics.

All this would have been enough for her to have been able to create an institution of exceptional richness in all genres. But she constantly pushed the limits of time, place, fashion: the "isms" of the day. She surrounded herself with specialists, many of whom were artists themselves, capable of asking the right questions and eliciting multiple answers. Casa de las Américas never limited itself to particular schools of art, styles of literature, tendencies in theater or any other art form. It sought many different representations and got them talking to each other.

Haydée, creatively quirky in her own right, appreciated artistic idiosyncrasy. Nothing escaped her inquisitive eye, and she played as passionately as she engaged. At the same time, she was highly disciplined. One by one, then in larger and larger numbers, she drew artists from the Americas and around the world to Casa, where their art was respected and they had the opportunity of experiencing firsthand this new nation in the making. Haydée talked endlessly with them. And she listened. Nothing was extraneous to her passion to connect.

In 1970 I was invited for the first time to be a judge in the poetry category of the Casa de las Américas Prize. Each of several genres—poetry, novel, short story, theater, and essay—had five judges, one Cuban and four from abroad. Rigorous anonymity surrounded each submission back then.

We received 198 books of poetry. All the judges were taken to a hotel on the Isle of Youth, given our manuscripts, and for a week did nothing but read and meet periodically to share criteria. Haydée spent a few days with us. She would appear at meals, interested in getting to know each of us individually and inquisitive about our lives. We all knew who she was, of course, and something about her extraordinary life. She was modest but forthcoming when anyone asked a direct question. She deflected attention and shied away from anything resembling a cult of personality. When she spoke about heroic events it was always "we," never "I." A magical quality seemed to envelop her.

I remember her breaking into raucous song with the Brazilian poet Thiago de Mello,[9] in earnest conversation with the French-Mexican anthropologist Laurette Séjourné,[10] commiserating with Haitian René Depestre,[11]

Casa's inauguration recital, July 4, 1959. Left to right: Armando Hart, Haydée, and US musicians William Warfield (bass-baritone) and David Garvey (pianist). PHOTO COURTESY CASA DE LAS AMÉRICAS.

and laughing with Roque Dalton from El Salvador. I also saw her in animated conversation with members of the dining room staff or with a hotel maid. No one was beneath her, no one unworthy of her complete attention. She would devise elaborate tricks, unexpectedly targeting anyone and everyone. When one of those tricks hit its mark, she screamed in delight.

In subsequent years, we met on a number of occasions. A prodigious memory, sparked by genuine interest, prompted her to ask about my children, inquire about my current writing project, ask for my analysis of some event that had taken place in the country of my birth. She easily picked up where we'd left off the last time we'd spoken. She wanted to understand every culture, every historic coincidence or anomaly. She was Casa's soul.

Haydée was so far ahead of her time that it became evident only long after her death how much she'd risked in pursuing justice in every situation. I've already talked about the role she played in protecting and promoting the members of *La nueva trova* and other marginalized artists. When it came to gender, race, or difference of any kind, her attitudes and actions were those

Haydée participating in painting a mural, Casa de las Américas. PHOTO COURTESY CASA DE LAS AMÉRICAS.

of someone born decades into the future. That conduct didn't come from reading a book or considering advances in the ways revolutionary movements were beginning to look at issues of inequality. In fact, at the time most such movements believed that dealing with class difference would eventually mitigate all other differences. Haydée chose justice every time because that's who she was.

In 2011 I was invited back to judge another Casa literary contest, this time in the more recent category of testimonial literature. One of the prize's organizers laughed and said they had decided to issue me an invitation every forty-one years. By now, Haydée had been gone more than three decades, but her legacy remained firmly in place. New contest categories had been added: Brazilian literature, English literature of the Antilles, writing by Latinos

Gathering of musicians at Casa, 1972. Chilean singer-songwriter Víctor Jara, at left, would be tortured to death a year later. Puerto Rican musician Aponte Ledeé is at right. PHOTO COURTESY CASA DE LAS AMÉRICAS.

inside the United States, among others. Plans were in progress to establish a department devoted to *las culturas originarias*—the native cultures of the American continent. Now, instead of Haydée greeting the judges and telling us our only concern should be for literary excellence, it was Roberto Fernández Retamar[12] who issued those instructions. Not having been in Cuba or Casa for many years, when I walked through the main door Haydée's presence shook me to my core.

Her presence was palpable in memory but also in the attention to detail, democratic working relations, and horizontal leadership I felt in every part of the institution. The old guard, mostly retired now, comes in a day or two a week to lend experience and continuity. Each department is headed by a young person—lots of women, lesbians and gay men, people of color and from many different cultures, all experts in their fields—who work together to carry on a tradition of excellence. All major events draw on the cooperation of specialists from every area.

Many of the older people worked closely with Haydée; her spirit lives in them. The youngest have seen her only in pictures or read about her at school, but they have a consciousness of what she meant to the institution, the revolution, and beyond.

Haydée's correspondence with hundreds of the world's most cherished artists and writers was passionate and intimate, timely and aware. Those letters, many of them handwritten in her round, almost childish hand, are archived at Casa. They provide a map not only of her numerous friends and colleagues but also of her rapidly evolving sophistication. The earliest letters contained common errors of spelling and punctuation. Quickly, these disappeared.

Someone with whom I spoke remembered how Haydée loved using new words. When she discovered one, she would use it again and again. An example was *syntax*. But her daughter, Celia María, said she used that word with dismay, claiming she lacked proper syntax when she spoke or wrote. Celia María assured her that her syntax was marvelous, that she wrote as she spoke, with an energy and magic that were uniquely her own.

In 2009, in tribute to its fiftieth anniversary, the institution published *Destino: Haydée Santamaría*, edited by Silvia Gil, Ana Cecilia Ruiz Lim, and Chiki Salsamendi.[13] This is a compendium of letters from artists and writers throughout the world to Casa's extraordinary founder over a span of two decades. Nobel Prize winners and incipient poets are represented, the famous and the unknown. They express delight at having met her and gratitude for her generosity of spirit. They equate Casa with the Cuban Revolution and speak of how the former gave them access to the latter. They talk to her easily, about their children, their creative plans, their problems. They tell stories. There are telegrams, notes, and lengthy missives. They speak freely of contradictions and disappointments, losses and gains. Some are typed, while others are handwritten or accompanied by spontaneous sketches. Many address the recipient as one would a mother or longtime friend. And this in spite of the fact that none but a very few had spent more than hours or days in her presence. All correspondence in those days traveled via the regular postal service, with the additional problems incurred with mail to and from Cuba.

Moving as this collection is, it is only half the picture. Missing are the letters written by Haydée. As I say, she wrote hundreds, more accurately thousands, between 1959 and her death in 1980. People from all walks of life corresponded with her, about anything and everything. Some were distant relatives or friends of friends. She didn't receive correspondence only from artists and intellectuals; a Cuban from the countryside, still moved by her enormous dignity at the trial that followed Moncada, might write to thank her for being who she was or to confide in her about a sick child.

People were as likely to ask for a piano as to beg her to intercede in a judicial problem, help them find a job, or get medical attention. She was principled in her refusal to use her position to grant favors. She would answer each request by first sincerely commiserating with the letter writer, then explain why influence or nepotism had no place in revolution, and then—and only when she felt it was appropriate—direct the person to try for a solution through proper channels. Only very occasionally, only when a child was involved, did I find evidence that she tried to help and never in a way that circumvented revolutionary law.

One letter that shows who she was, in terms of her gender consciousness as well as her overall sense of justice, impressed me profoundly. It has no year but was almost certainly received—in light of the references it contains—early in 1968. It is addressed to a woman named Berta, probably a member of a family connected in some way to Haydée's, perhaps someone related to Boris Luis Santa Coloma. Haydée's letter begins:

Dear Berta: I received your letter of December 28, a few days after the Congress and just months after [losing] Che. For these reasons I couldn't answer right away, as would have been my impulse perhaps more than my desire. I say this because of what you wrote in your letter: "It seems as if you have forgotten the friendship that linked us when you weren't so important." At first this hurt me, then it angered me, and I am angry as I write to you now.

In response to that paragraph, I will tell you that when you knew me I was important, so important that I had just gone through a monumental episode in our nation's history, in spite of the horror and without my courage deserting me for a second. I think you are confused about what it means to be important. You met me shortly after one of the most important events, not for me alone, but for our country. That's what I call important. But you call having a position and great responsibilities important, position and responsibilities that come precisely from having taken part in actions such as the one on July 26, 1953 [. . .]

Haydée continues to berate Berta for asking her to use her influence to help solve a series of personal problems. She refuses, saying that she believes in revolutionary justice, that the family member in prison is there for a reason and has an opportunity to rehabilitate himself, and that she is confident that this rehabilitation will be effective. She says she understands why Berta has written to her in this way but assures her that she rejects such requests "from wherever they may come."[14]

This was Haydée, attentive but evenhanded with family, friends, and strangers.

With artists and writers she operated under identical principles but developed a style more attuned to their characteristics. She was careful to separate her appreciation of their work from her concern for their well-being, especially when that well-being was threatened by the dictatorial forces of the era. She never flaunted her own role or the Cuban revolution's extraordinary exploits, making each person she wrote to understand that she saw him or her as an individual within a unique set of circumstances. In May 1977, as the Sandinistas' final offensive was beginning in Nicaragua, the poet Ernesto Cardenal was contemplating returning to his country. She wrote him:

> Right now it seems as if going home might endanger your life. You will have to decide what to do, in accordance with your conscience. But remember, there are times when being cautious is not a sign of cowardice but of strength, the strength each of us finds at a given moment and in a particular circumstance. And if you feel you shouldn't return right now, don't forget that you, like every Latin American revolutionary, has another homeland: Cuba. And that we will always welcome you here, with open arms and hearts, in your Casa de las Américas.

In July 1969 she wrote to Uruguayan poet Mario Benedetti and his wife Luz:

> Dear Mario and Luz too: Although there wasn't even a note for me, I'm writing to you (yet one more confirmation of my thesis) [that] all we humans get our feelings hurt, but I also believe that those who get hurt the most are those who are the best at caring and being cared for. This is a joke (sort of).
>
> I've read your letters: the one for everyone, and those to Beba and Roberto. I'm answering the collective letter. We are delighted to know about your lives and especially to know that you cannot live fully without us. Here in this Casa we feel the same. At our first directors meeting we weren't sitting around a table; rather it seemed we were bidding farewell to a corpse. This tells you that we can't keep on bidding farewell to that corpse. We need to continue at our round table, in conversation with the

living. I hope Beba, Mariano or Roberto has written to you about the changes we've made. What a shame you weren't here, because you would have enjoyed these changes, or reorganizations as I call them, but the professors on our board of directors, such as Galich[15] and Retamar, don't accept that, they say it's not reorganize but organize. This is our argument these days, we need your vote to see who wins [. . .]

The letter continues, talking about different writers they hope to invite to be part of the various contest juries and emphasizing the need for a broad representation from as many countries as possible, not concentrated in only one or two. In 1970, the literary contest, traditionally held in January of each year, would be delayed until July, because 1969 and part of 1970 would be designated an 18-month "year." The young revolution felt that it could adjust anything, even time. All efforts were aimed at achieving a major sugar harvest in which Cuba hoped to cut ten million tons of cane. That lofty goal proved impossible, and the inordinate effort ended up adversely affecting many other areas of the national economy in 1969/70.

In November 1965, Arnaldo Orfila Reynal, an Argentinian living in Mexico, was given hours to vacate his position as director of El Fondo de Cultura Económica, the prestigious publishing house he founded and led for many years. The Mexican government disapproved of the publication of a book that exposed the poverty of a city ghetto in the country's capital and another that urged the United States to leave the Cuban revolution alone.[16] Haydée immediately wrote to Orfila:

It shocked us to learn that you've been forced to abandon the very important work you were doing at El Fondo de Cultura Económica. I believe, and I speak as well for our government and Party, that the prestige El Fondo attained in recent years was due in great measure to your skill, and above all to a spirit that refused to be swayed by ideological limitations or conventionalisms of a political or economic nature. That generous spirit, open to all the currents of universal thought and to all aesthetic positions, guided only by the quality of the work, bears the mark of your personality. We believe your ouster was due precisely to that attitude, which made the publishing house what it was and gave it such a good name.

Haydée's letter continued, inviting Orfila to come to Cuba and use his talents to start a publishing house there. She ended by saying: "In short, Cuba's doors are open to you and you would be valuable and necessary to Cuba."

Awarding 1969 Casa literary prizes. Left to right: Manuel Galich, Roque Dalton, Onelio Jorge Cardoso, Efraín Huerta, José Agustín Goytisolo, and Haydée. PHOTO BY ASTUDILLO, COURTESY CASA DE LAS AMÉRICAS.

Arnaldo Orfila didn't move to Cuba, although he visited often. And Siglo XXI, the new publishing house he founded with the support of a large number of Mexican intellectuals and writers, would work closely with Cuba's publishing programs. In 1968, when Che Guevara's campaign diary from Bolivia was found and reproduced simultaneously in a number of different languages, its Mexican publisher was Siglo XXI.

In March 1969, Haydée wrote to Antonio Saura.[17]

I would like to have been able to talk to you more about the Galeria del Siglo XX (Twentieth-Century Gallery) idea, but as you know I had some health problems when you were here. In any case we've discussed it with Mariano,[18] and agree that you are the ideal person to help us with this. I know it's not an easy job, but it's worth giving it our all. We could write to Picasso, Tapies, Miró, Max Ernst, Appel, Calder, etc. If they understand what we have in mind, I think they'll be enthusiastic [. . .]

Salvador Allende's Popular Unity government, which held such promise in Chile beginning in 1970, was brutally put down when Augusto Pinochet staged his military coup in 1973. Haydée felt a deep attachment to the art of Chilean singer-songwriter and fabric artist Violeta Parra, a beautiful spirit who wrote "Gracias a la vida" (Thanks to Life) and then took her own life in 1967. She was also close to Violeta's daughter, Isabel. On September 17, 1975, she wrote to the younger Parra:

Dear Isabel: I received your September 7th letter today. We've all been following you, me in particular, precisely because I felt bad that I never said good-bye. I was the one who avoided saying good-bye, and that made me feel even worse. I always try to be brave, but I wouldn't have felt good about the kind of good-bye we would have had. What could I have told you? I knew the pilgrimage that awaited you, hard times, and even family problems; and I know from my own experience that when faced with such times the best thing is simply to approach them head on. Still, letting you go without telling you that wasn't something I felt good about either.

Your letter made me very happy, not only because it brought me everyone's news, but because in deciding to write you took your time, and that's also good. You can be sure I never saw you as ungrateful. Perhaps at another time I would have noted the artist's lack of gratitude, but in your case I was only concerned with the human's pain. I understand the great responsibility you have with all those close to you: your daughters, Angel, El Pato. You are, and must be, the strong one. Life has given you some difficult challenges, not only as a revolutionary but also as a woman, and if you make an effort and are able to deal with both sides of that equation, you will have your reward. The day will come when you will understand that all this has made you stronger, better, more understanding, much more human, a more effective communist. [. . .]

Be patient, especially with Angel. Because of their education over thousands of years, men are proud and there are times when they are unable to find their way. And, although they may not realize it, they need a mother, a sister, a woman. I don't know Angel well, but I think he must always have suffered his quota of loneliness. It's hard for a young boy to grow emotionally without a father at his side, and with a mother who is ahead of her time. And after all that, when he matured, having to live far from his country: the only real mother, his homeland. Well, Isabel, I always say that in matters such as these, advice is superfluous. But if I didn't

Haydée with Betita Martínez and Stokely Carmichael of the United States, 1970s.
PHOTO COURTESY CASA DE LAS AMÉRICAS.

offer my advice it would be like when I didn't want to say good-bye, and there wouldn't be a letter. I want there to be a letter.

I'll tell you that I'm feeling okay about all this. I can see that you are doing your best: finding the necessary energy in your work. But always remember the strongest weapon with which you can help your people is your voice in song. Try to devote some time to studying music. Create beauty from all that pain. You have talent and legacy. This is a privilege that life has given you. How many times have I wanted to sing to life, to the struggle, to the pain, to those who are no longer here? And when I opened my mouth, all that came out was a moan. You must give "thanks to life" every minute for that privilege. You are living in a better time than the woman who gave us that other "thanks to life." Conditions and comprehension today are totally favorable to women. Today, if we learn to understand the role we have to play, we can and must do more than men. [. . .]

Isabel, I want you to understand this letter, what I'm telling you and also what I've left unsaid. With all my love, Haydée Santamaría.

On November 29, 1967, less than two months after losing Che, Haydée wrote to the Chilean painter Roberto Matta.[19]

> Dear Matta: when we received your letter and you told us all about your trip to Chile, we thought about writing you. Since you know us so well, I won't make excuses.
>
> We gave your letter to Fidel. Do you want to know what he said? (Don't tell anyone, not even the people at Casa de las Américas.) He said: "Matta understands and loves us like he does because he's as mad as we are." I know he's right, because to understand and love us you have to mount the train of this great Cuban madness. We typed a copy of your letter, and of course we gave Fidel the original, that's the one he read. He understood it perfectly, because you also have to decipher what he writes. He found every bit of it interesting. [. . .]
>
> Think about it, Matta, everything here is big and beautiful. Now we must live in this terrible and beautiful insanity of having and not having Che. If you could have seen our people, out of their minds, shouting at the wake that was supposed to have been a solemn night of silence, before that impressive multitude, maybe the only thing you could feel was Che's breathing problem, the rasp of his anti-asthma inhaler every now and then, before that multitude, everyone remembering his difficulty breathing and knowing he wouldn't need his inhaler now, his little *aparatico* as he called it, beneath our stars and looking at our palm trees, that sad and grandiose night when Fidel bestowed Che's final rank on him: *Artist*, artist fallen on the battlefield, at the moment of his greatest creation.
>
> Do you know what I mean, Matta? All this, it is all pain, great joy, infinite, the pain of no longer having him here with his eyes open, the joy of having him more than ever showing us the way, waking so many, encouraging those who have begun so they will keep on going, and those who haven't so they will begin. To believe more than ever that the revolution is truth and to die for truth is to live. And not to betray what he told us: "The duty of every revolutionary is to make the revolution." What greatness, what pain, infinite love to the artist who gives his life in order to produce his enduring work of art, art that we all want to make because it is beautiful, and true.

This was Haydée's style, when she wrote and when she spoke: passionate, alive, wandering and then returning to the essence of what she had to say, sentences running together, sometimes stumbling over each other, phrases

Exposition by Feliza Bustyn, 1980. Left to right: Mariano Rodríguez, Feliza Bustyn, Haydée, and Gabriel García Márquez. PHOTO COURTESY CASA DE LAS AMÉRICAS.

separated by commas and then again lacking even those brief stops. This was the Haydée of Encrucijada, of Moncada, of the war years, and finally Casa de las Américas.

Again in April 1980 Haydée wrote Matta:

Dear Mad One: Here I am, here you have me. Saint Peter doesn't want me, and all those who love me say I'm pretty. I feel stronger than ever and close to Casa with its homebodies, women and men, we are doing well and keep on loving you and expecting you as always. More and more love from Haydée Santamaría.

She would end her life three months later.

Haydée's correspondence with multiple writers and artists wasn't limited to problems they might be having in their countries of origin, projects they would embark upon together, or personal issues their friendship gave her permission to discuss. With Peruvian novelist Mario Vargas Llosa there is a particular exchange of letters that is worth quoting extensively. It shows her fierce defense of the revolution and also her principled stance when attitudes or actions clashed with what she knew the revolution meant.

The Padilla affair was sadly typical of a repressive period in Cuban revolutionary history, one that has since been revisited. It was a bad turn, not the revolution itself. Such an incident couldn't happen today. I cannot help but wonder if Haydée approved of the way it was handled; it certainly wasn't her style. But she was a disciplined party member, and didn't always get to make the decisions.

In 1971 the poet Heberto Padilla was picked up, held incommunicado for a month or so, and then released. He delivered a long mea culpa, criticizing himself for having lied about the Cuban process to a series of foreign journalists. It was an embarrassing speech and did not sit well with a number of intellectuals who had previously supported the revolution. Some of these intellectuals would remain wary. Some would break with Cuba. Some who had voiced their concern felt they had acted hastily and reconsidered.

Inside Cuba, many writers and artists were also uncomfortable not only with the revolution's treatment of Padilla but with its attitude toward artistic expression itself. It would take several years before an ambience of respect overcame those remnants of Stalinism and longer still before this sad chapter was discussed openly. Those willing to wait eventually got the necessary debates and reassurances. Outside Cuba, though, a number of artists took incidents out of context and were quick to disavow the revolution.

Vargas Llosa was among the most vociferous attackers, and the Padilla affair marked his definitive break with the Cuban revolution. From ostensibly leftist politics, he moved farther and farther to the right, until he became a vocal enemy of liberation movements, especially those in Latin America. He began to embrace neoliberal politics, praising such as Margaret Thatcher for "her audacious and worthy efforts to carry out a great liberal revolution in Great Britain," and even ran for president of Peru, losing to the extreme right-winger Alberto Fujimori in 1990. In 2010 Vargas Llosa received the Nobel Prize for Literature.

But I'm getting ahead of my story. Back when Vargas Llosa initially launched his attack against the Cuban revolution, he made a dramatic show of breaking with Casa de las Américas and its literary magazine, a publication on the editorial board of which he had served. At that time, Haydée wrote to him:

Mr. Vargas Llosa: You know that the editorial committee of *Casa* magazine, from which you supposedly resigned, no longer exists [. . .]. In January of this year, in a declaration you yourself signed, we decided to replace it with a broad list of contributors. We made this decision in view of the growing discrepancies among some of the writers involved. The vast majority sustained revolutionary positions, but some did not. You were among the latter. Out of human decency, we thought it best to handle the situation in this way [. . .] rather than simply dispensing with those such as yourself who had shown an increasing commitment to imperialist manipulation. We still believed a young man like you, who has written such beautiful novels, might change his mind and use his talents in defense of the peoples of Latin America. [. . .]

You, better than most, know that it has never been our custom to criticize people gratuitously. In April 1967, you wrote asking what we would think if you accepted the Venezuelan Rómulo Gallegos award from the Leoni administration, a government that has distinguished itself by assassinating, repressing and betraying our peoples. We proposed a brave act, one without precedent in Latin American cultural history: that you accept the prize and give the money to Che Guevara's guerrillas. You didn't take us up on our suggestion. You kept the prize money for yourself, thereby passing up the extraordinary honor of aiding Che Guevara, if only symbolically. [. . .]

Haydée's letter goes on. She refers to the Padilla affair, saying she hadn't criticized Vargas Llosa publicly for the position he took at the time, although she felt that neither he nor the other intellectuals who voiced concern had understood the issue and, far from where things were happening, had been hasty in their condemnation. She reminded him that she hadn't criticized him in 1968, when he'd published an article, in *Caretas*, attacking Fidel Castro's position on Czechoslovakia. She mentioned his having committed to being a judge at Casa's 1969 prize and then simply failing to show up because he'd accepted an invitation to a US university.

Needless to say, because of all these incidents, we didn't really think you would come to teach the course about which we'd spoken informally. If you came in 1971 it was above all to obtain support from Casa de las Américas—which we didn't give—for *Libre* magazine, which you planned on launching with money obtained from Patiño.[20] And if several writers associated with this Casa de las Américas discussed these matters with you privately or publicly, it was never in the form of an insult.

The insult, Vargas Llosa, is your own shameful letter: it shows you for who you are, the living image of a colonized writer, who disrespects his people, who is vain and convinced that as long as you're a good writer you will be forgiven for acting as you have. That you will be permitted to judge a grand process such as the Cuban Revolution which, in spite of its human errors, is the greatest effort to date to install a process of justice in our countries. Men like you, who put your own miserable interests ahead of the desperate interests of what Marti called our "pained republics," are really superfluous to this process. [. . .][21]

Haydée's letter ends after a few more lines in the same vein. Mario Vargas Llosa dropped his supposed concern for the needs of Latin America. His neoliberal positions were now well known. But these were not to be the last words between Casa de las Américas and Vargas Llosa. In 1986, the Peruvian writer spoke publicly of the exchange with Haydée about the Romulo Gallegos prize and accused her of having been dishonest in her proposal. As she could no longer defend herself, Roberto Fernández Retamar responded in her name.

In an interview given to his son Alvaro, which appeared at the end of May in the daily *Expreso* of Lima, [Mario Vargas Llosa] includes a surprising attack on Haydée Santamaría, dead now six years. The following is taken verbatim from that interview: "The Rómulo Gallegos incident was one of the things that led to [my break with Cuba]. When I learned that *The Green House* was one of the finalists for that prize, I asked Haydée Santamaría, then director of Casa de las Américas where I formed part of the editorial board, for the Cuban revolution's opinion of it. Alejo Carpentier delivered her answer to me personally in London. Haydée proposed that I go to Caracas to accept the award, and then to Cuba where, in a public act, I donate the $25,000 dollars to Che Guevara who was then in Bolivia. [. . .] To that point her response made sense. But Haydée said she would then return the money to me discreetly. In other words I would have enjoyed the glory of the revolutionary gesture and the money too. This suggestion offended me. I would have had to be a real cynic to accept.

Retamar writes that Vargas Llosa's interpretation of the exchange is all the more suspect since, had it been true, there were a number of occasions on which he would have mentioned it: among them, when he received the prize itself or later, when he publicly broke with the revolution. He

Casa de las Américas Prize, 1978. Left to right: Haydée, Mariano Rodríguez, Roberto Fernández Retamar. PHOTO COURTESY CASA DE LAS AMÉRICAS.

reaffirms the Peruvian novelist's right to the award, for the high quality of his work, but not his right to lie about a woman who could no longer speak for herself.

By this time Haydée and Alejo Carpentier (her messenger) were both safely gone; they died in 1980 within three months of one another. Retamar goes on to say that Vargas Llosa could have questioned Haydée's suggestion at the time, taken her up on half or all of it, or in whatever way made public his disapproval. Instead, he waited until he thought his version would go unchallenged to allege a conclusion as arbitrary as it is incorrect.[22]

For those of us who knew Haydée or have visited Casa de las Américas, these letters and articles sound against a familiar backdrop. For those who have not had that direct contact, it may be useful to read the words of one of Cuba's great cultural critics, Ambrosio Fornet,[23] with regard to the pattern of agency-repression-resistance-renovation that has characterized the revolution's half century, in hard times and in those less difficult.

Two things have *never* been in short supply here, even during the worst moments of the current [economic] crisis: imagination and ideas. The

lack of material and financial resources has affected our cultural production only in quantitative terms (fewer books, exhibitions, concerts, films),
but our creative impulse and intellectual drive have persisted and even
intensified in certain areas despite the exodus of numerous writers and
artists. [. . .] If *resistance* was the watchword in political discourse, it was
equally clear that writers and artists were also resisting in their own way,
that is, practicing politics by other means. [. . .] The art and literature
of the Revolution, equally fostered by audacity and caution, in a climate
of trust or tension, has maintained an equilibrium that is not typically
expressed in declarations or manifestos but in daily practice. [. . .] It is
clear that a cultural movement such as ours—one that has thus far proved
immune to market forces and has been supported, regardless of the form
it takes, by a substantial and enthusiastic public—can develop for the
most part in accordance with its own dynamic and in a climate of enviable
freedom.[24]

Haydée Santamaría was an architect of this climate of enviable freedom.

I wanted to talk to the old-timers at Casa, those who began their professional
careers working with Haydée and couldn't have imagined the association
would end so abruptly. Roberto Fernández Retamar told me he and Haydée
met right after the war, when he was working at the Ministry of Education
with Armando Hart. But he didn't really get to know her until a year or so
later, when he went to work at Casa: "It was a very intimate relationship," he
told me. I knew he meant engaged, intense, profound.

> You know, Haydée didn't have an extensive formal education; she'd only
> been able to study through sixth grade. Her brilliance came from her life,
> her experience, her generosity. Yet she was able to develop the most pro-
> found relationships with the world's greatest intellects. Many of them
> related to her as a mother, and I think a lot of people who knew her felt
> that way. I don't know if you've read the poem by Fina García Marrúz,
> written about a month after Haydée's death.[25] It has that line: "Those who
> loved her have been orphaned."
>
> I've always believed it was Haydée's nature that brought her to the
> revolution. It wasn't the revolution that made her who she was. And for
> her there was a difference between politics and Revolution. The Revolu-
> tion wasn't only political to her, but deeply human. After Moncada, she

focused her love on Fidel. She was able to transfer the great love she had felt for Abel and Boris, to Fidel. And that kept her going.

Roberto and I talked about a number of moments of dramatic conflict in the revolution's cultural history, among them the Padilla affair. I wanted to know if Roberto could remember Haydée having taken a stand with regard to Padilla himself.

> Haydée was never close to Padilla. But he was a friend of mine. The Padilla affair led, as you know, to a backlash in the cultural world here, what we now refer to as *el quinquenio gris* (five gray years). That was a hard time. I'm absolutely sure there were those in the revolution's leadership who put pressure on Haydée to leave Casa then, maybe abandon the whole cultural milieu, which seemed so suspect to some. She did just the opposite: she dug in her heels and became all the more protective.
>
> Looking back, I can say that both Mariano and I might have fared little better than Padilla had we not had Haydée's solid endorsement. She didn't hesitate to defend anyone she felt was genuine. Perhaps, if Padilla and Haydée had been close, he would have evolved differently, and there wouldn't have been a Padilla affair. The revolution made some mistakes with all that. Looking back, we call it *La hora de los chacales* (the time of the jackals).

It seems absolutely clear to me that what Haydée knew, beyond the issue of a single disaffected poet or the revolution's unfortunate handling of his case, was that much more was at stake than artistic freedom, important as that undoubtedly was. The *quinquenio gris* proved as detrimental to the social sciences—philosophy, sociology—as to the arts. The University of Havana's philosophy department was shut down. The most important magazine of political thought, *Pensamiento crítico*, was forced to close. If not reversed, such repression is dangerous to a country's future. Cuba, with that sad chapter now behind it, more than most countries uses the social sciences to solve its myriad problems. Visionaries like Haydée made this possible.

Inevitably, Roberto and I talked about Haydée's suicide:

> I believe she was mad. I remember when Che died, she told me "I can't live anymore, I can't." In so many ways, she was the last victim of Moncada. She needed psychiatric help but wouldn't hear of it. A psychiatrist friend of mine said all those who commit suicide are mad in their final

moment. Haydée's daughter, Celia María, didn't accept that analysis, but it's the only conclusion I can come to.

And then that scene at the funeral home! We should have been able to say good-bye to her at the Plaza de la revolución, not at an ordinary funeral parlor. But the next morning, when they took her body to the cemetery, the cortège wasn't made up of cars. Everyone just started walking. And people joined that procession, hundreds at first, then thousands. Whatever one thought of suicide—and we weren't as forgiving about it back then as we are now—the people themselves had already forgiven her. They were wiser than the revolution.

I wanted to know what it had been like, at Casa, to go on living and working after Haydée's death. Roberto said it was terribly painful.

But she herself left us the necessary tools. No one could take her place, but she left a work style that continues to this day. And it wasn't only her deep intelligence. She had a unique sense of justice. She treated the employee who swept the floor with the same kindness and concern as she did her closest collaborators and all the artists and writers who came to the revolution through Casa's broad door.

Many with whom I spoke mentioned Haydée's tolerance for people's deficiencies, as long as they were not ill intentioned. Many also emphasized the fact that she rarely spoke badly of anyone. When Roberto remarked on the kindness with which she treated every person with whom she came in contact, irrespective of that person's class or culture, I was reminded of a story I heard from someone else at Casa. It seemed a janitor once worked there who managed to irritate just about everyone. Nobody liked him, and complaints were frequent. When Haydée heard someone criticizing the man, she said: "Don't be so hard on him. If he did his job the way you think he should, he would be the director!"

Silvia Gil is another of the old guard. She started working at Casa in 1964. She was at the National Library when Haydée called to ask if she would like to come to help reorganize the library at the institution; they needed people familiar with Latin American literature. "As of this past March [2014]," Silvia said, with a sigh that contained both pride and wistfulness, "I've been here fifty years."

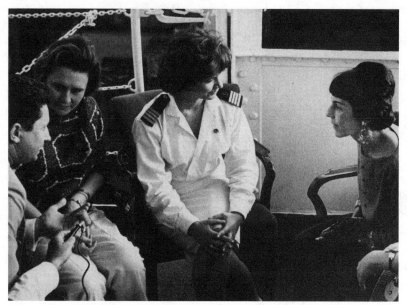

Haydée and Celia Sánchez with Soviet cosmonauts Yuri Gagarin and Valentina Tereshkova, 1961. PHOTO COURTESY CASA DE LAS AMÉRICAS.

Silvia talked about how extraordinary it was for a provincial woman, at mid-twentieth century, to do the things Haydée did:

> I grew up in Bayamo, not far from Santiago de Cuba. I was a young girl when the attack on Moncada took place, and I remember hearing that two women had been involved. My first thought was that they must be prostitutes who happened to be hanging out with the men! It didn't occur to us then that decent women could do such things. But it didn't take long for us to learn the truth. Understand: I am talking about our mentality back then.

Silvia shared some illuminating stories about Haydée's leadership style. Like others, she reiterated the heroine's refusal to limit the idea of revolution to party membership:

> "Being a revolutionary," she used to say, "is more than having a party card." I'll tell you a story about when the first party cells were being established in workplaces here. Haydée resisted and resisted. She was afraid that the beautiful collective we'd developed would be adversely affected

when some attained party membership and others, inevitably, were left out. Finally she had no choice but to initiate the process.

I wrote her a letter, in which I told her I didn't want to put myself up for membership. My parents had left the country, they were living in New Jersey, and you know how it was back then: party militants were expected to cut all ties with family on the outside. Even though I wasn't that close to my parents, I wasn't prepared to stop communicating with them. So I wrote that letter explaining this to Haydée and telling her that if it meant I had to resign from the board of directors, I would.

She never answered my letter. But when the party nucleus was established she made a passionate speech. I knew she was talking to me, and to two others who had decided to pass. I wish we had a copy of that speech; we recorded it, but somehow it got lost. Haydée was vehement as she expressed her conviction that to be a revolutionary you didn't need to be a party member.

Silvia's voice broke, as she sat for a moment or two with the memory.

I think of some people back then telling me they'd cut ties with their family members in exile—as if it was something to be proud of. Those same people began traveling the moment the revolution eased its restrictions. Many of them live in Miami now themselves! Yet back then we thought the world would collapse!

Silvia and I talked about the repressive period that cost so many such hardship:

We called it *el quinquenio gris*, because it started in 1971 and the thaw didn't begin until 1975, when Armando Hart was named minister of culture. But that was only the beginning of the thaw. Some people prefer to call it *el decenio negro* (ten black years). The problem was, the power struggle between the old Partido Socialista Popular [PSP, People's Socialist Party; a Moscow-oriented Communist party] and the July 26 Movement was still going on at the time. The PSP had some very old-fashioned ideas about culture and the people who make it.

I remember that during those difficult years Haydée spent a lot of time at Casa. Before that she might only show up a couple of times a month. She took care of business mostly over the phone. But when things got rough, she began coming to work almost every day. She defended the institution fiercely, with her great prestige. One day she sat down with a

Participants in 1972 gathering of visual artists. Haydée converses with Julio Le Parc, Tilsa Tsuchiya, Alfredo Rostgaard, and Miguel Rojas Mix, among others.
PHOTO COURTESY CASA DE LAS AMÉRICAS.

few of us. I remember her saying: "We have to be very careful for a while, so the tornado moves on by without doing us permanent harm."

We came to the moment of Haydée's suicide. Silvia echoed the shock and pain I'd heard from others. She said she was so upset at the funeral parlor that she went up to someone in charge and questioned the decision to hold the wake there rather than at the base of the grand statue of José Martí in the Plaza of the Revolution. "I remember Lilia Carpentier saying: 'They mourned Alejo in the Plaza; why not Haydée?'[26] But the Cuban people had the last word. Thousands of them accompanied her to Colón Cemetery; they filled every street."

I was glad to be able to sit down with Marcia Leseica, not only because she worked at Casa from its inception, but because as a teenager Haydée recruited her to the July 26 Movement and she remained a close confidante until her death. From a wealthy family, as a young girl Marcia took guitar classes at a private school in Havana. One day she noticed a young woman with a white handkerchief in her hand, sitting in the corner during class. Someone said her name was María. Later she learned that María had brought some students around to stay at that house. Marcia remembers being struck by her eyes:

> She looked at you, but it was as if she inhabited another dimension. There was such sadness in those eyes.
>
> That was 1957. And my life changed completely. Before that, I was your typical bourgeois student, fun loving, frivolous. There have been a number of times like that for me, when everything changed from one moment to the next. And this was one of them. I carried out some actions for her. And I continued to participate. My entire family left the country; I was the only one who stayed. I didn't see my mother again until 1993, when she fell ill in the United States.

Marcia told me she called Haydée María until she came to work at Casa, in 1959:

> Casa opened its doors in April of that year, and she contacted me in July. I came to work in September and remained until 1967, when I decided I needed to be in the countryside and went to work at a forestry project in Pinar del Río. I came back in 1990. But I always kept in touch with Haydée. I visited her often, and was with her in all her crises. She talked and talked: monologues really. I remember telephone conversations in which one of my ears turned red from having the receiver stuck to it so long. Just one ear!

Like so many others who knew her well, Marcia emphasized Haydée's singular sense of justice:

> You didn't see it only in the great heroic acts, but in the smallest details. She was never rancorous. Justice was the leitmotif of her life. And that gave her great moral authority, and an ability to bring people together. Which was why they sent her to Havana during the war, to deal with the different organizations. And why they sent her abroad, to deal with the factions in the exile community; you know, there were people there from all the different tendencies, even a couple of ex-presidents, and she was able to get them to act in concert—at least for the moment.

And Haydée was obsessive. She had to be, to get so much done. She was an avid reader, particularly of novels. She read biographies and liked poetry, but I don't remember her reading much in the area of the social sciences. She loved artistic expression in general, especially the visual arts. Although I spent many hours with her in her room, I don't remember her listening to music there. And she wasn't particularly interested in classical music. She entered the world of music through the guitar. But she got interested in those of *La nueva trova* because she could tell they were revolutionaries who were being unjustly persecuted, who had talent and needed help, not so much because of their music.

Marcia, too, pointed out that Haydée was the only woman who participated in every phase of the struggle against Batista: the attack on Moncada, the preparation for the revolutionaries' return from Mexico, the war in the Sierra, the underground work in the cities, and the important task of organizing the exile community in the United States—every single arena. She stressed her enormous sensibility and intuition: "Aside from her concept of justice, she was sensitive to the smallest details."

When our conversation got to the inevitable questions about Haydée's suicide, Marcia had no doubts:

Moncada's wounds simply never healed in her. Never. I know, because we were very close, and I accompanied her through her crises. Right after the revolution came to power, she took to her bed. And she took to her bed periodically throughout the rest of her life. She always needed help to shake off those depressions. She was able to do all she did because of her deep commitment and extraordinary strength. But it took everything she had, everything. From time to time she would just collapse. She would spend long periods in bed, reading, reading.

Many people tried to get her to see a psychiatrist. But what psychiatrist could have understood what she'd endured at Moncada? She was too smart for them, but her suffering also came from having lived through experiences they couldn't understand. She took medication, and it helped from time to time, but it never really got to the root of her problem. And even if we had known how close to the edge she was, I don't think any of us would have been able to have done anything about it anyway. She always lived her life exactly the way she wanted to.

I'm absolutely convinced that at the end she was out of her mind. Had she been in control, with her concept of motherhood, the way she adored

Haydée with Angela Davis and unnamed translator, 1972. PHOTO COURTESY CASA DE LAS AMÉRICAS.

her children, she never would have killed herself with them in the house. No matter what anyone says, it was a moment of madness. But the question really isn't why or how she killed herself. It is how she managed to live as long and generously as she did.

Immediately following Haydée's death, her colleagues at Casa memorialized her in the pages of *Revista Casa*. And there were other memorials on the fifth anniversary, the twentieth, and on what would have been her ninetieth birthday. Intellectuals and service workers gave their testimonies. Poets and artists and others around the world sent messages and poems. Here is a very brief selection, from among the many who loved her:

Trinidad Pérez[27] said:

The first time I saw her I was caught off guard. I'd imagined her the way you might a mythic figure: distant, serious. And I discovered that she was anything but. Haydée would arrive, stop and talk to everyone, and then make her way upstairs. Someone was painting a mural, and she'd pause and observe the artist at work. [. . .]

For me, the most important thing about Haydée was the connection she had with artists and service workers alike. She was so human. She always said she didn't know anything about art, but that wasn't true at all: she had a tremendous capacity for appreciating every artistic manifestation. I can't forget how she responded to poets reading their poems: Roque Dalton, Retamar, Benedetti. Or when she looked at one of Violeta Parra's tapestries. When she listened to popular or so-called classical music. She said she didn't know anything about art, but I think she knew a great deal. The sensibility with which she approached a given work allowed her to express herself with great depth. I was always impressed by how she related to the artists; I don't see that in many others. If there was a concert, for example, she was always right there, in the front row. If she went to the theater and there wasn't much of an audience, she'd go out in front and invite people in: "Hey, come on in and hear Viglietti,[28] or Mercedes Sosa!"[29]

When Haydée appeared at Casa, everything changed. The atmosphere became more animated. She imposed respect, not fear. We all admired her, but none of us felt pressured. She respected anyone who was knowledgeable about anything: the artist or the technician. She let everyone do his or her job. She could spot an error you might have made, but she supported you and that was a great stimulus. She gave people strength, made them strong. She might call you in later to discuss something. But she never abandoned anyone. [. . .]"

Alicia Aguiar[30] responded to a request that she speak about Haydée with these words:

One of the things I liked about Haydée was that she always considered the worker. She talked with everyone, and never demonstrated those painful differences. She was such a good person, so good. No one here forgets her. I'm telling you no one forgets her, and I remember her with love. Once she brought me a beautiful length of cloth so I could get a new uniform made. And I've never, ever, worn that dress. I can't wear it knowing she isn't going to be able to see it on me. It's green gingham, really beautiful. I had it made up just the way I wanted. But oh my no, I just can't. I wanted her to see me in it.

María Regla Averoff[31] had this to say:

Look, Haydée would arrive in the morning and come to my house, the little place where I live behind Casa. She'd just drop by to see how I was doing. She'd come around lunchtime, lift the lid from one of the pots on my stove, and breathe in the scent of whatever I was cooking. "Oh, that's good!" She'd ask me if it was gizzard, or what it was. And she'd ask if she could taste a little. She was a boss and a comrade. A friend of all the workers. You'd tell her: "Ay, Haydée, what a pretty dress you're wearing," and wham! Right away she'd want to give it to you. No, no, no, no, I'm telling you, Haydée was a wonderful person. One thing I'll always remember: around eleven in the morning, if she had a moment, she'd come and sit over there in the doorway, and it could get to be two in the morning and she'd still be talking to us! And she'd say: 'Well, I can see from your faces that you're tired!" And she'd go. That's why I feel her here in my house, day and night, just like you can feel her in Casa de las Américas.

Lesbia Vent Dumois[32] said:

It's as if you asked me to talk about my mother. What can one say about a mother? That's what Haydée was to all of us, because it's no coincidence that we speak of Casa as if it were our home. It's no coincidence that we have become a family. . . . She could as easily sit at the top of the stairs as take your arm and start talking to you about an idea she had. That was Haydée: human, simple, and also fire. A whirlwind of action and joy.

Like intellectuals and artists all over the world, when he heard about Haydée's death Pedro Orgambide[33] sent a heartfelt message:

I woke up this morning thinking about Cuba and about Haydée Santamaría. Life, death, and survival suddenly came together, maybe because on days like this one tends to think about what one has done or failed to do, one takes stock as a way of understanding oneself better. What happened, Roberto? What happened to us all with the loss of Haydée? She was (is) one of the most beautiful figures of the Revolution, which is to say of life.

Chiki Salsamendi[34] had this to say:

Haydée was like a mother to me, like a combination mother and older sister. She was always so concerned about my problems, what was happening in my life, in my personal as well as my work life. What she meant to me is beyond my power to describe.

I began to work here at Casa de las Américas on October 2, 1962. And could she talk! She was a great conversationalist, a great conversationalist.

She could talk about anything. It was so easy to communicate with her. She was always kidding around, always making jokes. But when she had to be serious, she could do that too. She had all that in her. She was extraordinary, capable of seeing things one couldn't even imagine. I wouldn't see her for a while, and we just picked up where we'd left off. There was no sense of time having passed. She was always right there.

Like these testimonies there are thousands, in archives, publications, and in the memories of those who may not have spoken publicly but hold Haydée in a special place in their hearts. Those who knew her well, say the relationship was one of the great privileges of their lives. Those who knew her slightly still burn with the spark of that contact. Casa de las Américas, without doubt one of her greatest accomplishments, continues to radiate her brilliance, creativity, respect for diversity, and pursuit of justice.

# 8 TWO, THREE, MANY VIETNAMS
## *Haydée and Che*

At the vortex of the political and the spiritual lies a renewed sense of function, even a mission, for art. [. . .] It can mean a new way of looking at shared experience.
—Lucy R. Lippard, *Mixed Blessings*, 14

One might ask the same question about Haydée that she asked about Ho Chi Minh: was he who he was because he was Vietnamese, or were the Vietnamese who they were because they had him as a leader? Haydée embodied certain very Cuban qualities—the worldview of an islander, small-nation pride, and the inventiveness and creativity of those forced to compete on the world stage with citizens of larger, more powerful countries—but she had these qualities to an inordinate degree. Something of her uniqueness rubbed off on everyone she touched.

By 1959, when Fidel Castro and his rebels took power in Cuba, the US Central Intelligence Agency (CIA) had a long and criminal history of invading its southern neighbors or provoking the overthrow of democratically elected governments throughout the region. During the first half of the century, US troops invaded Caribbean countries at least thirty-four times, briefly occupying Honduras, Mexico, Guatemala, and Costa Rica and remaining for longer periods in Haiti, Cuba, Nicaragua, Panama, and the Dominican Republic. It had designs on other Latin American countries as well. In fact, its

*Hasta la victoria siempre!* Commission of Revolutionary Orientation (ORI),
Antonio Pérez González (Niko), serigraph, 1967. USED BY PERMISSION.

interference throughout the world was legion. But most calamitously, it was waging a war in Vietnam that had divided that Southeast Asian nation, had no end in sight, was rapidly becoming a worldwide symbol of US imperialist reach, and would define an era.

In 1973, US money and covert military maneuvering brought down Salvador Allende's government in Chile, the first socialist project on the American continent to have been elected by popular vote. In 1980, the year of Haydée's death, the Reagan administration initiated its Contra war in Nicaragua and ten years later succeeded in defeating the Sandinistas. In the eyes of people throughout the world, the United States was the great bully: destabilizing by covert and overt means and establishing trade agreements that always favored its own interests at a devastating cost to those it claimed to be helping. It invaded, occupied, murdered or attempted to murder foreign leaders, spread animal and crop diseases, and pillaged for its gain. All of which makes Cuba's resistance all the more impressive.

Cuba's solidarity with Vietnam was especially profound. I remember the thousands of young Vietnamese studying in the country when I lived there in the 1970s. The girls all had long braids; they vowed not to cut their hair until the invaders were routed from their precious land. The Cuban revolution supported liberation movements across the globe, including some within the United States. This support was reflected in material aid and training, as well as through conferences, invitations to visit the island, shortwave radio broadcasts, and exciting art.

The Cuban revolution, thumbing its nose at arrogant power and like a slap in the face so close to US shores, represented the first successful opposition to US dominance and control. A small group of ragged but audacious revolutionaries had ousted a dictator backed by a succession of US administrations. As outlined in the first chapter of this book, the revolution had wasted no time in reclaiming its banks, sugarcane, and most important, its dignity. Cuba had become an example that standing up to the bully was possible. The guerrilla methodology that had proven successful in the Sierra Maestra, the idea that a small group could take up arms, earn popular support, and eventually take power, was known as the *foco* theory. It never really worked again as it had in the Sierra Maestra.

Régis Debray, a young French political theoretician, wrote *revolution in the revolution?*, which became the *foco* theory's central text. Casa de las Américas published the treatise and also a critique of the Right's response. A Mexican publisher brought out a panel discussion, *Diez años de revolución*,

George Jackson poster, Organization of Solidarity with the Peoples of Africa, Asia, and Latin America (OSPAAAL), Rafael Morante, 1971. USED BY PERMISSION.

in which several important Latin American revolutionary writers debated Debray's proposal.[1]

Ernesto "Che" Guevara, the Argentine doctor who joined Fidel in Mexico, fought in Cuba, and envisioned similar liberation struggles throughout all of Latin America and the subjugated world, was the most visible proponent of the *foco* theory. He wrote about it, lived it, and was murdered in his attempt to carry it out. His cry of "Two, three, many Vietnams!" urged people everywhere to rise up against imperialist domination, thus weakening that control by spreading it thin as it tried to defeat increasing worldwide opposition to imperialism.

This cry was the theme of Guevara's message to the first Tricontinental Conference of Solidarity with the Peoples of Africa, Asia and Latin America (OSPAAAL), held in Havana at the beginning of 1966, and became a rallying call in many parts of the world. In Che's absence the following year, Haydée presided over the continuation of Tricontinental: the 1967 Latin American Solidarity Conference (OLAS), where the Cuban leadership reaffirmed armed struggle as the "fundamental path forward" for the continent's revolutionaries.

Haydée and Che met in the Sierra during the Cuban war. They were friends and comrades and shared an intensity of revolutionary identification unique even in such situations. Many men and women made the Cuban revolution. Many were consumed by its demands. But few possessed the clarity, even purity, of these two. They shared ideals illusive to others. Haydée's daughter Celia remembered that "from the moment she saw him, my mother understood [his] enigma, the unique myth his hopeful image has become for generation after generation. She got it long before he became the Heroic Guerrilla."[2] And on hearing the news of his tragic death, Celia said, her mother was inconsolable. Inconsolable and angry: "What a *machista*, what an outrageous *machista*. He promised he would take me with him to make the revolution in the rest of America. He promised but he went without me."[3]

Haydée was as passionate about Che's dream of a liberated continent as she had been when she followed her brother Abel and Fidel into battle at Moncada, when she resisted the horror of being shown her brother's eye and fiancé's testicle by refusing to give her torturers the information they wanted, when she called on every bit of will and composed herself in order to speak truth to power at the trial following that epic action, and throughout the rest of the war: in prison, in the underground, in the Sierra, in every other arena of Cuban struggle.

She was passionate, as well, in her belief that art is the highest expression of revolutionary social change. At Casa de las Américas she created the perfect venue in which to demonstrate the role that art and culture can play in creating a new society. Her vision, as we have seen, was always inclusive, never narrow or limited to the safe and stereotypical socialist realism recipe being pushed at the time by Soviet communism. At Casa she wooed the best artists and writers from many different schools and tendencies. She valued creative integrity and urged the judges at each year's literary contest to consider quality over political content. She frequently defended writers, artists, and musicians misunderstood or victimized by rigid party functionaries.

In the United States, throughout the 1950s McCarthyism cast a deep chill on artists and intellectuals. Left-leaning writers, filmmakers, and others were blacklisted. Many lost jobs or entire careers. Among those who were called before the infamous House Un-American Activities Committee (HUAC), some refused to testify while others turned state's evidence. The country's cultural institutions—universities, Broadway, Hollywood studios, publishers, funding agencies, radio, and incipient television—proclaimed that "political" art was not art; meaning social concerns were off-limits as subjects of creative work. While artists in other parts of the world felt free

CANCION
PROTESTA

encuentro agosto 1967 casa de las américas/cuba

Poster for protest
song event, Casa
de las Américas,
Alfredo Rostgaard,
serigraph, 1967. USED
BY PERMISSION.

to take a multiplicity of journeys, US artists were encouraged to stay within
a safe zone of provincialism.

The 1960s brought a thaw in the United States, and creative rage reas-
serted itself. With it came a new cultural rebellion. Important movements
in the worlds of poetry, music, the visual arts, and theater (including street
theater) came to the fore. The American war in Vietnam gave birth to Artists
and Writers Protest and Angry Arts (both based in New York), the Artists
Protest Committee (Los Angeles), and many similar groups.

Abstract artists continued to make work without discernible social content, but many of them were also unwilling to be told by government what
subject matter to embrace. In 1968 fourteen of them donated works to ben-

efit the Student Mobilization Against the War. They raised $30,000. Art historian Lucy R. Lippard explains:

> the organizer's statement offered the abstract artists' rationale:
> These 14 non-objective artists are against the war in Vietnam. They are supporting this commitment in the strongest manner open to them by contributing major examples of their current work. The artists and the individual pieces were selected to present a particular esthetic attitude, in the conviction that a cohesive group of important works makes the most forceful statement for peace.[4]

The US civil rights / black freedom movement produced powerful art, particularly in the genres of photography and song. Hundreds of "little" magazines (meaning independent of institutional support), underground newspapers, graphic comics, and wallpapers began publishing. And the personal was becoming political. The Art Workers Coalition (AWC) formed in 1969, essentially to protest injustice within the art world itself. The second wave of feminism burst on the scene, and women artists began to get together to protest their exclusion from museums and galleries; Heresies was an exciting collective that functioned from 1977 to 1992. But residual discomfort remained, and there was confusion about what constituted "real art."

Again, as Lippard has written:

> The older New York artists harbored taboos against social content inherited from the days of Stalinism and McCarthyism, and the younger artists were unaware that art *could* be politically effective. They had been trained to understand that all political art was corny and old-fashioned—barely art in the highest sense—and few had the political sophistication to combat these dominant views.[5]

Thus, every creative space was contested, particularly from the grassroots. Social insurgencies always produce new art, and in the United States, throughout the 1970s and 1980s, these included farmworkers, Native Americans, autoworkers, women, and members of the LGBTQ community, among others.

It may be relevant today to point out that neoliberalism objectifies and commodifies the most popular artistic manifestations, understanding all too well that authentic cultural expression expands social horizons and allows people to visualize a different world. After the implosion of the socialist bloc, in 1989, when neoliberalism became hegemonic, capitalism authored new and more sophisticated cultural strategies and introduced them into the developing world by every means possible.

The Cuban Revolution understood the importance of culture from its inception. It was alive with what we called "Marxism in Spanish": an innovative, sometimes raucous expression that drew on the country's Spanish and Afro-Cuban traditions, as well as respecting the new and producing an exciting amalgam of artistic output that was communist and utopian, tropical and astute. If the Russian and Chinese revolutions had painted themselves in steel gray, the Cuban Revolution exploded onto the scene in brilliant color.

Soon after its victory, news about the island stopped appearing or was grossly distorted in the mainstream US press. The United States attempted to erect a cultural blockade in tandem with its economic and diplomatic counterparts. It was largely due to Haydée that the first was never as successful as the other two. Her brilliant work at Casa broke through all sorts of barriers.

Although the US news blackout of Cuba has been ongoing, hundreds and then thousands of young people defied government restrictions and traveled to the island—so near and yet so distant. The Venceremos Brigade, an independent organization begun in 1969 by Students for a Democratic Society (SDS), took 9,000 mostly young people on yearly trips. They had to travel through Czechoslovakia, Mexico City, or Montreal and spent up to a month working (cutting sugarcane or building schools), getting to know the revolution's achievements, and meeting with representatives of people's movements from Latin America, Africa, and Asia. These brigades continue today in conjunction with Pastors for Peace.

Many of those who visited Cuba, either with the Venceremos Brigade or on other delegations, were journalists, artists, and writers. Some had alternative publications and galleries or belonged to collectives that promoted socially conscious art. They became the conduit through which some of Cuba's posters, books, and music arrived in the United States. And Cuban music had a tremendous impact on the world music scene. The posters, in particular, proved important. Many of them were in solidarity with US political movements.

In this perfect storm produced by the challenges of having to remake society in a context of scarce resources but with a burst of revolutionary energy, posters in Cuba took off—in directions as varied as the styles of the artists who designed them. Soviet and Polish poster art were inspirations. Their destinations and impact "went viral," as a later generation would say.

The US government was quick to castigate US citizens who disseminated information about Cuba or shared the human stories of how the revolution had or hadn't changed people's lives. New York poet Susan Sherman, who edited *Ikon* magazine, an important cultural political forum for social change, lost her university teaching job upon her return from the island in 1968. The distributor that had handled the magazine dropped it at the same time. Her FBI file—which she managed to obtain many years later—was filled with lies that some paid informant had told about what she was supposedly doing on the revolution's behalf. Many of these informants simply made things up in order to justify their shameful pay.

First published in *Casa de las Américas* magazine, Roberto Fernández Retamar's 1971 essay "Caliban: Notes toward a Discussion of Culture in Our America" had an impact on progressive writers in the United States and throughout the world.[6] It was one of the first Latin American texts that offered a view of cultural priorities from the perspective of the global South. Testimonial literature, or oral history, also got a boost from the revolution. It was called *testimonio* back then. Casa's yearly literary contest began including a category devoted to the genre. The revolution raised the consciousness that ordinary people, not only the "experts," could and should tell their stories.

In the 1960s, before my own move to Cuba, Mexican poet Sergio Mondragón and I edited *El Corno Emplumado / The Plumed Horn*, a bilingual literary journal out of Mexico City. We attended a gathering of poets in Cuba in January 1967[7] and brought back some of the new Cuban poetry and artwork. Our issue 23, appearing in July 1967, was completely devoted to Cuba. Much to the surprise of some US readers, most young Cuban poets weren't writing specifically about political issues. "We don't need to write about the revolution," one of them said, "we are the revolution."

The Pan American Union, cultural arm of the then US-dominated Organization of American States (OAS) warned us against publishing a letter that referenced that anthology. We defied the threat, and the institution canceled its five hundred subscriptions. In 1968 Mexico's student movement emerged with significant power, and the government (about to host the Olympic games) repressed it violently.[8] Our magazine defended the students, and I was also active in the movement. The following year I suffered a political repression, was forced underground, and had to leave Mexico. It was then that I moved my family to Cuba.

It wasn't long before Cuba's cultural ideas began to have an impact on young artists in the United States and in other parts of the world. Politically conscious painters, photographers, writers, musicians, singer-songwriters, dancers, and theater people began calling themselves cultural workers. This came out of an ideological identification with the working class and was an attempt to avoid the rarefied status bestowed upon artists by a commodity-oriented society.

From the mid-1960s through the early 1980s, Cuba produced some of the most powerful revolutionary art anywhere in the world. We've already seen the influence wrought by Casa's yearly literary prize, but the country's publishing program was much broader. The 1961 literacy campaign had all but eradicated illiteracy in the country and left a population hungry to read. Books were heavily subsidized, and title followed title, in editions for a country of 11 million that would have seemed impossibly large in one with a population twenty times its size. And these editions sold out quickly; news of a new title had people lining up for hours to obtain a copy. I remember my oldest daughter standing in line all night for the next in her favorite mystery series. A few books that were classics of world literature merited especially large editions; a million copies were printed of Cervantes's *Don Quijote*, and Malcolm X's *Autobiography* was an early bestseller.

Like most poor countries, prerevolutionary Cuba didn't have much of a film industry. Under the direction of Alfredo Guevara, the Cuban Institute of Cinematographic Arts and Industry (ICAIC) began its wild run of extraordinary films—classics such as *Lucía*, *Memories of Underdevelopment*, and *Strawberry and Chocolate*.[9] Eventually a school for filmmakers opened on the island, and Havana's yearly international film festival began making headlines. Visual artists, too, flourished with the revolution; many were subsidized so they could commit to their own work, and the state provided materials when scarcity became a problem.

Cuba has always had rich traditions of music and dance. With the revolution, young singer-songwriters such as Silvio Rodríguez, Pablo Milanés, Sara González, and Noël Nicola—many of them discovered and supported by Haydée—joined the old-timers, aging troubadours whose talents the new society also recognized and brought to renewed prominence. The great Cuban ballerina Alicia Alonso, famous before the revolution came to power, stayed on, created a new school of ballet that took into account particular Cuban body types, and in a still macho society encouraged young boys who were interested to study the discipline.

In addition to the dozen or so theater companies that existed in Havana

Poster for *Lucia*,
Cuban Institute
of Film Art and
Industry (ICAIC), Raúl
Martínez González,
serigraph, 1968.

and other Cuban cities, a new type of theater developed out of the revolutionary struggle itself. The Escambray Mountains harbored a counterrevolutionary movement long after the war was won. A theater group called Teatro Escambray sent its members out to live among the poor farmers in the area, learn their problems, and together write plays that would showcase those problems followed by discussion aimed at resolving them.

A National Arts School drew talent from the most remote regions of the country. Scouts traveled to rural areas, issuing calls to young people interested in studying a variety of artistic genres, and brought them to Havana for professional training. Eventually, each of the country's provinces would have its own art school. And art was also an important component of the revolutionary curriculum being developed throughout the system of public education. But Cuban posters, like no other expressive form, conveyed a rejection of the old order and invitation to the new.

In the context of the Cuban revolution, posters acquired a life and vitality of their own. From the early 1960s through the mid 1980s, Cuban poster art may have had as great an influence on rebel movements in the United States and throughout the world as any other artistic genre. A number of institutions produced their own: among them Casa de las Américas, ICAIC, and the Organization of the Peoples of Asia, Africa and Latin America (OSPAAAL). Great Cuban artists, such as René Mederos (whose silk screen images of Vietnam remain iconic), Alfredo Rostgaard (whose haunting protest song poster of a stylized rose, a drop of blood dripping from its single thorn, has been reproduced worldwide), Nelson Ponce, Lilia Díaz, Asela Pérez, and Umberto Peña (who designed Casa's posters and publications for years), are among the artists who created those unforgettable images.

Because of its commitment to global social change and its strong internationalist bent, Cuban posters addressed the struggle for black power in the United States, Puerto Rican independence, freedom for Angela Davis, defiance after the murder of George Jackson,[10] and the liberation struggles being waged throughout the Third World, among others. They honored figures such as Vietnam's Ho Chi Minh, Puerto Rican nationalist Pedro Albizu Campos,[11] Colombian priest and guerrilla fighter Camilo Torres,[12] and of course Che Guevara in every possible iteration.

The great Cuban writer Alejo Carpentier has written:

With the Cuban revolution a new mechanism was established for production, distribution and consumption, eliminating the legitimacy of the traditional advertising poster that, particularly for cosmetics, drinks or the cinema, would often arrive ready-made, printed in the United States. It was then that our design artists, engravers, decorators and typographers were called into action. Those who previously (with rare exceptions) had been shunted to the sidelines in the advertising industry [. . .] were given the opportunity of working on posters conceived for historical and cultural purposes. And because of its high quality, the poster was converted into an intrinsic vehicle for the spread of culture and a permanent expression of a new reality, continually reinventing itself and accessible to all.

At the same time, we must emphasize the importance these posters acquired in our people's political consciousness. Every commemoration, every event, every aspect of our collective lives were reflected in posters that, in a certain sense, through the images they projected, make up a living and contemporary chronicle of the revolutionary process.[13]

A sad commentary on how our world has changed between that era and the present is how these posters were regarded in the 1960s–1980s period and how they are regarded now. Back then, they applauded courage, showed solidarity, educated for social change, and encouraged liberation in many different cultures and situations. Cuban posters have now become valuable items displayed in special collections and sold on eBay. Capitalism's consumer-oriented society has reduced them, like so much else, to objects of market worth.

The counterrevolution understood all too well the power of that art. I remember when the CIA removed every copy of a poster honoring the Black Panthers[14] from between the pages of Cuba's *Revista Tricontinental*, replaced it with a significantly altered knockoff that carried a message designed to divide, and then resealed the envelope and sent magazine and poster on their way.

From December 1972 through January 1973, US painter and muralist Jane Norling spent two months in Havana working half days at OSPAAAL's design studio. I was living in Cuba at the time. Jane was a member of the People's Press collective in San Francisco. Because the collective produced a quarterly digest of OSPAAAL's *Tricontinental* magazine in English, the Cuban organization invited one of its members down to have this experience. Studio director Alfredo Rostgaard asked Jane to design a poster for the Day of World Solidarity with the Struggle of the Puerto Rican people.

Jane remembers:

> The poster had international distribution. It was a tremendous honor for me. I was 25 and extremely naïve politically and internationally, but I did speak Spanish. Frankly, I don't remember much about working at the all-male design department other than Rostgaard's gentle wit, encouragement, conversations about political art making in the US, and general wisecracking and practical joking.
>
> I do recall a discussion about signing the poster. As a member of a collective, I adamantly believed that if the name of the artist appeared on the work, the names of all the producers of the piece should also appear, from copy camera operator to stripper and printer. I asked why in socialist

Jane Norling's poster in solidarity with the struggle of the
Puerto Rican people, designed for OSPAAAL, 1973. USED BY
PERMISSION.

Cuba only an artist's signature would appear with the image. Rostgaard
said: "People want to know who did it. However collectively produced a
published piece, the hand of the artist, the eye of the designer, belongs to
that one person. Its use is collective."

Cuban poster art informed the civil–rights-fueled social justice organizations of the 1970s, consciously or just because we absorbed it. The vi-
suals that exemplified the young Revolution educated US artists eager to
use our hands and eyes to build a just society. Cuba turned the successful
blend of word and image to sell capitalism against capitalism, and did it

with wit and a "fuck you" that thrilled us 50 years ago and roars forward today in the Occupy posters.

Haydée Santamaría and Che Guevara promoted "Two, three, many Vietnams" in different ways: she by facilitating revolutionary art, and he by making of his life the highest expression of that art. When Che was killed in Bolivia in October 1967, Haydée lost a soul mate, someone with whom she identified completely. Her anguish can be felt in her letter to Chilean painter Roberto Matta and in her own posthumous letter to the guerilla leader:

Che:

Where can I write you now? You would tell me anywhere, to the Bolivian miner, Peruvian mother, guerrilla fighter who is or isn't but will be. I know all that, Che. You yourself taught me, and anyway this letter isn't really for you. How can I tell you that I never cried so much since the night I heard they killed Frank [País]—even though when it was announced I didn't believe you were really dead. We were all sure you were still alive, and I said: "It's not possible, a bullet can't bring down that which is immortal. Fidel and you must live. If you don't, how can we?" Fourteen years ago I saw those die whom I loved most in the world—I think I've already lived too long. The sun isn't any longer so beautiful, the palm trees don't give me pleasure anymore. Sometimes, like now, although I love life so much, knowing it's worth opening one's eyes each morning if only for those two things, I want to close them forever, like you.

This continent doesn't deserve this, that's the truth. With your eyes open, Latin America would have found its way forward. Che, the only thing that might have consoled me would have been to have gone with you. But I didn't go. I'm here with Fidel. I have always done what he wanted.

Do you remember? In the Sierra you promised. You said: "You won't miss the coffee, we'll drink *mate*." You were an internationalist, borders didn't exist for you, but you promised you would send for me when you were finally in your Argentina. I never doubted you would keep that promise. Now it cannot happen, you couldn't, I couldn't.

Fidel said it, so I know it's true. How sad. He couldn't say "Che." He drew on all his strength and said "Ernesto Guevara." That's how he broke the news to the people, your people. What tremendous sadness. I cried for the people, for Fidel, for you, because I can't take it anymore. And later, at your wake, when our great people wondered what rank Fidel would confer upon you, he said "artist." I felt that any rank would have been too low, inadequate, and Fidel as always found the right one.

Everything you created was perfect, but you created something unique: yourself. You showed us that a new human being is possible. Everyone could see that this new being is real, because he exists, he is you.

What more can I say, Che? If only I knew how to speak like you did. Once you wrote me:

I see that you have become a writer with a talent for synthesis, but I confess I liked you best that New Year's day, with guns blaring all around and all your ammunition spent. That image, and our time together in the Sierra—even our fights back then are precious memories—are what I will carry with me for my personal use.

That's why I can't write about you, and you will always have that memory.

Until victory always, dear Che,

Haydée.

Artist. That's what Fidel called Che at his wake, and as Haydée reiterated in this letter and on many other occasions, it was the highest accolade in her vocabulary, the most honorable rank or condition to which she believed a person could aspire. In life, Che too was known for his love of art and respect for the creative process. In "Man and Socialism in Cuba" (1965), he devotes significant space to the revolutionary nature of abstract art.[15] In his guerrilla campaigns he often carried books of poetry in his backpack, even when it meant less room for ammunition or medicine.

The Cuban revolution showcased a series of convictions that, although present in earlier cultures, periods, and struggles, were strongly emphasized in its narrative, especially during its first two decades. These included confidence in the feasibility of a small group of rebels being capable of routing an entrenched regime fully supported by a powerful neighbor, a belief that social change is primarily human rather than simply political, an appreciation of culture and art as driving forces in the new society, and internationalism at a level never before seen.

Haydée and Che embodied these beliefs in a way few others did. Haydée gave all her energies to struggle before it was even visible on Cuba's mid-twentieth century horizon. She committed herself to that struggle when she was one of a handful of revolutionaries and of an even smaller number of women. She broke international barriers with her work at Casa. She embraced all that was authentic in the arts—and the artists who created that authenticity. She defended creative Cubans engaged in similar activity. And she linked her work to internationalist concerns at every level.

Che developed his internationalism after leaving his native Argentina, honing it as a very young man traveling Latin America on a beat-up motorcycle. He brought this consciousness with him when he met Fidel in Mexico. In a matter of hours the two men joined forces. Che was one of the few survivors of the ill-fated voyage on the *Granma* and proved himself during the war in the mountains, becoming a leader long before the 1959 victory. Although he stayed on in Cuba for almost a decade, lending his brilliant and innovative mind to projects such as the National Bank and Ministry of Industry, the idea of work as a constructive force, and culture as an imperative to change, he never intended to remain in Cuba.

Fidel was destined to become the statesman, charged with leading a country, carrying on diplomatic relations with other nations, and resolving the problems inherent in bringing Cuba out of underdevelopment in a bipolar world. Che was destined to take his dream of national liberation across borders, to die in the service of that dream, and to become an enduring symbol of resistance—even for generations too young to know his history. Haydée was like a bridge between the two, embodying some qualities of each and adding her own.

Meaningful social change, free education from kindergarten through postgraduate work, universal health care, internationalism, culture, arts, and sports made accessible to all: these are the rights and responsibilities the Cuban revolution has prioritized from the beginning. Che and Haydée wanted these achievements to come better, faster, more creatively and permanently. Each gave his or her life in that effort.

Haydée at a Communist Party assembly in 1977.
PHOTO COURTESY CASA DE LAS AMÉRICAS.

# 9 THE WOMAN BENEATH THE MYTH

She was not
an instrument
for you to play,
already radiant as she was
with death's empty light,
the way death is its own
effortless not doing.
—V. B. Price, "Orpheus the Healer"

Haydée Santamaría came from the obscurity of provincial life on a Cuban sugar plantation and grew up during the most oppressive half of the last century to take her place among her nation's heroes. She was known by her first name in households all over the island, and anyone old enough still refers to her as Haydée.

To revolutionaries she became a legend in her lifetime. But even those who were less than enthusiastic about the political change wrought by her and her comrades were drawn to her warmth and authenticity. Just as some in this latter category might pinpoint Fidel and others as targets of their resentment, they would speak about Haydée as an exception, citing a kindness she had bestowed upon them or a story they had heard. Revolutionaries troubled by the rigidity of certain officials or the repressive excesses in periods during which difference was disdained looked to her for understanding and protection. They were not disappointed. And for anyone beyond Cuba's borders, anywhere in the world, if we had the privilege of knowing her it was a gift.

Like all girl children in a world controlled by men, Haydée achieved her survival at great personal cost. She learned where she could, detecting teachers and turning them into mentors. She apprenticed in all directions and with an energy that set her apart: from the teacher in the provincial schoolhouse of her youth, from her country's greatest rebels (dead and alive), from field hand or Nobel laureate, innovative musician or neighbor child. Her brother Abel, with whom she developed a deep bond in their common pursuit of justice, led her to Fidel, Celia, and Che, figures who remained the essential points on her compass.

Her gender consciousness was raw and deep. She came up long before feminism's Second Wave swept the Western world, pointing to a new analysis of power and designing a more equitable dynamic that would challenge institutions as well as individuals. She wasn't someone who studied theory; she simply had a highly developed sense of right and wrong. Attitudes others may have espoused out of an ideological stance, she expressed naturally. And she came to many feminist ideas before theoreticians or activists wrote about them.

Her consuming involvement with changing society as a whole left little time for thinking about a particular sector: women, people of color, lesbians and gay men, the differently abled, or others. Her pursuit of justice for everyone caused her to demand equality for all groups. She saw the challenge as a single task and positioned herself on the front lines of all these struggles simultaneously. When she felt an injustice had been committed, she undoubtedly railed against it in high-level party meetings. She also took what measures were possible on her own. Singer-songwriter Silvio Rodríguez attests to the fact that she went to the reeducation camps set up to "make men out of homosexuals" in 1965 and personally removed a number of artists whom she then continued to encourage and protect.[1]

Haydée's ideas about womanhood were not without contradiction. On the one hand, she looked to uniquely courageous women as models and had an unusually developed sense of her own female self. In response to the longtime acquaintance who'd accused her of being too important now to remember old friends, she wrote that the woman was mistaken and, outraged, declared she'd been important years before when she'd risked her life at Moncada, not later when having done the right thing gave her status and responsibilities. As I read that letter, I expected her to express the self-effacing modesty so typical of women at the time and insist that she wasn't as important as the woman thought. Instead, she owned her true importance with a confidence rare in women then—and even now.

On the other hand, she held marriage as sacred and divorce unacceptable. The sanctity of marriage, for her, didn't come from state or religious authority; she was not a believer and her attitude toward organized religion ran from disinterest to rejection. Rather, it was her understanding of loyalty—the commitment one human being makes to another—that made it so difficult for her to contemplate dissolving such a union.

Several of my interviewees made it clear that Haydée believed that a wife's place was with her husband. She clearly felt that men need women, not as servants or for pleasure, but because women are more emotionally developed and could be helpful when men might flounder. And she said her era favored female strength and sensibility. At the same time, she couldn't bear a man standing in the way of a woman's (or anyone's) creativity, work, or goals. Life's great projects came first: the revolution, internationalism, children, culture, and art. In her view, art was as important as the more practical forms of nourishment, and I think her belief that culture is the highest form of politics informed everything she did, as well as all her relationships.

Haydée had strong family ties and cherished motherhood. Despite her vast professional and political responsibilities, she always found time for her children and the children of others. And this time was far from perfunctory. Everyone with whom I spoke, very particularly those who had been mothered by her, talked about the time she spent with her children, on all their important occasions and in the everyday.

She lived at a time when men and women together attempted to change the world and when men almost always led in that endeavor. It was a monumental goal, requiring full commitment. And she was of a generation in which many of us, myself included, found it difficult to mother our own children well while working to make life better for all the world's children. Yet she managed that balance admirably.

Haydée's concept of family was large and inclusive. Along with her two biological children, she added the children of family members to her household whenever necessary. She hosted children from the Cuban countryside

Haydée enjoying Casa de las América's twentieth anniversary celebration. PHOTO COURTESY CASA DE LAS AMÉRICAS.

who came to study in the capital. And she and Armando took in a number of Latin American children whose parents were on the front lines of struggle or in prison or had died in the various efforts to liberate the continent.

Norma Ruiz told me that at mealtimes there could be as many as fourteen sitting around her dining room table. And Haydée's daughter Celia María wrote about how the number of her brothers and sisters varied year by year. Haydée was also deeply interested in the family situations of everyone with whom she worked and many she met along the way, keeping up with their children, aware of particular problems, and always ready to help.

Dolores Pérez ("Lolita"), a childhood friend of Haydée's who was a great support during the underground struggle in Havana, remembers how she

> adored plants and animals, to say nothing of humans whom she loved above all else. She imbued everything with life, making the simplest gatherings into something more, so that the smallest act seemed like a great event. One of her notable characteristics was her ability to embellish a project with a series of little details that turned it into something special. Her solid leadership characteristics never separated her from others, or made her seem one-dimensional.[2]

Fashion? Haydée disparaged consumerism and industry fads, even as her position at the head of Casa de las Américas and as an official representative of the Cuban revolution abroad required she use an appropriate style of dress. She knew that in this respect more was expected of her as a woman than if she were a man; and she raged against gender discrimination as expressed in the dress code of the day. Her appreciation of art and craft drew her to indigenous weavings. She was vain about her hair, which she thought of as thin and inelegant, and innovated wigs and other head coverings to deal with the problem. She also delighted in dressing up and masquerading to play elaborate tricks on others.

But her most profound statement about dress and its implications came, as we have seen, when she appeared at a PCC Central Committee meeting dressed as a man. As one of very few women in an upper-echelon world that was predominately male, she was sick of the lack of respect she suffered when she received engraved invitations addressed to "Comrade so and so and wife" or when the instructions for correct attire listed "bring wife" below "medals" or "tie."

Haydée was very much a woman of her time, shaped by the history and culture of Cuba as it filtered through class, race, and gender at mid-twentieth century. She was also a woman who defied her era. She sought justice in ways that served as an example to many and proof of her *locura* (craziness) to some, depending upon the person's own broad-mindedness and moral compass. People from all walks of life were drawn to her, especially those who favored authenticity over social pretense. Those who loved her tended to be the great creative spirits and others who shunned pretense or unnecessary formalities. Timid apologists for social hypocrisy, those who defended imperialist politics, opportunists, and social climbers were uncomfortable in her presence, fearing the implacability of her truth.

There are numerous stories that show her defending a person or idea, even if hers was the lone dissenting voice against a high-level chorus of opposition. A concrete example of the way in which Haydée defied pressures to go along with conformist cultural strategies can be found in the following piece of history. In the late 1950s and immediately following the victory of the revolution, several newsreels made by different companies were documenting recent Cuban events. One of these was José Guerra Alemán's *Cineperiódico*. When Alfredo Guevara founded ICAIC and began producing *Noticiero latinoamericano*, he made sure the latter replaced the former.

*Cineperiódico* had its own anti-Batista history. It had gained a reputation for independence and professionalism from its 1951 reportage on Eduardo Chibas's suicide and had produced *Cuba 1959* and *El gran recuento* (The Great

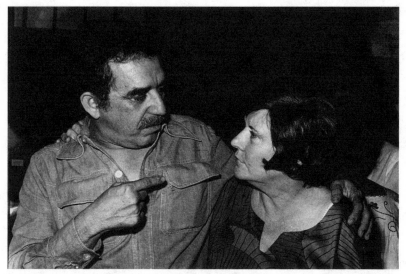

Gabriel García Márquez and Haydée, Colombian Exhibition, Casa de las Américas, 1979. PHOTO COURTESY CASA DE LAS AMÉRICAS.

Story)—both excellent portrayals of the revolutionary saga. *Noticiero latino-americano* was rooted in more traditional Communist ideology; *Cineperiódico* was denied space and disappeared from Cuban theaters. Guevara clearly wanted absolute control of the new Cuban film.

Alemán supported the revolution and had contact with members of its leadership. Haydée appreciated his honesty, political commitment, and professionalism. In an interview with Emmanuel Vincenot, Alemán remembers that "Haydée was a godmother to us." Vincenot writes that Haydée's support of Alemán was decisive and that she defended him publicly, not only in opposition to Guevara but against the opinion of her own husband, who was minister of education at the time.

Eventually, many of those who worked in *Cineperiódico* emigrated, indicative of many such losses in periods in which the revolution seemed to have room for only one cultural manifestation at a time. There is no doubt that both Alfredo Guevara and Haydée Santamaría thought outside the restrictive box, but I believe Haydée was by far the more adventurous and greater risk taker. I do not know of an instance in which she put a particular line before her multifaceted and comprehensive respect for a variety of voices.[3]

Haydée rarely spoke ill of anyone. She was immensely understanding of the many levels of human capacity, and although quick to criticize a bad

Haydée with
Alejo Carpentier.
PHOTO COURTESY
CASA DE LAS
AMÉRICAS.

decision or a job poorly done, she attacked the act rather than the person. Silvio Rodríguez has written:

> Haydée would not permit bad-mouthing of any sort. When you heard her insisting on someone's virtues, you knew that person was in the funeral chapel, so to speak. She was a great teacher of humanity in a small body and with the voice of a flute. But no one was fooled as to the character that resided in that body. [. . .] For me, Yeyé was the mortar that bound those random bits and pieces still floating within me.[4]

When she died, Marcia Leseica, who was one of her closest friends and colleagues, remarked that for the first time they wouldn't be able to count on her exquisite sensibility when collectively preparing a document issued by Casa: "We will miss her tact in choosing just the right word, or eliminating a phrase that might have been hurtful to someone."[5]

According to Louis Pérez Jr., Cuba's suicide rate has always been high, probably among the highest in the world and certainly the highest in Latin America. For whatever reasons of geography, climate, temperament, socialization, or an intensely tragic sense of life and death, just as in several of the Nordic nations, women as well as men on the tropical isle have historically opted to end their lives. Although in Cuba the numbers of suicides rose during the Special Period in the early 1990s, this has not been a phenomenon of the revolution. It has been true from the late colonial period into the early republic, under capitalism as well as socialism.[6]

All those who knew or worked with Haydée describe her as joyous, loving a good time, and delighting in arranging encounters that would be entertaining to others. At the same time, no one failed to note the deep sadness in her eyes, the horrendous memories she carried with her from Moncada on, and the great losses that continued to assault her for as long as she lived. Some used the word "depression" or "depressive state." One of my interviewees confided that she periodically took to her bed and always needed help to get up again.

Post-traumatic stress disorder (PTSD) was not widely understood when she was alive, but with what we now know it doesn't seem an exaggeration to say that she suffered from the condition, at least beginning after Moncada. I sensed a depressive personality dating much farther back, perhaps inherited from gender configurations in her family of origin, where strong women had to fight their way from restriction to agency. It may have been written into their genetic makeup.

Escape from her parental home wasn't easy for Haydée. And it wasn't obtainable without cost. She never envisioned for herself an escape that would simply allow her the freedom to study, work, choose a husband, or follow the life-sized dreams most women of her time nurtured. Her dream was always much larger than life: nothing short of changing the power relations in the country she loved so deeply—and the world.

The fact that Haydée was known for her joyous enthusiasm, for dressing up and playing tricks on people, or for throwing a party at a moment's notice, doesn't belie her darker side. Both elements lived and struggled within her,

Haydée with Cuban writer Dora Alonso, 1980 Literary Prize. PHOTO COURTESY CASA DE LAS AMÉRICAS.

each constantly vying for the upper hand. It is painful to consider how hard she must have had to work to keep her demons under control.

Haydée led by transgression, by which I mean she led by following her own exquisitely developed sense of justice, irrespective of the people she had to challenge, the rules she had to break or the ways in which she had to veer from the official line. But hers was never a rebellion for rebellion's sake. She was as adept at knowing when staying beneath the radar was the more propitious course as she was at taking a visible stand when that was called for. She knew how to choose her battles.

Understanding power is essential to understanding society. Few movements for social change have considered power itself as a political category. Almost invariably, those who sacrifice everything to take power will do anything to hold onto it, even when that means relinquishing some of the ideals on which they base their struggle.

Long after Haydée's death, we finally have an example in the Zapatistas of southern Mexico, who claim their goal is not to take state power and have given us lessons in indigenous forms of consensus and decision making. In May 2014 Zapatista leader Subcomandante Marcos announced he would step aside to make room for younger leadership. This was not the tradition Haydée inherited. She was part of the communist paradigm with its Leninist principles of party organization and democratic centralism. Yet her ultimate decision, in some strange way, may also have been a passing of the baton—as well as a definitive rejection of rigid party morality.

Haydée had a very different view of power than most of Cuba's other revolutionary figures. To some extent this was gender-based. Celia Sánchez was another woman in the Cuban leadership who adamantly rejected self-glorification; even to the extent of refusing to appear in public or call attention to herself in any way. Over a period of fifty-five years, I know of no woman entangled in any of the power plays that occasionally destroyed their male comrades. But in Haydée's case I don't believe gender alone was involved. It was part of the picture, but she simply had no use for self-aggrandizement.

In Haydée's worldview, it wasn't the person who was important, but what that person gave of herself, what she did. And she saw people in all their complex dimensions. If someone she considered limited was able to overcome those limitations and shine, she never failed to encourage and applaud. All she asked of those around her was honesty and dedication. The work itself was important, not the honors or medals. In her contact with the world's great personalities, she had to learn to consider position and rank. But in the collective she established at Casa de las Américas she promoted a uniquely collaborative model, shunning competition and drawing on people's strengths. She was as good at listening as at giving orders. Many of those who worked with her emphasized how they had felt empowered.

It was impossible for the revolution, even for those in her most intimate circles, to understand someone of Haydée's vitality and creative energy choosing suicide. The communism of her time considered it betrayal. The psychiatric community deemed it pathological. Those who loved and needed her naturally experienced overwhelming loss. Dying on the front lines of

Haydée with President Ho Chi Minh, Hanoi, 1968. PHOTO COURTESY CASA DE
LAS AMÉRICAS.

revolutionary struggle would have been the ultimate sacrifice—as it was
when Che Guevara met his death in Bolivia or any Cuban internationalist
gives his or her life on a foreign battlefield. To succumb to illness, as in Celia
Sánchez's case, couldn't be blamed on the individual. Taking one's own life
was not on the list of heroic acts in 1980. It still isn't.

Haydée Santamaría and Celia Sánchez, among many outstanding women
of the Cuban Revolution, were unique and uniquely similar. The revolution
treated them differently in death, but in life they represented a rare duo, sen-

sitive and wise beyond their time. Alfredo Guevara has said: "Losing Haydée and Celia, both in 1980, changed everything. After they died the revolution continued to be the revolution, but it was the revolution without them."[7]

And yet the discomfort around Haydée's suicide was complicated. Nine years earlier, in June 1971, Comandante Eddy Suñol took his life at age forty-six. He left a note saying the chronic pain from wounds incurred during the war made it impossible for him to continue to carry out his revolutionary duties. In 1983, Oswaldo Dorticós, the country's president, also shot himself; he suffered from a chronic spinal affliction and his wife of many years had just died. Suñol was eulogized by Raúl Castro, and buried in his native Holguín with full military honors. Several people with whom I spoke pointed out that at least back then it was easier for the revolutionary leadership to accept physical rather than psychological pain as a valid reason for ending one's life. It wasn't only the leadership that failed Haydée in this respect. Extreme emotional anguish was not considered a legitimate illness by almost anyone at the time.

Only Haydée's daughter eventually wrote of the respect we must have for those who decide they would rather be dead than alive. And only a very few among the family members, colleagues, and friends with whom I spoke saw Haydée's suicide as an act of freedom. Yet in the context of who she was and what she did, I am inclined toward this interpretation.

Mourning a revolutionary heroine at an ordinary funeral establishment was linked to this lack of understanding but also raised other issues. It was palpably uncomfortable for those of us crowded into the commercial viewing space that night. Yet it did not and would not diminish her stature.

"In any case," Haydée's niece Norma told me, "the fact that my aunt wasn't laid out in the Plaza isn't worthy of the discussion surrounding it all these years. She wouldn't have wanted all that fanfare, and her family didn't care either. The pain of losing her was too great, and if there was ever a death felt in every social sphere it was hers. Intellectuals, as you know, are fond of speculating; they love polemics."[8]

A woman's sacrifice invariably means sacrificing for others, giving up her time or energy to make the lives of others better. I believe Haydée sacrificed the sun and palms she loved, the revolution and even her motherhood, because it finally hurt too much to wage that daily battle against overwhelming anguish. She was surrounded by ghosts. Perhaps their call had become too insistent. She also trusted the revolution and must have known that she had bequeathed the tools of social change to her colleagues, family, and friends.

Tribute to the New Song Movement. Haydée greets Silvio Rodríguez; Noël Nicola can be seen just behind Silvio to the right and Pablo Menéndez to the far right in the photograph. Casa de las Américas, 1979. PHOTO BY PIROLE, COURTESY CASA DE LAS AMÉRICAS.

Haydée herself left all the clues we need to understand why she took her life. On more than one public occasion she explained that, after Moncada, she remained alive because she needed to find out if Fidel had survived. She was convinced that if he lived, the unspeakable losses of her brother and fiancé and so many others would not have been in vain. Then she had to live to be able to tell Fidel that his second-in-command was dead but that it was all right because he had loved him—and that he, too, had believed that if Fidel survived, their revolution would succeed. Then she had to live to be able to give her testimony at trial.

Still in prison, Fidel had important tasks for Haydée and Melba: first to round up the comrades who had escaped Moncada or been unable to make it to the garrison, and gather them together in a single place. Then they had to receive and assemble the encoded pages of "History Will Absolve Me," decipher the text, raise the money, and arrange to have it printed and distributed throughout Cuba and the world: no small effort. A movement for amnesty had to be promoted. And once the July 26 leadership, now in Mexico, was ready to return to Cuba, the uprising in Santiago and support for the struggle in the Sierra had to be organized.

As the war progressed, other important tasks claimed Haydée's attention: in the cities, in the mountains, and even outside the country. I can imagine her, waking each morning and rededicating herself to each new effort. The feats demanded of her were challenging. They must have given her ample reason to stay alive. And she became an expert at doing so, often being the only one capable of escaping a police roundup or slipping through enemy lines.

Once the war was won, the real work began. Che Guevara and many others have emphasized that armed struggle is the easiest phase of revolution. Peacetime brings the much more complex job of creating a new society, with all that implies in terms of changing values and achieving equal opportunity. Basic rights such as dignity, work, equitable food distribution, housing, health care, education, and culture must be developed and made accessible across the board. In a revolution, there is no shortage of reasons to live. When the revolution becomes institutionalized, there may be fewer.

Haydée's main arena, Casa de las Américas, gave her ample opportunity to contemplate the fruits of her labor. In an extraordinarily short time, she was able to create a structure in which the world's great intellects and artists were introduced to what the Cuban Revolution was doing, and Cubans came in contact with the world's great art. Perhaps just as important, she put in place a working collective that showcased revolutionary values and relationships. For Haydée, desired ends never justified dubious means. She understood that the new society's values must be built into the process itself. Casa remains a brilliant example of her spirit and intelligence at work, when it comes to how power should be exercised, how democracy can function.


Historic necessity and her own highly developed commitment combined to give Haydée a succession of reasons to open her eyes each morning, following an event so traumatic that death surely must have seemed the easier choice. In their last minutes together, Abel himself had impressed upon her that his death would be the easier of their destinies; by far the more difficult would be hers to live. And that was what she must prepare herself to do. In a fragment from one of her talks, quoted in this book, she wonders if Abel was even still alive in her memory of their last conversation. Her uncertainty speaks to the intensity of the moment.

Having to find reason after reason to go on living, though, requires an energy few can sustain. Eventually exhaustion takes over.

And if we feel compelled to die, there is no space in which we can talk about the option—not in the society in which Haydée lived nor in most places now. Perhaps in some saner future we will come to a greater rationality with regard to the right to determine how long each of us wants to live and when and why life may no longer feel acceptable.

A very few countries and a couple of US states practice death with dignity when experts agree it is warranted in specific cases. Up to now, this has always been linked to terminal physical illness. In the more advanced societies, we have achieved a woman's right to make such a decision with regard to an unborn child. And almost all nations have protocols for putting an animal out of its misery when its life is no longer viable.

The mere whisper of suicide, however, by an adult who is loved and perceived as vital elicits immediate efforts to prevent that person from killing herself. Life is simply believed to be the only moral choice. Despite all evidence to the contrary, it is always presumed the person can be made to feel better and should be enticed to keep on living. There are thousands of cases each year of those who, unable to complete the act themselves, force law enforcement to do it for them.

Haydée was always absolutely sure of what she needed and wanted. Once her mind was made up, there was no deterring or seducing her to an alternative decision. This aspect of her character could be observed in the largest acts of choice and follow-through and in decisions as seemingly insignificant as where a piece of furniture should go, how a painting should be hung, or what to cook for dinner. She let others do their jobs, but she was meticulous in doing hers.

We cannot know the emotional pain she endured day in and day out, from Moncada to the moment of her death. What we do know, much more fully than thirty years ago, is how intimately mind and body are linked and how emotional and physical pain move and metastasize between apparently separate poles.

We talk about suicide from the outside. Most of those who pronounce themselves against it have never experienced the overwhelming need to choose death. In the vast majority of humans and animals, the life force is stronger than any other. But we must remember we are outside, not in. When we say: "If she had been in her right mind, loving her children as she did she would never have done such a thing," we fail to understand how extreme pain can rearrange or even erase priorities. No one would think of accusing a woman dying of cancer of leaving her children because she didn't take them into consideration or love them enough.

Haydée's funeral cortege making its way from the funeral home to Colón Cemetery. Juan Almeida is two removed from Fidel on his right, and Nicaraguan Sandinista Comandante Dora María Téllez is to Almeida's right. Behind them are thousands of Cubans. PHOTO COURTESY *GRANMA* AND CASA DE LAS AMÉRICAS.

Having defended Haydée's right—more accurately *need*—to end her life, I must also defend the anguish and even anger of those she left behind. Her children, first of all. Finding his mother in her death agony surely affected Abel Enrique for the rest of his life. Celia María, despite eventually coming to such a mature appreciation of her mother's decision, also suffered horribly. Haydée's sisters were profoundly unbalanced by her suicide, Ada to the point of going a similar route twenty-three years later. Haydée's niece Niurka, more than three decades farther on, still wept with rage and grief when speaking of her loss.

At Casa de las Américas the women and men who worked with Haydée every day, who were in the midst of projects and looked forward to upcoming plans, were shaken to the core. Very suddenly, they found themselves without their guiding force, the person they had gone to with every problem, personal as well as professional, and upon whom they had depended in the complexity of their work.

For all these family members, friends, and colleagues, the tragedy of loss was compounded by the terrible dilemma of how to mourn someone their revolution told them had committed an unacceptable act. It was disconcerting to have to grieve her at a funeral parlor, rather than at the foot of the great Martí statue in the Plaza of the Revolution. Breathing was difficult, comprehension impossible.

Going forward, how to honor Haydée's memory also comes into question. Casa de las Américas has organized periodic tributes, but none with the unfettered homage that would have permitted the nation to take part. For Haydée there was no great public act as there had been for Che. Schoolchildren do not toss flowers into the sea each year, as they do for Camilo.[9] Yet there is no question she was of their stature. Perhaps the absence of a large public demonstration also has to do with gender, for Celia doesn't receive this sort of nationwide anniversary tribute either.

Although attitudes toward suicide have changed in the years since Haydée's death, few public buildings bear her name, and her magnificent life has yet to be memorialized as it should. Contested opinions have kept film production, theater, and books from proliferating as one might have expected. There is the sense that all these hesitations and doubts are fading with time. What cannot be undone is the unnecessary pain still burdening those who knew and loved her best.

The woman for whom the revolution meant creativity and diversity, the woman who never judged a person by a single act but saw each in his or her full dimension and appreciated and honored lives in their totality, was punished at the hour of her death because of a single decision. The revolution, to which she gave her all, could not take into account her pain or overwhelming need. I understand how slowly cultural values change, but at key moments I believe it's always better to err on the side of inclusivity than condemnation.

The poet Walter Lowenfels once said: "It is not a choice between madness and suicide—that's only the way it appears. The real choice, historically, is to be heard or not to be heard. To accept the vast silence that surrounds us or to scream intelligibly."[10] For Haydée it was never a choice. Or she chose it all. There are those who say she was mad but her madness, if that's what it should be called, was illumination. No one can deny that she screamed intelligibly, that she was heard. What she left behind more than testifies to that.

A life such as Haydée's speaks for itself. Gradually (too gradually for some, myself included), the Cuban revolution has focused more on who Haydée was for fifty-seven years than on her final seconds. Hopefully, the monuments and films, books, and songs will come. And I hope they will honor her in all her complexity.

The question shouldn't be "Why did she kill herself?" but "How did she manage to live so fully and for so long and give so much?"

# 10 IMPOSSIBLE POSSIBILITY
## *Elegy for Haydée Santamaría*

*. . . was there a place*
*that could hold you as you opened yourself*
*to it as you went where no one else*
*could follow where no one else could see . . .*
—SUSAN SHERMAN, "DEFINITIONS," PART 4

*Under or above the words she exchanged with us,*
*she was always speaking with the dead*
*she carried within her, speaking with death itself.*
—ROBERTO FERNÁNDEZ RETAMAR

1
Where is the door I can open
to go to you?
Where do your luminous molecules
assemble, shatter and reassemble?
Where can I forgive you that instant
when turning back was no longer an option,
forgive you although unable to forgive myself?

You don't look back at me from T-shirts
or bravely-painted walls:

myth defacing reality on every map.
Your image remains a reflection on water,
your features shimmering
through breaking waves of memory.

Yeyé to your familiars,
Haydée to the rest of us
as Fidel has always been Fidel,
you freed yourself from the storyline
that blinks or winks:
not quite the last laugh.

I go back to your first thunderous death,
not the bullet to the head
by your tired hand
when release was the only escape
unhinging a broken scale,
but to those earlier deaths
visiting in the dark of night.

The deaths that stalked you at Moncada
27 years before,
messengers urging you not run from
but toward those enemy soldiers
as you tried to protect the ones
you knew must live.

The deaths that left raw wounds and fragile scars,
followed you into the *Sierra*,
entered your secret places
from a beach where Royal Palms
bend beneath grief
against a storm-streaked sky.

2
I don't believe in a soul or afterlife
and I'm sure you didn't either,

but your presence was so intimately tender,
so stoic and steel strong
we cannot imagine not finding comfort
in your piercing eyes,
creative passion
where your absence leaves us naked and bereft.

Your body forever stooped beneath such murderous blow
yet your embrace renewed unstoppable energy
pushed you to cliff's edge,
a territory you understood.
Embodying such fear
you were never afraid,
a contradiction few deciphered.

Thirty-three years since that Havana night,
July 28, 1980,
when hundreds crowded your wake
in the funeral home at *Calzada* and K,
too many flowers
overwhelming the scent of such a loss,
too much for the small body
arranged in your casket,
lids drawn over fierce eyes,
hands clasped across spent lungs.

Two minutes suspended in that inner chamber
standing guard at your casket
I could not take myself
from your recomposed features,
questions snagging bruised underside of skin.

3
Numb to time's displacement,
memory's history
spun me beyond myself:
your visionary life unspooled

from your birth at La Constancia sugar mill,
Encrucijada, Las Villas, 1922,
introduced to Cuban poverty
through the prism of small privilege
and a brother's indignation.

*Constancia*: the word evokes decision
as *encrucijada* spells dilemma
or doubt:
the first your leitmotif
while you never allowed the second
anywhere close.

A grade school diploma,
though even that uncertain
in the one-room schoolhouse
where learning crumpled
like a bird too hurt to fly.
How you put yourself
where you knew you had to be.

One of five siblings:
fairytale names
from fairytale operas,
until you and younger brother Abel
went to Havana to change the world,
rented the tiny apartment at 25 and O
where Fidel was the tall man
who flicked his cigar ashes
on your clean floor.

4
When you kept your date with Moncada,
July 26, 1953,
you and Melba the only women
among that determined crew of men:
sisters and lovers,

natural mothers,
more than muses
never quite leaders.

They say when the battle was lost
they brought your brother's eye
and lover's mangled testicle
to break your spirit,
a useless exercise.
*If you did that to them and they didn't talk,*
your proud response.
Legend or fact,
does it matter at all?

Prison and underground,
clandestine struggle
where ordinary looks and perfect composure
kept you and your comrades safe.
You traveled to the hated North,
recruited soldiers for an invisible army,
collected more than a million dollars,
bought Mafia arms
and sewed bullets for home
into the folds of 1950s poodle skirts.

In the city you ordered only those
you knew despised the task
to place the necessary bombs:
*I never wanted them to get used to it,*
you said,
and throughout your life
repeated how much you hated killing
or violence of any kind.

You believed if Fidel lived
Cuba would live
and become that country of sun and palms

you dreamed again each painful dawn.
And when the new nation rose
in distressing risk
and David and Goliath fragility,
you were among the handful who knew
love is the only tool to change the world.


5
I still hold the curve of sweaty plastic in my palm,
see the pale blue sheen of that tiny inhaler
and taste the sugary mist you handed me,
explaining its use
before a breathing crisis took the reins.
We'd only just met
when lifetime sufferer took newcomer's hand,
asthma our filial connection.

I hear the early echo of your words:
*Of course it's absurd to say HIM*
*when we mean HIM AND HER*
*or HIS for THEIRS,*
years before women's rage
caught up with a revolution
where barren rhetoric
dubbed gender consciousness
a weapon to divide the working class.

You needed no imported theory,
knew justice
because you paid attention,
listened to all the stories,
embraced all those within the radius
of your lightning field.

When you sent me to judge Miss Carnival Queen 1970,
embarrassed, head pounding, revulsion-choked,
I sputtered *why me*

when any man would have reveled at the chance
to pick the prettiest face,
most sensual body.
Until years later when I asked
and you said *because I knew you would help put an end
to those awful contests,*
and I did.

6
Imagine Simone de Beauvoir's independence
sewn with Joan of Arc's pure sinew
but vulnerable to tropical storms
and any disloyalty,
a passion uniquely yours
in a time when women were only supposed
to want to clean and serve.

Imagine careful and daring in a single human,
immensely caring,
savory like *yucca en mojo de ajo*
or cyclone against the helpless coast,
founding and heading a place
worthy of the greatest artists,
breaking a blockade meant to isolate, destroy.

The woman who looked into those artists' eyes,
held their hands
and cherished their creativity
modeled possibility across any border,
cast solidarity
in a rainbow of 42 countries,
knew any defeat could be turned to victory.

You who never studied art or literature,
never attended university,
whose history hid in reconfigured skirts,
underground sleight-of-hand,

mountain command post
and indelible loss,

made *Casa de las Américas*
home to poetry and painting,
theater and song,
understood how art moves peoples
into a future of change,
no small-minded prejudice
or Socialist Realism
would jettison authenticity.

Your brilliant gaze embraced each artist
on their terms,
defied authority,
brought every work alive
in the space it filled,
made a family for troubadours
who threatened the status quo,
queer talent and misunderstood genius
in danger from bureaucratic hands
too power-crazed to see beyond crass ignorance.

7
By your visionary presence
you gathered us in,
created a place where we learned
and learn
what revolution means,
where each generation grows the next,
the end never justifies the means,
and no one is left behind.

That early lover gone,
you married a comrade wise as you,
gave birth to a son and daughter
and took orphans from every battlefield
into a family that always had room for more.

Your daughter remembered:
*The number of my siblings changed*
*year by year.*

In your farewell letter to Che,
brother among brothers,
you wrote:
*Sexist, unforgivable sexist!*
*You swore you would take me with you*
*to make America's revolution*
*but left me here,*
*alone,*
an ocean of tears eroding your shore.

Then the father of your children opted out
as men sometimes do
and you were left holding memories
no one should have to juggle —
island within an island.
I knew your choice was never that
of a woman jilted
or some midlife crisis
dragging you off to a decision
you might regret.

An accident had almost taken your life,
physical pain overlaying the deeper kind.
A terrible exodus drew vitriol,
hateful expressions you couldn't bear.
Some of those you trusted
drifted away,
and a sister in attitude succumbed.

8
It was exhaustion and too many deaths:
each beckoning from its ghost dance
—Abel and Boris, Che and Celia—
transparency and accompaniment spread thin,

disappointment in those you believed
inhabited the revolution with you,
so many of them
leaving you finally in the cold.

It was what a friend overheard you say
after one more public dialogue
about those early years,
sharing with the young ones what it was like,
giving voice to a history
fading among more recent histories:
*I can't do this again*, you said,
and wouldn't.

You were a small woman
at a time women relished
or were resigned to small,
plain mid-twentieth-century woman
whose skin could not contain
your passion for justice
or how you birthed the energy
that welcomes justice home.

What happens when an idea withers
along the fault line
rocked by those you trusted with your life
and the lives of others,
route to a new planet
where the music in your ears
excited such strange dissonance?

You were a woman plain and simple,
slim-boned,
great-hearted,
who thought a bus ride should cost 5 cents,
public pay phones be free,
health, education, shelter, food,
culture and art:

all that we need free,
bountifully free!

9
So long before,
in that apartment at 25 and O
you'd made pots of *cassoulet*,
enough for every mouth,
and then, with the same careful planning,
took your place at the constricted heart of struggle
and secret recesses of change.

You refused to go into exile
and return on the *Granma*,
afraid if you left you might not
find your way back.
Cuba ran in your veins
viscous with martyred blood.

No one could deny your courage then
or when victory came
and Fidel assigned you the job
of bringing every poet, writer, painter
musician and actor
to your triumphant revolution.

You opened its doors
wider than anyone could,
ignored the official institutions
groveling at power's feet,
sought poets in prisons and factories,
painters from indigenous tribes
along with those
who'd won the most prestigious prizes,
or would.

You looked into each one's eyes
and he or she looked back,

seen and understood,
wanting to give our best
to an experience shaped
by gravitational pull transformed.

10
You offered Cuba's impossible possibility
to those whose children were disappeared,
minds drugged by torture,
hands severed by generals,
diminished by the loneliness
of daring to dream beyond the ugliest schemes.

Moncada's deaths continued to claim your spirit,
endow you with strength,
never weakness:
explosive yet slow-burning fire,
suicide your last brave act.

At the precise moment
we were in danger
of losing sight and hearing
to smug opportunism or insidious drones,
when reduced to rote applause
for those who would rob us of memory,
condemn us to repeat lives
with neither past nor future,
you came along
and made us whole.

Haydée, in the magic of your hands,
twin wings of a tropical bird,
in your unexpected lessons
and perfect listening,
you took that death we fear
and laid it gently at our feet
where we may find it
when our time arrives.

# NOTES

CHAPTER 1. BEFORE WE BEGIN

1. Cuba's socialist constitution, approved February 24, 1976, by a vote of 97.7% of Cubans sixteen years and older, after a nationwide consultation of workers, military personnel, students, and others who modified 60 of its 141 articles.

2. This is the way the tiny mountain nation of Bhutan describes itself. In today's world, how countries describe their political systems bears little resemblance to what those descriptions once meant. China, e.g., still calls itself communist but has implemented numerous aspects of a market economy.

3. Susan Sontag (1933–2004) wrote memorably about Vietnam, Sarajevo, and other places where extreme conflict shaped culture, as well as on photography, illness, and identity.

4. Sontag, "Some Thoughts."

5. For an excellent overview, I recommend García Luis, *Cuban Revolution Reader*.

CHAPTER 2. WHY HAYDÉE?

1. Rubén Darío (1867–1916) was a great Nicaraguan modernist poet; 1967 marked what would have been his hundredth birthday. The gathering of poets and literary critics in Cuba that was hosted by Casa de las Américas was one of several held throughout the world that year.

2. In *Che On My Mind* there is a chapter called "Che and Haydée." In *More Than Things* there is an essay, "Shaping My Words," that focuses on her.

3. Randall, *To Change the World*.

4. Fidel Castro Ruz (b. 1926), born into an upper-class family in Biran, Cuba, became

a lawyer and eventually founded the July 26 Movement with the aim of overthrowing the Batista dictatorship that had grabbed power in 1952. After six years, his movement was victorious. He served as prime minister and then president of his country until his retirement from public life in 2008.

5. Ernesto "Che" Guevara (1928–1967) was an Argentine doctor who fought in the Cuban Revolution, went on to take several important peacetime positions in that country, and then left to wage guerrilla warfare in other parts of the world. He was murdered in Bolivia.

6. Celia Sánchez (1920–1980), Cuban revolutionary hero and Fidel Castro's closest associate until her death from cancer.

7. José Martí (1853–1895), Cuban revolutionary, prolific thinker and writer, considered the intellectual father of Cuban liberation. He is claimed by the revolution's detractors as well as its supporters.

8. The Cuban Orthodox Party was founded in 1947 by Eduardo Chibás in response to government corruption and lack of reform. It was nationalist in nature and pushed for economic independence. Fidel Castro was a member early on.

9. Fulgencio Batista (1901–1973) was the elected president of Cuba from 1940 to 1943 and grabbed power again in 1952. In 1959 he was overthrown by the Cuban revolution.

10. Jesús Menéndez (1911–1948).

11. Fidel Castro and his group attacked Moncada Barracks in Santiago de Cuba on July 26, 1953. They hoped to spark a popular resistance to the Batista dictatorship. The action was a military failure but political success; it initiated the revolutionary struggle that was victorious five and a half years later.

12. Randall, *Cuban Women Now*, 312.

13. Conversation with author, 1970s. My translation.

14. Young Silvio Rodríguez, Pablo Milanés, Noël Nicola, Sara González, and others were at first considered problematic. Their brilliant lyrics asked too many questions and were too critical for the revolution's hardliners. Haydée provided them a home at Casa, where they flourished and would soon become some of the country's greatest cultural assets.

15. Aida's daughter Niurka Martín Santamaría, interviewed later in this book.

16. Gloria Rolando (b. 1953) is a Cuban documentary filmmaker whose films include *Eyes of the Rainbow* (1998), about US revolutionary Assata Shakur; *Raíces de mi corazón* (2000), about the destruction of the Independents of Color political party; and many others on Afro-Cuban cultural traditions. Rolando made these remarks at a panel on her work at the Berkshire Conference on the History of Women, Toronto University, May 24, 2014.

17. Raúl Roa García (1907–1982) was a Cuban intellectual, politician, and diplomat. He served as the country's foreign minister from 1959 to 1976.

18. Carlos Rafael Rodríguez (1913–1997) was a member of the PSP who served in both Batista's and Fidel's cabinets.

19. Santamaría, *Haydée habla*, 37. My translation.

20. Santamaría, *Haydée habla*, 14. My translation.

21. Armando Hart Dávalos (b. 1930), follower of Fidel Castro, married Haydée during the war. They had two children and parented many more. Hart was the revolution's first minister of education, headed the 1961 literacy campaign, and later became minister of culture.

22. "Stalin," Hart's article, may be found online in several places, among them www.rebelion.org/noticia.php?id=10776. My translation.

23. Filmed by Esther Barroso Sosa. My translation.

24. Santamaría, *Haydée habla*, 8. My translation. Ernest and Thérèse Defarge are fictional characters in Charles Dickens's *Tale of Two Cities*. Celia Hart refers to the "Lafarges" rather than "Defarges," but in the context I believe it to be a misprint.

25. Santamaría, *Haydée habla*. My translation.

26. Santamaría, *Haydée habla*. My translation.

CHAPTER 3. EARLY LIFE

1. Epigraph: Haydée Santamaría, *Revista Casa de las Américas*, no. 138, May–June 1983, on the third anniversary of Haydée's death.

2. Interview with Jaime Sarusky, February 2, 1977, Casa archives. My translation.

3. Portuondo López, *La pasión*, 19.

4. Interview with the author, April 2014.

5. This is how Haydée herself described her family on a number of occasions.

6. Randall, *Cuban Women Now*, 317.

7. Interview with author, April 2014.

8. Portuondo López, *La pasión*, 21.

9. Portuondo López, *La pasión*, 20.

10. Interview with Rebeca Chávez for an unfinished film, 1978. Published in *La gaceta de Cuba*, no. 4, 2013. My translation.

11. Portuondo López, *La pasión*, 33.

12. Portuondo López, *La pasión*, 40.

13. Interview with author, April 2014.

14. Portuondo López, *La pasión*, 18.

15. Interview with author, April 2014.

16. Haydée Santamaría in a talk with outstanding cane cutters from Camagüey Province, July 19, 1969. Casa archives. My translation.

17. Interview with Rodolfo Alcaraz, May 21, 1968, Casa archives. My translation.

18. Rodolfo Alcaraz interview.

19. "The Permanence of Haydée," by Roberto Fernández Retamar, in Maclean, *Haydée Santamaría*, 76. My translation.

20. Roberto Fernández Retamar (b. 1930), poet, essayist, and literary critic; Casa de las América's current president and, as such, a member of Cuba's Council of State. He founded Casa's important literary magazine.

21. Fernández Retamar, "Permanence," 76. My translation.

22. Fernández Retamar, "Permanence," 74. My translation.

23. Carlos Manuel de Céspedes (1819–1874), Cuban revolutionary in the fight against Spain.

24. Ignacio Agramonte (1841–1873), Cuban revolutionary who played an important part in the Ten Years' War (1868–1878).

25. General Antonio Maceo (1845–1896), second in command of the Cuban Army of Independence in the war against Spain; called the Bronze Titan because he was black.

26. Interview with author, 2014.

27. Sarusky interview.

28. Eduardo Chibás (1907–1951) founded the Orthodox Party in 1947. He was active against the governments of Grau San Martín and Carlos Prío, predecessors to the Batista regime. Chibás's main issue was corruption. Although anticommunist, he influenced Fidel and Abel. Chibás had a popular radio program, and on August 5, 1951, during his regular broadcast, he shot himself in protest against the country's political situation. He died 11 days later.

29. Taken from a talk about the attack on Moncada Barracks given by Haydée Santamaría to the workers at Casa de las Américas on July 24, 1969.

CHAPTER 4. MONCADA

1. Antonio Guiteras (1906–1935) was a proponent of revolutionary socialism who participated in the radical government installed after the overthrow of right-wing President Gerardo Machado in 1933.

2. Melba Hernández Rodríguez del Rey (1921–2014), the only woman besides Haydée who fought at Moncada. She was active in the revolution and served as Cuba's ambassador to Vietnam and Cambodia.

3. Rodolfo Alcaraz interview.

4. Santamaría, *Haydée habla*, 15. My translation.

5. Santamaría, *Haydée habla*, 20. My translation.

6. Santamaría, *Haydée habla*, 2–3. My translation.

7. Lieutenant Pedro Sarría (1900–1972), the officer in Batista's army who captured Fidel Castro as he tried to escape from Moncada and refused to turn him over to the general of the garrison, who would have murdered him. After the 1959 victory, Sarría remained with the revolution. His bust is on display at Moncada.

8. Hart, *Aldabonazo*, 77–78.

9. Transcript of an interview with Rebeca Chávez, 1978. My translation.

10. Letter courtesy of Norma Ruiz.

11. Portuondo López, *La pasíon*, 313.

12. Marta Rojas, "Testimonio: De entrevistadora a entrevistada" (From interviewer to interviewee), *Santiago*, no. 11, June 1973, 123–148. My translation.

13. Haydée Santamaría, transcript of a conversation with outstanding cane cutters in Camagüey, July 19, 1969. Casa de las Américas archives. My translation.

14. Haydée Santamaría, "Que la vida es hermosa cuando se vive así" (Life is beautiful when you live it like this), *Casa de las Américas*, no. 273, October–December 2013, 5–19. My translation.

15. Haydée Santamaría, talk about Moncada given to workers at Casa de las Américas, July 24, 1969. From a transcript in the Casa archive. My translation.

16. "Una de las niñas de la foto en la cárcel de Guanajay" (One of the little girls in the photo at Guanajay Prison), by Marta Rojas, *Granma*, September 10, 1996.

17. "Si no puedo escribir algún día empiezo a coser," *Isla del Sur* online, August 8, 2008. My translation.

## CHAPTER 5. WAR

1. Stout, *One Day*, 140.

2. "Todo es una sola cosa," interview with Nils Castro in *Santiago* magazine, nos. 18–19 (June–September 1975): 15–56. My translation.

3. Stout, *One Day*, 173.

4. Nils Castro interview. My translation.

5. Nils Castro interview. My translation.

6. Rebeca Chávez transcript. My translation.

7. Stout, *One Day*, 81.

8. Rafael García Barcena (1907–1961) was a philosophy professor. He founded the National Revolutionary Movement (MNR), consisting largely of middle-class members, contrasting with the July 26 Movement's predominantly working-class support. Hart was a member of the MNR, but Haydée recruited him to the July 26 Movement.

9. Hart, *Aldabonazo*, 92–93.

10. Special to the Soviet news agency Novosti, reproduced in *El Mundo*, July 24, 1964. My translation.

11. Nils Castro interview. My translation.

12. Nils Castro interview. My translation.

13. Nils Castro interview. My translation.

14. Rebeca Chávez interview. My translation.

15. Nils Castro interview. My translation.

16. *Babalawo* (the word means the father or master of mysticism in the Yoruba language) is a Yoruba chieftaincy title that denotes a priest of Ifá. In Cuba's African religion it is a high priest's title.

17. Transcript of an interview with Haydée made by Rebeca Chávez for a film that has not yet been made. My translation.

18. More information on *Magín* can be found in Randall, *To Change*, 111–112.

19. Mariana Grajales (1808–1893) was Antonio Maceo's mother and a leader in her own right in the late 19th-century war against Spain.

20. Dated April 15, 2014. My translation.

21. Ismaelillo (b. 1878) was José Martí's son. Father and son were separated by Martí's revolutionary responsibilities. He felt a deep need for the boy and wrote a moving book of poems to him.

22. Cubans refer to José Martí as *el maestro*, which I have translated as "the Teacher." My translation.

## CHAPTER 6. WITNESSES

1. Interview with author, April 2014. My translation.

2. Interview with author. My translation.

3. Flores is the neighborhood where Haydée lived the last years of her life. Her home overlooked the ocean.

4. Franqui, *Libro*, 92.

5. Frank (1934–1957) and Josué (1937–1957) País were movement leaders in Santiago de Cuba. Frank worked closely with Fidel, organizing the November 30 uprising and funneling aid to the Sierra. The two brothers were gunned down by the police, first Josué and, soon after, Frank.

6. Vilma Espín (1930–2007), revolutionary leader in Santiago de Cuba, later headed the Federation of Cuban Women (FMC). She was married to Raúl Castro.

7. *El instituto cubano de arte e industria cinematigráfica* (Cuban Institute of Cinematographic Art and Industry, ICAIC), established in March 1959 and headed by Alfredo Guevara. It soon put Cuba on the map with its production of excellent documentaries and feature films. It now sponsors a yearly Havana Film Festival.

8. Sergio Corrieri (1939–2008), Cuban film star.

9. Lisandro Otero (1932–2008), Cuban novelist and journalist.

10. Santiago Álvarez Román (1919–1998) was a Cuban filmmaker who wrote and directed an oeuvre of important documentaries. His "nervous montage" technique of using found materials, such as Hollywood movie clips, cartoons, and photographs, is considered a precursor to the modern video clip.

11. Roque Dalton (1935–1975), Salvadoran revolutionary, poet, novelist, and political thinker; a victim of jealousies, he was murdered by members of his own political organization.

12. Francisco "Chico" Buarque de Hollanda (b. 1944) is a singer-songwriter and poet.

13. María Esther Gilio (1928–2011) was an important Uruguayan journalist, biographer, and lawyer.

14. Carlos María Gutiérrez (1926–1991), Uruguayan poet and journalist and winner of Casa de las Américas' 1970 poetry prize for his book *Diario del cuartel* (Prison Diary). He suffered prison and exile during his country's military dictatorships in the 1970s and 1980s.

15. Ernesto Cardenal (b. 1925), Nicaraguan priest, liberation theologian, and one of the most important living Latin American poets. He was Nicaragua's minister of culture during the years of the Sandinista Revolution.

16. Mario Benedetti (1928–2009), Uruguayan poet and novelist, who suffered years of exile during the military dictatorships that ruled his country in the 1970s and 1980s.

17. A more relaxed form of the Argentinian tango.

## CHAPTER 7. CASA DE LAS AMÉRICAS

1. Julio Cortázar (1914–1984), Argentine novelist and short story writer, one of the bright lights of the Latin American boom. *Rayuela* was titled *Hopscotch* in English.

2. Silvia Baraldini (1947) was born in Italy but came to the USA as a child. In the 1960s, 1970s, and early 1980s she was active in the black power and Puerto Rican independence movements. She went to prison in 1982, sentenced to forty-three years for conspiring to commit two armed robberies. She spent time at the infamous Lexington Control Unit, a sensory-deprivation prison wing that eventually was closed. She won extradition to Italy in 1999 and was released in 2006 thanks to a pardon law passed by the Italian parliament.

3. Alejo Carpentier (1904–1980), Cuban novelist and musicologist.

4. Fernando Ortíz (1881–1969), Cuban anthropologist and scholar of Afro-Cuban culture.

5. Alicia Alonso (b. 1921), prima ballerina assoluta, choreographer, and director of Cuba's National Ballet Company.

6. Nicolás Guillén (1902–1989), Cuban poet and journalist.

7. Mirta Aguirre (1912–1980), Cuban poet and critic.

8. Wilfredo Lam (1902–1982), Cuban painter and sculptor.

9. Thiago de Mello (b. 1926), Brazilian poet.

10. Laurette Séjourné (1911–2003), French-born Mexican anthropologist, whose visionary analysis of the thought and culture of ancient Mexico did not always sit well with the academy.

11. René Depestre (b. 1926), Haitian poet who lived in Cuba for many years in exile from his country's Duvalier regime.

12. Roberto Fernández Retamar (b. 1930), poet, essayist, and literary critic. Casa de las América's current president and, as such, a member of Cuba's Council of State. He founded Casa's important literary magazine.

13. Gil, Ruiz Lim, and Salsamendi, *Destino*.

14. All these letters, unless otherwise noted, are courtesy of the Casa de las Américas archive.

15. Manuel Galich (1913–1984), Guatemalan playwright and revolutionary who took part in the October Revolution of 1944, which put an end to a series of authoritarian governments. He was exiled in Havana, was one of the founders of Casa, and was active with the institution until his death.

16. Spanish-language editions of *The Children of Sánchez*, by Oscar Lewis, and *Listen, Yankee!*, by Waldo Frank.

17. Antonio Saura (1930–1998), Spanish artist and writer.

18. Mariano Rodríguez (1912–1990) was an important Cuban painter who took over the presidency of Casa de las Américas when Haydée Santamaría died. At Mariano's death, Roberto Fernández Retamar became president and remains in that position.

19. Roberto Matta (1911–2002), Chilean surrealist and abstract expressionist painter.

20. Antenor Patiño (1896–1982), Bolivian tin tycoon. He rid his country of organized labor after the 1952 revolution nationalized the tin mines.

21. *Rocinante*, Caracas, Venezuela, 1971.

22. *Revista Cuba Internacional*, September 1986.

23. Ambrosio Fornet (b. 1932) is one of Cuba's foremost literary and cultural critics. Recipient of his country's National Prize for Literature in 2009.

24. Fornet, *Bridging Enigma*, 10–12.

25. In Spanish the poem is called "En la muerte de una heroina de la patria" (On the Death of a Heroine of the Nation), and the line is "Los que la amaron, se han quedado huérfanos." Fina García Marrúz (b. 1923), a devout Catholic, is an accomplished Cuban poet with many books and awards to her credit.

26. Lilia Estéban de Carpentier was Alejo Carpentier's wife and an intellectual in her own right. She died in 2008 at the age of ninety-five. Alejo Carpentier died in Havana in April 1980, just three months before Haydée.

27. Trinidad Pérez, longtime colleague at Casa, who began working at the institution from the time she was practically a child.

28. Daniel Viglietti (b. 1939), Uruguayan singer-songwriter and political activist.

29. Mercedes Sosa (1935–2009), Argentinian folk singer and activist.

30. Alicia Aguiar cleaned Casa's physical plant and served coffee.

31. María Regla Averoff was one of the people in charge of cleaning the building.

32. Lesbia Vent Dumois (b. 1932) is a Cuban visual artist who worked at Casa for many years.

33. Pedro Orgambide (1929–2003), Argentinian writer.

34. Chiki Salsamendi (b. 1933), Cuban intellectual and longtime Casa worker who continues to collaborate with the institution.

CHAPTER 8. TWO, THREE, MANY VIETNAMS

1. Régis Debray (b. 1940) laid out his *foco* theory in *Revolution* (*Revolución en la revolución*) in 1967. Gutiérrez, *Diez años*, was the transcript of a 1969 roundtable composed of Carlos María Gutiérrez, Ambrosio Fornet, Roberto Fernández Retamar, René Depestre, Edmundo Desnoes, and Roque Dalton. In 1970 Dalton penned *Revolución y la crítica*.

2. Hart, *Haydée*, 22. My translation.

3. Hart, *Haydée*, 23–24. My translation.

4. Lippard, *Different War*, 18–20.

5. Lippard, *Different War*, 17.

6. Fernández Retamar, *Calibán*.

7. *Encuentro con Rubén Darío*, an event honoring the hundredth anniversary of the great Nicaraguan modernist poet. Hosted by Casa de las Américas.

8. The year 1968 saw student-led uprisings in Paris, New York, and Mexico. In the last country workers and small farmers joined the struggle. The government put it down ruthlessly on the evening of October 2, when up to 1,000 unarmed protestors were gunned down in Tlatelolco Square, often referred to as the Plaza of Three Cultures.

9. *Lucía* (1968) was directed by Humberto Solas and written by Julio García Espinosa and Nelson Rodríguez. It tells the stories of three Cuban women in three different eras. *Memories of Underdevelopment* (1968) was directed by Tomás Gutiérrez Alea and was based on a novel by Edmundo Desnoes. In 2012 *Sight & Sound* called it the 144th best movie of all time. *Strawberry and Chocolate* (1993) was directed by Gutiérrez Alea and Juan Carlos Tabío. It addresses the themes of homosexuality, Afro-Cuban religion, and emigration.

10. George Jackson (1941–1971) was an African American Marxist, left-wing activist, author, and member of the Black Panther Party. He was incarcerated at San Quentin prison for a teenage robbery and was shot to death by guards during an alleged escape attempt.

11. Pedro Albizu Campos (1891–1965) was a Puerto Rican attorney and politician and a leading figure in the Puerto Rican independence movement. He was the president and spokesperson of the Puerto Rican Nationalist Party from 1930 until his death. He spent 26 years in prison for attempting to free his island from US control.

12. Camilo Torres (1929–1966) was a Colombian socialist and Roman Catholic priest. An early exponent of liberation theology, he joined the National Liberation Army (ELN) and died in battle fighting with that organization.

13. Valdéz, *Cuba en la gráfica*, 6.

14. The Black Panther Party (originally Black Panther Party for Self-Defense) was a black revolutionary socialist organization active in the United States from 1966 until 1982. It developed free breakfast programs and schools and defended black neighborhoods. Eventually it was destroyed by US government repression, including the planting of informants and the murdering of key leaders.

15. Three years before his death, Guevara penned this document, considered one of his most important theoretical legacies. In the form of a letter, he sent it to Carlos Quijano, editor of the Uruguayan progressive magazine *Marcha*. It has been reproduced in many publications and languages.

CHAPTER 9. THE WOMAN BENEATH THE MYTH

1. The terrible UMAP camps (*Unidades militares de ayuda a la producción*, military units in aid of production) existed for a short time in 1965. Homosexuals and others were sent to them for "reeducation." Rodríguez spoke of Haydée's role in rescuing

gay artists from UMAP in Raysa White's film *Yeyé among Us*, as well as in other interviews and talks.

2. Conversation with author, April 2014. My translation.

3. The complete story of this complex history can be found in "*Cineperiódico*, la otra memoria filmada de la revolución cubana," by Emmanuel Vincenot, a paper delivered at the Latin American Studies Association (LASA) meeting, 2014.

4. Maclean, *Haydée Santamaría*, 123. My translation.

5. Collective tribute, fifth anniversary of Haydée's death. My translation.

6. Pérez, *To Die in Cuba*, 5.

7. Alfredo Guevara in *Yeyé Among Us*. My translation.

8. Letter to author from Norma Ruiz, June 19, 2014. My translation.

9. Camilo Cienfuegos (1932–1959) was a beloved Cuban revolutionary who died in a plane crash shortly after the war. As his plane was lost at sea on October 28, children honor him on that date by offering flowers to his memory.

10. Conversation with author, 1960s.

# BIBLIOGRAPHY

ARCHIVES, INTERVIEWS, AND ARTICLES

Archive of the Office of Historic Affairs of the Council of State, Havana.

Archives of letters, talks, and other documents, Casa de las Américas, Havana.

Document center, *Granma* newspaper, Havana.

Full-length interviews (18) and conversations, Havana, April 2014.

Magazine and newspaper articles (several hundred), Casa de las Américas Library, Havana.

BOOKS

Arango, Arturo. *Terceras reincidencias*. Havana: Ediciones Unión, 2013.

Bustos, Ciro. *Che Wants to See You*. London: Verso, 2013.

Cardenal, Ernesto. *In Cuba*. New York: New Directions, 1974.

Cushing, Lincoln, et al. *Visions of Peace and Justice: San Francisco Bay Area 1974–2007*. Berkeley, CA: Inkworks Press, 2007.

Dalton, Roque. *Revolución en la revolución y la crítica de derecha*. Havana: Casa de las Américas, 1970.

Davidson, Russ, ed. *Latin American Posters*. Santa Fe: Museum of New Mexico Press, 2006.

Debray, Régis. *Revolución en la revolución*. Havana: Casa de las Américas, 1967.

Espín, Vilma, Asela de los Santos, and Yolanda Ferrer. *Women in Cuba: The Making of a Revolution within the Revolution*. Edited by Mary-Alice Waters. New York: Pathfinder 2012.

Fernández Retamar, Roberto. *Calibán and Other Essays*. Minneapolis: University of Minnesota Press, 1989.

Fornet, Ambrosio, ed. "Bridging Enigma: Cubans on Cuba." Special issue, *South Atlantic Quarterly* 96, no. 1 (winter 1997).

Fornet, Ambrosio. *Narrar la nación*. Havana: Letras Cubanas, 2009.

Fornet, Jorge. *El 71*. Havana: Letras Cubanas, 2013.

Franqui, Carlos. *El libro de los doce*. Havana: Instituto del Libro, Ediciónes Huracán, 1968.

García Luis, Julio, ed. *Cuban Revolution Reader: A Documentary History of Fidel Castro's Revolution*. Melbourne: Ocean Press, 2008.

Gil, Silvia, Ana Cecilia Ruiz Lim, and Chiki Salsamendi. *Destino: Haydeé Santamaría*. Havana: Fondo Editorial, Casa de las Américas, 2009.

Gutiérrez, Carlos María, et al. *Diez años de Revolución: El intelectual y la sociedad*. Mexico City: Siglo XXI, 1969.

Hart, Armando. *Aldabonazo: Inside the Cuban Revolutionary Underground 1952–58*. New York: Pathfinder, 1997.

Hart, Celia María. *Haydée: Del Moncada a casa*. Buenos Aires: Nuestra America, 2005.

Hart, Celia María. *It's Never Too Late to Love or Rebel*. Edited by Walter Lippmann. London: Socialist Resistance, 2006.

Herman, Judith Lewis. *Trauma and Recovery*. New York: Harper Collins, 1992.

Lippard, Lucy R. *A Different War: Vietnam in Art*. Seattle: Real Comet Press, 1990.

Lippard, Lucy R. *Mixed Blessings: New Art in a Multicultural America*. New York: Pantheon 1990.

López Vigil, María. *Cuba: Neither Heaven nor Hell*. Washington, DC: Epica, 1999.

Maclean, Betsy, ed. *Haydée Santamaría*. Melbourne: Ocean Press, 2003.

Pérez, Louis, Jr. *To Die in Cuba: Suicide and Society*. Chapel Hill: University of North Carolina Press, 2005.

Portuondo López, Yolanda. *La pasión que me llevó al Moncada*. Havana: Casa Editorial Verde Olivo, 2013.

Price, V. B. "Orpheus the Healer." In *Broken and Reset: Selected Poems 1966–2006*, 20. Albuquerque: University of New Mexico Press, 2007.

Puebla, Teté. *Marianas in Combat*. Edited by Mary-Alice Waters. New York: Pathfinder, 2003.

Randall, Margaret. *Che on My Mind*. Durham, NC: Duke University Press, 2013.

Randall, Margaret. *Cuban Women Now*. Toronto: Women's Press, 1974.

Randall, Margaret. *More Than Things*. Lincoln: University of Nebraska Press, 2013.

Randall, Margaret. *To Change the World: My Years in Cuba*. New Brunswick, NJ: Rutgers University Press, 2009.

Rojas, Marta. *El juicio del Moncada*. Havana: Ciencias Sociales, 1988.

Santamaría, Haydée. *Haydée habla del Moncada*. Melbourne: Ocean Press, 2005.

Sherman, Susan. "Definitions." In *The Light That Puts an End to Dreams*, 8. San Antonio: Wings Press, 2012.

Sontag, Susan. "Some Thoughts on the Right Way (for Us) to Love the Cuban Revolution." *Ramparts*, April 1969, 6–14.

Stout, Nancy. *One Day in December: Celia Sánchez and the Cuban Revolution*. New York: Monthly Review, 2013.

Valdéz, Reyna María. *Cuba en la gráfica*. Milan: Ediciones Gianni Constantino, 1992.

Weiss, Rachel. *To and from Utopia in the New Cuban Art*. Minneapolis: University of Minnesota Press, 2005.

# INDEX

Cold War, 6, 8, 19

communism: anticommunism in Cuba, 2, 210n28; Castro's Cuban Communist Party (PCC), 19, 21, 208n18; Haydée's definition of, 21, 25, 48, 166, 186; the influence of Trotsky's writing on Cuban, 26; the July 26 followers formation of Cuba's PCC, 12, 19, 21; "Marxism in Spanish", 6, 166; Moscow-oriented followers of in Cuba, 5; opposition of to suicide, 25, 186; People's Socialist Party (PSP) of Cuba, 151, 163, 182; power struggle between the PSP and the PCC, 5, 151; rejection of feminism by the, 21, 100

Communist Party of Cuba (PCC), 12, 22, 25, 35, 78, 181

Constancia: Santamaría family at, 50, 51–52, 60, 65; sugar refinery at, 24, 32, 34, 38–40, 46, 48

counterrevolutionaries, 2, 8, 22, 169, 171

Cuadrado Alonso, Joaquina (mother), 33, 42, 65, 69

Cuba: 1974 Family Code, 100; Afro-Cubans, 166, 208n16, 213n4, 215n9; artistic expression in, 143, 146–48, 168–73; Bay of Pigs attack by the US, 6; corruption in, 9, 54–55, 208n8, 210n28; counterrevolutionary activities against, 2, 5, 8, 22, 85, 169, 171; Cuban cultural and literary critics, 146, 209n20, 213n7, 213n12, 214n23; dance in, 23, 168, 213n5; economic plight of individuals and families before the Cuban revolution, 39, 41, 50–51; economy of before Cuban revolution, 3, 16, 99; economy of under Castro, 5, 93, 100, 137, 146; education in Castro's, 5–6, 26, 28, 100–103, 120, 168–70, 190; education in pre-Castro, 3, 40, 46–47, 99–100; emigration from, 9, 22, 101, 182; exile community in the US, 17, 22, 85, 151, 153, 154; filmmaking in, 20, 121n7, 147, 168, 181–82, 193, 208n16, 212n10; food rationing in, 5–6, 64; foreign students in, 20; gender equality in Castro's, 8; health care in Castro's, 5, 9, 100, 102, 175, 190; health care in pre-Castro, 3; inequality as a major social problem in

Batista's, 16, 34; internationalism in Castro's, 7, 19, 20, 23, 111, 113, 170; labor and employment in, 8, 38, 40, 47, 58, 99–101; leadership of in revolution, 7, 20, 58, 136, 162; literacy campaign in, 5, 28, 100, 168, 209n21; nationalism as an ingredient of the revolution, 19; nationalization of business and industry in, 5, 6; people of color in, 20, 47, 100, 133, 178, 208n16; Playa Girón attack by the US, 6; poverty in, 7, 8, 100, 168, 169; President Carlos Prío Socarrás, 55; President Gerardo Machado, 210n1; President Grau San Martín, 47; provinces, 32, 209n16; racism in pre-Castro, 47; reestablishment of diplomatic relations with the US, 9; relationship of with Vietnam, 18, 161, 170, 187; religion in, 2, 25, 52, 211n16, 215n9; repression of creativity in, 20, 121, 143, 146–48, 151–52, 193; strikes in, 67, 86, 104; suicide in, 181–82, 184, 188, 191–93; uprisings in, 4, 17, 86, 189, 212n5

Cuban revolution: as a continuation of earlier struggles, 55, 56; free education as a priority of, 8, 175; Haydée's actions on the day of triumph (December 31, 1958), 96–99; internationalism as a value of, 20, 173, 174, 175; leaders of, 15; participants in Cuba's war against Spain, 210nn23–25, 211n19; participants in the revolution against the Batista dictatorship, 174, 212n6; and revolutions elsewhere, 7–8, 58, 136, 166; role of culture in, 166; smuggling by rebels during Batista's regime, 17, 57, 85, 93, 94; social equality as a value of, 6, 8, 100, 101; Time of the Jackals (La hora de los chacales), 148; torture of rebels by Batista's forces, 17, 62, 64, 77, 133, 163; underground activities of rebels in Havana and Santiago, 4, 17, 86, 180; underground activities of rebels throughout Batista's Cuba, 4, 17–18, 67, 76–77, 81, 101, 154; universal health care as a priority of the, 6, 8, 60; women's benefits from, 91, 102. See also revolutionaries; underground activities

nationalism: as a motivating factor of the Cuban revolution, 19, 48, 208n8; problematic nature of, 19, 22

Nicaragua: Cuba's internationalist ties to, 111, 207n1, 215n7; military activities of the US in, 2, 159, 161; Niurka Martín Santamaría's work in, 111–12; Sandinistas, 20, 136, 161, 192, 212n15

Nicola, Noël, 78, 118, *119*, 168, *189*, 208n14

Obama, President Barack, 9

OLAS (Latin American Organization for Solidarity), 21, *115*, 162

Orfila Reynal, Arnaldo, 137–38

Orgambide, Pedro, 157, 214n33

Orthodox Party, 3, 17, 48, 51, 208n8, 210n28

OSPAAAL (Organization of the Peoples of Asia, Africa and Latin America), 162, 170, 171, 172

Our America, 23, 167

Padilla affair, 143–44, 148

País, Frank, 81, 83, 86, 88, 119, 173, 212n5

Parra, Isabel, 139–40

Parra, Violeta, 12, 139, 156

Pastors for Peace, 166

Pérez, Dolores ("Lolita"), 55–56, 180

Pérez Mujica, Elda, 57

Pérez, Trinidad, 155–56, 214n27

*Plumed Horn, The* (*El Corno Emplumado*), 167

posters: as a merging of art and commentary, *160*, *162*, *164*, *169*, *172*; as political statements, 166, 170–74; popularity of in revolutionary Cuba, 128, 166, 170

PSP (People's Socialist Party), 5, 151, 208n18

Puerto Rico and Puerto Rican independence, 133, 172, 213n2, 215n11

racial inequality, 8, 16, 19, 20, 47, 91

reeducation camps, 178, 215–16n1

Regla Averoff, María, 156–57, 214n31

*Revista Tricontinental,* 171

revolutionaries: Batista's imprisonment of Cuban, 17, 21, 28, 119, 180; Batista's torture and murder of, 17, 58, 61–62, 64, 77, 163;

centers of activity of Cuba's, 55; defining traits of pure, 15; educational backgrounds of the Cuban, 3, 4, 58, 89; the exile of Latin American, 212n14, 213n11, 213n15, 213n16; the exile of the Moncada to Mexico, 67; Haydée on being a revolutionary, 12, 25, 91, 141, 150–51, 163, 190; imprisonment of non-Cuban, 212n14, 213n2, 215nn10–11; imprisonment of the Moncada, 4, 17, 56, 58, 64, 93, 104; movements before the Cuban revolution, 208n8, 210n28, 211n8; movements by throughout the world, 7, 12–13, 23, 161–62, 166–67, 180; nineteenth century leaders, 208n7, 210nn23–24; revolutionary art, 166–71, 173, 174; student groups, 5, 166, 167; support and protection of by Cuban public, 5; thinkers, 26, 48, 208n7, 212n11; transformation of the Cuban, 4–5; twentieth-century leaders, 55, 99, 170, 208n6, 210n1, 212n6, 213n15, 216n9; in the twentieth-century United States, 208n16, 215n10, 215n14. *See also* Cuban revolution; underground activities

Rodríguez, Silvio: on Haydée, 27, 78, 118, 178, 183; musical work of, *119*, 168, *189*, 208n14

Rojas, Marta, 68–71, 78–80, 99, 123, 211n16

Rolando, Gloria, 20, 208n16

Ruiz, Norma (Ada's daughter), 34, 36, 113–19, 180, 188

Salsamendi, Chiki, 40, 134, 157–58, 214n34

Sánchez, Celia: friendship of with Haydée, 12, 28–29, 111, 116, 123, 178; role of in Castro's government, *150*, 186, 187–88, 193, 208n6; role of in Cuban revolution, 15, 88, 95, 99, 102, 208n6; in Sierra Maestre guerrilla camp, *83*, *90*, *92*, 97

Sandinista Revolution, 20, 136, 161, 212n15

Santa Coloma, Boris Luis (fiancé): revolutionary activities of, 64–65, 75–76, 81, *82*, 94, 116; torture and death of at Moncada as a permanent trauma for Haydée, 12, 17, 27–28

Santamaría Cuadrado, Abel (brother): animosity of toward Batista, 47, 55; apartment at 25 and O, 47, 53, 55; bond of to Haydée as a fellow revolutionary, 17, 21, 42, 45, 48, 51, 60; close bond of with Haydée, 16, 38, 42, 47, 48, 52, 178; Constancia sugar refinery renamed to honor, 24, 34, 40; corruption and inequality as factors that shaped, 17, 34, 41–42, 45, 47; death of following the attack on Moncada, 12, 17, 43, 58, 81; early life of, 30, 34, 38, 43, 46; family home established as a museum to honor, 36–37, 39; and Fidel Castro, 55–57, 63–65, 73, 76; at Moncada, 60, 63–65, 67–68, 71–73, 75–76, 163, 190; political thinkers and activists who influenced, 47, 55, 210n28; torture and death of at Moncada as a permanent trauma for Haydée, 12, 27–28, 63

Santamaría Cuadrado, Ada (sister): birth and death of, 34, 44, 60, 117, 192; relationship of with her sisters, 45, 111, 115, 121; revolutionary activities of, 60, 118

Santamaría Cuadrado, Aida (sister): early life of, 30, 34, 42, 46, 51; relationship of with her sisters, 43, 45, 48, 59, 117, 121

Santamaría Cuadrado, Aldo (brother), 30, 34, 42, 43, 44, 46

Santamaría Cuadrado family, 33–34, 35–38, 40–46, 111, 121

Santamaría Cuadrado, Haydée: actions of on the day when the revolution triumphed, 96–99; apartment at 25 and O, 53–55, 59, 65, 91; artistic sensibilities of, 18, 23, 129–30, 154–56; asthmatic condition of, 13–14, 200; attitudes of toward religion, 116, 179; automobile accident, 112; on being a revolutionary, 12, 25, 91, 141, 150–51, 163, 190; on being important, 135–36; Casa years photos, 10, 49, 106, 119, 126, 129, 132; childhood and family photos, 30, 33, 36, 39, 40, 45–46; the childhood of, 32, 41, 45–48; communism of, 25, 48, 163, 186; concerns of with the welfare of children, 13, 25–27, 102, 113–14, 116, 179–80,

209n21; corruption of mill bosses as an influence on, 41–42; courage of, 64, 81–86, 94–96, 99; court testimonies regarding the events at Moncada, 75–76; depression, 12–13, 32, 50, 113, 123–24, 154, 184; *Destino: Haydée Santamaría*, 134; education of, 16, 18, 23–24, 48, 50–51, 115, 129, 147; egalitarianism as a motivating value of, 20, 149, 178, 181; elegy references to the early life of, 198, 201; elegy references to the experience of at Moncada, 196, 198–99, 206; elegy references to friendships of with fellow revolutionaries, 203–4, 206; elegy references to the marriage and family of, 202–3; elegy references to the public mourning of, 197; elegy references to the sociocultural ideas of, 200–201, 204–5, 206; elegy references to the suicide of, 196; elegy references to the work of for the Cuban revolution, 199–200, 201–2, 205; elegy reference to the work of at Casa, 201–2, 205–6; eulogies and testimonies regarding, 15–16, 43, 155–58; evasion of capture by, 12, 32–33, 64, 84–86, 94–95, 104, 190; family as a motivating concern of, 26–27; fears of about leaving Cuba, 19, 71–72, 95, 96; and feminism, 13, 21, 178, 179; friendship of with Marta Rojas, 68–71, 78–80; funerary rites for, 25, 112–13, 123, 149, 152, 188, 192; and gender discrimination, 20, 101, 131–32, 178–79, 181; humanitarianism of, 18, 131, 134–36; imprisonment of following Moncada, 17, 56, 64–65, 68–70, 78–80, 88–91; inclusivity of, 15, 18, 101, 131, 163, 179; international correspondence of, 116, 134, 136–43; internationalism of, 20, 22–23, 121, 175, 179; interpretation of the suicide of by daughter Celia María, 27, 117; interpretation of the suicide of by Marcia Leseica, 154–55; interpretation of the suicide of by niece Niurka Martín Santamaría, 111–12; interpretation of the suicide of by niece Norma Ruiz, 117; interpretation of the suicide of by Rebeca Chávez, 123–24;

interpretation of the suicide of by Roberto Fernández Retamar, 148–49; interpretation of the suicide of by Silvia Gil, 152; justice as a motivating value of, 12, 32, 104, 118, 131–32, 153–54; as the last victim of the Moncada attack, 12, 148; leadership in OLAS, 21, 115, 162; leadership in the Cuban Communist Party (PCC), 12, 21–22, 176; leadership in the Cuban revolution, 88, 193; leadership of Casa de las Américas by, 12–13, 18–19, 22–23, 128–32, 146–47, 151–52, 190; letter exchange of with Mario Vargas Llosa, 142–46; letter to Che, 173–74; letter to Isabel Parra, 139–40; "Life is beautiful when you live like this" ("Que la vida es Hermosa cuando se vive así"), 71–77, 211n14; loyalty as a motivating value of, 12, 19, 22, 116, 179; on marriage and divorce, 13, 111, 113, 115, 116, 179; marriage and family photos, 37, 103, 109; memorializations to by colleagues, 155–58; Moncada as a life-changing hallmark for, 62–63, 77, 85–86, 147–48; Moncada commemorations as a reliving of the attack for, 25, 28, 50, 53, 62; participation of on the assault of Moncada, 17, 65, 71–74, 102, 154; PCC photos, 115, 122, 124, 176; photos taken with fellow revolutionaries, 74, 82; police file photos, 59, 61, 66; prison photos, 56, 69, 79; protection of artists by, 12, 118, 131–32, 148, 163, 178; provincial origins of, 11, 47, 50, 51, 123, 150, 177; reading habits of, 48–49, 110–11, 115, 129, 154; rebellious character of, 19, 42–43, 185; recruiting functions of, 86, 88, 152–53, 211n8; rejection of the provincial life by, 39, 42, 51; role of in establishing the Cuban Communist Party, 21; role of in planning and organizing the attack on Moncada, 11, 102, 154; Sierra Maestra photos, 83, 87, 89, 90, 92, 97; on social hierarchy in Batista's Cuba, 48; sugar plantation life as an influence on, 41–42, 46–47, 51; sugar plantation origins of, 16, 39, 48, 53, 123, 129, 177; suicide of, 12, 27–29, 123, 149,

193; suicide of as a political discomfort for the PCC, 20–21, 25, 186–87, 193; surreptitious visit of to see her husband in Boniato Prison, 86; torture and deaths of Abel and Boris as permanent scars for, 12, 17, 27–28, 63; torture of at Moncada, 154, 163; transgression as a motivating value of, 12; travel by on behalf of the Cuban Revolution and the PCC, 17, 153; urban underground activities of, 17–18, 21, 44, 86, 102, 163; use of disguise by to facilitate her activities as a rebel, 64, 85–86; on violence, 17–18, 22, 81; willingness of to challenge injustice, 19, 165, 185; writings of José Martí as an influence on, 48, 49, 50, 55–56, 115; as Yeyé, 39–40, 43, 84, 105, 117, 183, 215–16n1

Santamaría Fernández, Benigno (father), 33–34, 37, 40, 45–46

Santiago de Cuba: attack on the Moncada Barracks at, 3, 11, 17, 37, 208n11; Castro's return to Cuba via, 86, 99, 189; Haydée's smuggling of arms for the attack at, 64; as the place where the Cuban Revolution began, 57, 60; residents of as witnesses to revolutionary event, 77; the revolutionaries' plan for the attack at, 67, 73; revolutionary underground of, 4, 21, 55, 86, 95, 120, 212nn5–6; trial at, 68–69, 75

Sarría, Lieutenant Pedro, 67, 210n7

Siboney, 60, 61, 65, 76

Sierra Maestra mountains: Haydée's revolutionary training in, 87, 89, 90, 92, 97; Haydée's trips to and from, 83–88, 189; revolutionary encampment in, 4, 95, 98, 101–2, 161–63

Siglo XXI, 138

smuggling, 17, 57, 85, 93, 94

social change: as a driving force for revolution, 55, 59, 93, 185–86; as a primary goal of Cuban revolution, 5–6, 8, 170, 171, 174, 175; exploitation as a motivating force for, 3, 16, 34, 39, 42, 45, 58; Haydée's desire for, 12, 16, 23, 26, 130, 163, 188; inequality as a motivating force for, 16, 20, 34, 132 socialism: in Allende's Chile, 161; Che Guevara's "Man and Socialism in Cuba", 7, 174; in Cuba, 1, 5–7, 9, 104, 207n1, 210n1; Cuba's ties to the Soviet bloc, 8, 165–66; differing interpretations of among Cuba's political parties, 151; in pre-Castro Cuba, 47; realist or Soviet version of, 18, 130, 163

songs and songwriters. See music; Casa de las Américas

Soviet Union, 6, 8, 18, 26, 100, 130

Spain: Cuba's wars for independence from, 210nn23–25, 211n19; Galicians who migrated to Cuba from, 32, 40, 42, 44; Haydée's familial connections to, 32, 40, 42, 45, 46, 65; Marxism in Spanish, 6, 166; migration from, 44

Special Period (1991–1995), 100, 184

Stalin and Stalinism, 26, 143, 165, 209n22

Stout, Nancy, 83, 88

*Strawberry and Chocolate,* 215n9

students: activities of Venceremos Brigade of SDS, 166; international hosted in Cuba, 20; opposition of to United States involvement in Vietnam, 165; Orthodox Youth, 48, 51; participation of in formulating Cuba's socialist constitution, 207n1; revolutionaries, 55, 88, 167, 215n8; Students for a Democratic Society (SDS), 166

sugar: communal life of workers, 46–47, 51; corrupt practices in the industry, 41–42; mill at Constancia, 24, 34, 37–38, 40, 41–42, 46–47, 65; plantation life for the Santamaría Cuadrado family, 16, 39, 48, 53, 123, 129, 177

suicide: in Cuba, 181–82, 184, 188, 193; the impact of on surviving family and friends, 191–92

Suñol, Comandante Eddy, 101–2, 188

Tabor, Robert, 84

ten black years (*el decenio negro*), 148, 151

theater, 22–23, 128, 130, 156, 168–69, 193

Torres, Camilo, 170, 215n12

Trotsky and Trotskyism, 26

"Two, three, many Vietnams", 7, 162, 173

UMAP military camps (*Unidades militares de ayuda a la producción*), 178, 215–16n1

underground activities: at Havana, 17, 21, 86, 88, 180; Haydée's involvement in, 17–18, 21, 44, 86, 102, 163; at Santiago, 4, 86, 95; throughout Batista's Cuba, 4, 17–18, 67, 76–77, 81, 101, 154. *See also* Cuban Revolution; revolutionaries

United States: 1960s cultural rebellion in, 164–65; CIA activities against Cuba, 2, 159, 171; Cuban counterrevolutionaries in, 2; cultural blockade against Cuba by, 12, 18, 22–23, 128, 166–67; cultural rebellion in, 163–65, 167–68, 170, 172–73; diplomatic blockade against Cuba by, 9, 18, 129; economic blockade against Cuba by, 7–8, 18; invasions of Latin American countries by, 159–60; McCarthyism in, 163–64, 165; news reporting on Cuba, 4, 84, 166; reestablishment of diplomatic relations with Cuba, 9; restrictions of against travel to Cuba, 8

Uruguay, 114, 136, 212nn13–14, 214n28, 215n15

Vargas Llosa, Mario, 142–46

Venezuela, 98, 114, 144–45

Vent Dumois, Lesbia, 157, 214n32

Vietnam: Cuba's links to North Vietnam, 161, 170, 210n2; Haydée's visit to North Vietnam, 18; Ho Chi Minh, 15, 18, 159, 170, 187; Susan Sontag's writings about, 15, 207n3; "Two, three, many Vietnams" slogan, 7, 162, 173; US military interference in, 161, 164–5

Vincenot, Emmanuel, 172, 216n3

Vinceremos Brigade, 166

violence: in Cuba, 22, 55, 91, 167; Haydée's attitudes toward, 17–18, 22, 81

visual artists, 152, 154, 164, 168, 214n32

women: access of to education, 38; access of to health care, 102; artists, 165; in Castro's Cuba, 5, 21, 24, 102; dress codes and behavior protocols for Cuban girls

Elizabeth Betita Martz
— Diberman

Hist
3600 Fall

Cuba
* Randall
* Cuba Reader
* Chomsky